Elementary Education

Elementary Education

Editors

Monica Tomar
D.S. Srivastava

ISHA BOOKS
DELHI-110 033

Elementary Education

ISBN: 81-8205-169-X

Reprinted in 2011 in India by
Isha Books
B-63, Ist Floor
New Gupta Colony
Near DDA Market
Delhi-110009

Printed at: G. Print Process, Delhi

Preface

Elementary education is the first years of formal, structured education that occurs during childhood. In most countries, it is compulsory for children to receive primary education though in many jurisdictions it is permissible for parents to provide it. It generally begins when children are four to seven years of age. The division between primary and secondary education is somewhat arbitrary, but it generally occurs at about twelve years of age (adclescence); some educational systems have separate middle schools for that period.

Typically, primary education is provided in schools, where (in the absence of parental movement or other intervening factors) the child will stay, in steadily advancing classes, until they complete it and move on to secondary schooling. Children are usually placed in classes with one teacher who will be primarily responsible for their education and welfare for that year. This teacher may be assisted to varying degrees by specialist teachers in certain subject areas, often music or physical education. The continuity with a single teacher and the opportunity to build up a close relationship with the class is a notable feature of the primary education system. Over the past few decades, schools have been testing various arrangements which break from the one-teacher, one-class mold.

The major goals of elementary education are achieving basic literacy and numeracy amongst all their students, as well as establishing foundations in science, geography, history and other social sciences. The relative priority of various areas, and the methods used to teach them, are an area of considerable political debate.

In India, since independence, the central and state governments have been expanding the provision of primary formal and non-formal education to realise the goal of Universalisation of Elementary Education (UEE). Several central and state level initiatives have been in operation from the early 1980s. While the design of these projects vary substantially, all of them address the objectives and strategies of the National Policy on Education 1986. They pay special attention to increasing girls' enrolment, improving educational outcomes, strengthening community involvement, improving teaching and learning materials and providing in-service teacher training.

The current status of primary education in India is well reviewed in the present volume. The constitutions provisions, planning, policy framework and various initiatives for elementary education are discussed in detail. Conceptualized and written in a lucid and readable style, this book will be an essential reading tool for educationists, policy makers and teachers.

Editor

CONTENTS

1

ELEMENTARY EDUCATION IN INDIA

The universalization of elementary education in India has been a long-cherished but unrealized goal which India has been striving towards ever since her independence in 1947. As the British government expanded its rule in India, education for Indians gradually became their concern. However, their main purposes were, as stated in Macaulay's infamous Minute on Education in 1835, creating a class of people who would be interpreters between the British rulers and the Indian masses, and preparing government employees to bolster and further the imperialist aims of the raj. Sir Charles Wood's Education Despatch of 1854 suggested that the government should abandon the strategy of providing only higher education and promote mass education. However, teacher training for elementary education progressed at a very slow pace.

Indigenous Indian elementary education, whose features were popularity in the community and flexibility in its setup, was on the decline under the sluggish expansion of modern elementary school system. Although many reports under the British rule stressed the importance of elementary teacher training and recommended establishing more normal schools, elementary schools were woefully insufficient.

In the final analysis, the British Government never accepted responsibility for educating the masses in India, and the problem of wastage and stagnation in school education remained unsolved. Further examination on the educational policy after independence for universalization of elementary education requires careful consideration regarding the historical background of school education in India.

RECENT TRENDS IN ELEMENTARY EDUCATION

— Elementary Education is recognised as a fundamental right of all citizens in India. The Supreme Court of India in its judgement in Unnikrishnan's case has held that all citizens have a fundamental right to education upto the age of 14 years. The Government of India has introduced 83rd Constitutional Amendment Bill in Parliament in 1997 to make education a fundamental right of all children up to the age of 6-14 years.

— Greater emphasis on Decentralisation of educational planning and administration. The 73rd and 74th Constitutional Amendments have provided a statutory base for decentralised educational planning.

— Multi-sectoral holistic approach to Universalisation of Elementary Education (UEE).

— Greatest stress on creation of conditions that would encourage increased community participation in effective school management and supervision.

— Re-examination of relationship among the government, NGOs and private institutions to harness potential of non-governmental institutions in pursuit of UEE.

— Recognition of limitations of market forces in ensuring equity and equality in elementary education. The Government is committed to enhance financial allocation for education to 6% of GDP.

— Greater thrust on community-based support structures, educational planning and monitoring & evaluation to improve delivery of elementary education.

There is a strong consensus today about the importance of elementary education in Indian public policy. It is hard to imagine how productivity and income growth can come about for the 45 per cent of India which is illiterate. Going beyond economies, there are significant returns to education as far as social development and politics are concerned. It is hard to imagine how social progress can be obtained with 45 per cent illiteracy.

From this perspective, one common theme that has emerged is that while the liberalisation of the 1990s has involved taking the State out of myriad aspects of the Indian economy, there remains a major role for the State in elementary education. Indeed, the withdrawal of the State from other areas should help free up resources for education and health.

Why is elementary education special? Why should the State spend on elementary education? A common reason that is supplied is that poor people are too backward to invest in education by themselves; hence the only way to ensure that their children grow up educated is through large government interventions. This argument is highly suspect. The second, and more defensible rationale for public expenditures for elementary education is based upon the "externalities" of education. Each educated person generates myriad benefits for all those around him, and he, individually, cannot capture the full benefits of his education that accrue to society. Hence, individuals have an incentive to underinvest in education, generate these positive benefits, and take away part (but not all) of these benefits as taxes.

These arguments justify public expenditures on elementary education, and these expenditures have grown enormously in the 1990s. Yet, educational outcomes have not improved sharply. Illiteracy is still substantially with us. Children fail to enroll in enormous numbers and the drop-out rate is very high amongst those that do.We must shift focus from the inputs, such as public expenses on education or the number of schools, to outputs, which are educational outcomes. If elementary education is important, then we should focus upon outcomes, measured in terms of literacy rates, and school enrollment rates at age 7 and 15. If the educational system is badly functioning, then adding money as an input is an inefficient way to improve outcomes.

India's educational outcomes are a spectacular failure when compared with dozens of countries which achieved complete literacy in a generation after 1945. Part of this problem is rooted in low public expenditure on education in India. But an even more important problem lies in the inefficient State-dominated education system. The public sector is a highly inefficient producer of educational services (just as it is inefficient in producing watches, or banking services, or telecom services). In keeping with the spirit of liberalisation, we should try to obtain better educational services by using competition in the private sector.

Writing in the book Agenda for Change recently produced by the Rajiv Gandhi Institute for Contemporary Studies, Parth J. Shah has an elegant and simple idea which goes to the heart of this problem. At present, the government spends roughly Rs 3,000 per year per child in primary schools. This money is spent on the (inefficient) production of educational services by the public sector. Instead, a totally different approach should be used. The government should completely get out of the production of educational services; all schools should be run by the private sector and charge fees. Parents should be provided with coupons worth Rs 3,000 per child per year which they pay to the school of their choice. Coupon distribution is efficiently implemented, for example, by giving parents 12 coupons when a child is born.

The essential desirable features here are choice by consumers, and competition in the private sector. The private sector would work to run profit-making schools, charging fees of Rs 3,000 a year and above. Parents would be able to select between multiple competing schools. Some schools would offer teaching at the floor price of Rs 3,000 per year, other schools would charge higher fees where parents supplement the government subsidy by their own funds.

In this proposal, parents are empowered. If a school produces a poor education, parents would move their children to a competing school. This will be the most important ground-level check upon the quality of educational services and hence educational outcomes. Parth J. Shah describes a remarkable idea that has been used in Kerala. The government reimburses the transportation costs faced by children in commuting to school. This measure increases the choices available to parents, and avoids the problem of a local monopoly. This proposal is criticised on the grounds that poor people are so ignorant that they will give their vouchers to scamsters who will make off with the Rs 3,000 and not supply any education. This assumes that poor people are uninterested in the education of their children.

Parth J. Shah offers powerful evidence which shows that the poorest quintile of India — households which earn under Rs 3,000 per capita per year — spends between 10 per cent and 36 per cent of their family income on the education of their children. This is in a regime where primary education is supposed to be free. These poorest of the poor choose to supplement the low quality educational services, that the government supplies them, with additional services which they buy. This is sharp evidence about the extent to which the poor of India care about the education of their children.

In this sense, the evidence about low enrollment rates and high dropout rates is quite likely to be related to the poor quality of the education which public sector schools provide. If parents were given better schools that their children could attend, it is very likely that enrollment rates would rise. Private sector schools, competing for enrollment, would think innovatively in trying to produce better educational services. One simple example which Parth Shah offers is that of the timings which schools use. The timings are presently chosen in a way which is convenient for government employees.

In rural areas, a schedule such as 2 PM to 8 PM would be highly convenient, since it allows children to work on farms in the morning and then attend school. When educational services are produced by the public sector, as they are at present, there will be no effort at trying to think about the customer and improving the quality of services from his perspective.

If all parents are armed with coupons worth Rs 3,000, private sector production of educational services will blossom in quality and customer orientation. This will lead to better education, and better educational outcomes. Educational outcomes in India can be dramatically improved, without enlarged public expenditure on education, by the simple idea of putting parents in complete control of the Rs 3,000 per child per year that we currently spend in the country.

During the eighth plan period several international agencies are expected to pour in funds for the improvement of primary school education in about 200 districts in India. The origin of this trend goes back to 1983, with the implementation of the Andhra Pradesh Primary Education Project. The project receives funds from the Overseas Development Administration. There have been smaller externally funded projects to address specific concerns like teacher training, material development, nonformal education, etc. It is well known that the Government of India has been resisting pressures from international agencies to allow them to fund primary education in India.

However, the scenario changed sometime around 1988 when the Bihar Education Project was being formulated. The project envisaged comprehensive Intervention in primary education in 20 districts and has an outlay of Rs. 3540 million. About half of it is expected to come from international agencies. Since then the Swedish International Development Authority began funding similar projects in Rajasthan (Lok Jumbish - 25 development blocks - and Shiksha Karmi - 70 blocks projects). The World Bank got into the act with the Uttar Pradesh Basic Education Project envisaging similar intervention in 10 districts with a total outlay of Rs. 7280 million for 1993-2000. The World Bank has sanctioned a soft loan of US $163.1 million for this.

The most extensive intervention of them all has come in the form of the District Primary Education Programme (DPEP) the primary education component of the Social Safety Net Adjustment Credit financed by the IDA. This "safety net" seeks to cover the risks which the client governments are expected to run into during the initial years of 'structural adjustment' due to the withdrawal of expenditure from the social sector. Under this another 110 districts are to be covered. Needless to say all these are supposed to be the most 'backward' districts of the country.

It is not that the imperialist powers were not in favour of investing in Indian education earlier, but rather that the Indian Government did not agree to allow them a hand in so important a sphere as primary education. It was the adverse foreign exchange situation, the acceptance of the structural adjustment programme and the collapse of the USSR which must account for the capitulation in the early 1990s. While earlier the Indian Government formulated its policy and plan and outlined its financial requirements and then approached the international agencies for funds, in the case of the various district primary education programmes the international agencies participated in drafting the policies, plans etc. from the outset.

Some of the salient features of these district plans are of interest. The most significant feature of these programmes is the insistence of the funding agencies that separate autonomous bodies be set up to receive the funds and run the programmes. These bodies continue to be under the control of the various state governments with the Chief Minister of the state being the chairperson, and ministers and various bureaucrats *ex officio* members but are significantly exempt from the rules governing the expenditure of government funds.

The autonomous bodies set up at the state level go down to the block level. As of now they are composed of government officials and their nominees and some elected members of local bodies (panchayats). These bodies include representatives from various departments, from elected bodies (MLAs, MPs, Panchayat members, non governmental agencies etc.). The idea is to short circuit usual governmental procedures where interdepartmental coordination is so difficult.

On the face of it this seems a rather innocuous attempt at rationalizing and streamlining the governmental organization. However, the potential ties it opens for future intervention by the funding agencies is enormous. Even now the bodies set up under the programmes have been wielding enormous powers vis a vis normal government departments not only in allocation of funds for the districts in question but also in determining the content of education in all the districts.

When we view this in conjunction with the fact that the funding agencies have set up stringent procedures for evaluation and monitoring of the programmes (the monitoring teams though ostensibly set up by the Government of India, include nominees of the funding agencies and needless to say these experts enjoy much greater clout than their Indian counterparts) it is clear that a pathway has been cleared for the international agencies to intervene right down to the block level in all matters including the content and process of teaching. These projects seek to ensure that all habitats have access to school facilities, all schools have a minimum number of teachers and a minimum of educational materials, teachers are appropriately trained and the quality and standards of text-books and other teaching materials improved.

For those who visualise imperialism as an evil force with an evil face, allying with the most reactionary forces in the country, the plan outlined for the country's education may come as a surprise. The emphasis has been on the following unexceptionable principles:

1. Ensuring quality education for the most depressed sections of the society, the SCs STs, and women.
2. Involving the local community in defining its educational requirements and control of the public educational institutions - and within the local community mobilizing the most deprived sections.
3. Incorporation of liberal and democratic methods and contents into the teaching materials and methods.

This incorporation of a democratic agenda within an imperialist sponsored programme requires serious study and analysis. More so because these projects seek to harness the liberal intelligentsia, the left of centre voluntary groups, in short the democratic petty bourgeoisie. It is not a rarity to hear what used to be songs of revolutionary movements in the previous decades being sung in teacher training camps and perhaps even in the schools under these projects. Material prepared under these projects seek to treat social and economic issues in a critical light - agrarian relations, caste and gender issues and a critical evaluation of the development of the last 40 years is no longer a taboo.

This poses what may be called the 'Bengali Babu Syndrome'. The Bengali intelligentsia and middle class of the early nineteenth century found itself with the limited option of supporting either the decadent Mughal ruling class or the British who seemed to be ushering in a liberal, rational, scientific and democratic era and most of them willy nilly chose to support the British. Almost a century and a half later a similar situation seems to be in the offing and democratic and revolutionary trends need to study this phenomenon carefully and outline their policies. It may therefore be worthwhile to review the state of education in India and the various social forces at work in it.

One need not begin with the truism that the state of education in the country is rather dismal. We will be using some of the government data here and it is important to remember that the reliability of these data is rather poor. The official data tell us that out of every 100 children of school going age only 90 get enrolled in schools. Of these 90 about 45 drop out before reaching class V and we are left with about 32 children in class VIII. How many of them eventually complete 12 years schooling is anybody's guess.

It is quite another question as to who these 32 fortunate children are and who the other 68 children happen to be. We cannot expect the official sources to provide us with an analysis of the class composition of the 32 and the 68. They would rather operate with social categories like SC/ST/ girls/boys. However it does not require much imagination to figure out which social classes these children are likely to belong to. Several studies of the achievement levels of children who complete class V have been done - they add to the dismal picture. Of the 45 attending the class only about 15 manage to read and write and even less to do simple arithmetic operations.

In other words we are managing to provide rudimentary education to only 10% of our children! Once again who these 10% are or will develop into is anybody's guess. This failure of 'Independent' India's attempt at universalization of elementary education has other surprising aspects. An NSS survey went into the reasons for non enrolment and drop out from school. The results are revealing: 10% did not enrol because there were no proper schools nearby. About 34% did not enrol in school because they had to augment family income or the family could not afford to educate their children. Significantly 30% did not find the school education interesting.

Experts have been reading these figures differently, sometimes to argue that poverty is not a reason for non enrolment or drop out but rather the dreariness of class room transactions, and sometimes to argue that economic reasons do play an important role in the problem. "Lack of interest" is a vague term and can imply both dreariness of class room transaction and non-relevance of the content to the child's life requirement - a different way of saying that they cannot afford the luxury of such an education.

The fact remains that educating their own children comes rather low in the list of priorities of the mass of the people. We can propose two hypotheses to explain this apparently strange phenomenon. Firstly, formal education does not seem to help in the productive activities of the mass of people. Designed mainly to produce a bureaucratic middle class with enormous emphasis on memorizing tomes of useless information such education cannot be of much use for any real life situation unless of course one is trying to join the ranks of the ossified bureaucracy.

On the other hand given the use of traditional technology in the economy as whole with the notable exception of a few sectors the production process also does not yet seem to demand much from the formal education system. Thus the mass of the working population can do without any formal education. Secondly, to most people formal education is not essential to do their normal work better, but a means of upward social mobility, into higher social strata. And this costs a lot and little wonder few people opt for it.

While formal education is low on the agenda of the mass of the people, educating the mass of the people is increasingly becoming a matter of concern for the imperialists, their Indian partners, the middle classes, etc. Why this should be so is a matter of interest. Once again we can proffer only some hypotheses. Imperialist powers have seriously been concerned by the fact that the population of the underdeveloped world, the weak links in the chain of world imperialism, is far larger than that of the imperialist countries, and continue to grow at a rather fast rate. They seem to fear that this trend will be potentially dangerous in the long run.

Hence the serious attention being given to population control measures. Statistics seem to demonstrate that there is a strong correlation between literacy rate/ educational levels of the population (particularly the female component of it) and the rate of population growth. Educating the people therefore seems to be a cheaper and a more peaceful way of controlling the growth of population in the potentially dangerous regions of the world.

This angle in universalizing education is seldom concealed, and in fact no opportunity is lost to highlight it. Likewise the curriculum in formal education is expected to contain material which locates the reason for poverty and deprivation of the masses in the uncontrolled growth of population. Expanding such education serves both strategic and ideological functions of controlling the population growth and convincing the masses that they themselves are the cause of their poverty.

Secondly, though it is somewhat old fashioned, one may remember Marx and Engels's prophecy that capitalism will bulldoze all bastions of pre-capitalist relations and modes of productions and establish the sway of capitalism. With the collapse of the remnants of the USSR and the seeming annihilation of a socialist alternative imperialism seems to have entered a new phase of expansion and attack on the pre-capitalist survivals. Formal education is likely to spread capitalist ethos, build a manpower equipped to handle the new technology, and shape up a receptive market for its products.

The social strata which is expected to collaborate in the new capitalist/ imperialist educational effort is the middle class. The last few decades have seen the growing presumption of the middle classes in India. They have appropriated for themselves the nationalist cause (read the anti-Pakistani cause), the religious cause (read the anti-minority cause) and now the cause of educating and bringing light to the dark world of the working people. One only needs to peruse through the literature produced by the literacy movement to gauge the contempt and scorn and self-righteousness with which the middle class views the language, culture and the wisdom of the working people. These mass education ventures give employment to this middle class which by heaping insult and scorn on the working people at the same time tries to establish its social leadership over them..

Little wonder then that the reluctant mass of people are being engulfed with propaganda persuading them to get educated and educate their children. A major conflict within these initiatives springs from the attempt of the urban middle class to impose its norms and pace of learning upon all children through the so-called "Minimum Levels Of Learning". Such an imposition will ensure the leading position of the middle class and to a large extent force the children of lower rungs of the society to drop out being unable to cope with the demands being placed upon them.

As pointed out above given the complexity of the issues involved, the democratic forces are faced with a serious dilemma: imperialist intervention in education is a foregone conclusion by now; this intervention for the sake of efficiency and also to neutralise opposition seeks the cooperation of those very same democratic forces.

What should be the attitude of the democratic forces to this imperialist sponsored venture? There can be no doubt that it is imperative that those who stand by democracy must needs fight the further penetration of imperialism in all spheres of education. The democratic forces must compel the government to fulfil the directives of the Indian constitution which required the state to provide *by 1960* 'free and compulsory education for all children until they complete the age of fourteen years'. In those areas of elementary education where international funding has secured a dominant position resistance has to take different forms.

The role assumed by the 'specialists' appointed by the international agencies in determining the educational needs of the Indian people must be fought tooth and nail. This has to be done by a careful monitoring of the content and methods of education, timely criticism and posing of alternatives. To cite two examples, the increasing pressure to incorporate in the school curriculum imperialist wisdom on the relation between population and poverty needs to be squarely opposed. Similarly, the pressure to revise the curriculum to suit the requirements of the middle class elite to the detriment of the first generation learners needs to be opposed.

The Indian government has to be pressurised to continue to provide funds once the international agencies withdraw support. In the meantime it would appear that these imperialist-backed projects will lead to specific changes. The reach of school education will expand in terms of more school buildings and teachers, the children of the poorest of parents will receive increased access to education, feudal opposition to the education of the poor will be weakened, a different climate will emerge to up-date curriculum and teaching methods to make them more child-centred.

For those who have worked in the sphere of education the dichotomy between producing a few 'brilliant' scholars and educating the mass of the children is a well-known issue. Education of the mass of children requires enormous flexibility, acceptance of different paces of learning, adoption of a variety of methods rather than one uniform method, placing greater emphasis on skills and processes of the production of knowledge than on information memorising and processing, which would enable children to build upon their own experience, reflect upon it and articulate their experiences and visions. In contrast to this philistine pedagogy heaps the dead weight of accumulated knowledge in the form of information upon the primary education of children and thus deadens their ability to produce and articulate knowledge.

The situation calls for both a careful study and monitoring of the developments in the sphere of education but also educating the labouring people of the potential dangers in such projects and opposing their retrogressive aspects. It is here that the absence of interest in education matters among Marxist-Leninists poses a serious problem. It is time serious attention is paid to educational questions as they go a long way to shaping the thinking of the people.

The first seperate department for education was created in 1910 to look after the education in India. But it was after India achieved its Independence on 15th August 1947. A full fledged Ministry of Education was established on 29th August 1947. The nomenclature and responsibilities of the Education Department has undergone some changes since Independence. The present Department of Education is one of the four constitutent departments of the Ministry of Human Resource Development which was created on 26th September, 1985.

Education has been in prime focus throughout India's development plans. Its importance can be gauged from the fact that it is included as a part of the Directive Principles of State Policy in the Constitution, which states that " the State shall endeavour to provide within a period of ten years from the commencement of this Constitution, for free and compulsory education for all children until they complete the age of fourteen years".

Educational policy and progress are reviewed in the light of the goal of national development and priorities set from time to time. The National Policy on Educatuion was formulated in 1982, and was later updated in 1992, where specific responsibilities for organising, implementing and financing its proposals were assigned. The total budgetary expenditure on Education by the Education Departments of the Centre and States has increased from Rs. 644.6 millions in 1951-52 to Rs. 300,000 millions in 1995-96. There are, at present 130 plan schemes in the Department with a total Eighth Plan outlay of Rs. 74430 Millions.

The state of political and economic affairs too are responsible for determinig the educational policy. For example, in the second five year plan (1956-60) when heavy industries became the basic industries, the socialistic education was given and was put emphasis on conversion of basic education and secondary and higher educations. Also, when India saw the economic crisis and the school attendance rate fell in 1960's a big reconsideration on the whole education was done establishing the advisory committee including foreigners.

Today the system which was decided by the international conference party is revolved. It has 10-2-3 system and in some states it has 5-3-2 system or 4-3-3 system. The elementary education is divided into the first term and the latter term. The secondary education is divided to the first term and the latter term, and the first term is for studying the extention of elementary education and the latter term is divided into the college entering course and vocational education course to study. It is the characteristic that scientific education and talent education are done. The rate of the students to enter the first term is 24.6%. For the higher education, 137 higher educational systems aim at the improvement of the qualities of education and research in scientific technology.

2

Constitutional Provisions for Universalisation of Elementary Education

Universalisation of Elementary Education (UEE) is a constitutional provision and national commitment in India. Elementary education is recognised as a fundamental right of all citizens in India. The directive principles of state policy envisage UEE as one of the major goals to be achieved and mandated in a timeframe of 10 years. Though still unachieved, the achievements are significant as reflected by the rising national and state literacy rates.

The Supreme Court in its judgement in the Unnikrishnan case (1993) has held that all citizens have a fundamental right to education up to 14 years. The Government of India introduced 83rd Constitutional Amendment Bill in Parliament in 1997 to make education a fundamental right of all children of 6-14 years. The 73rd and 74th Constitutional Amendments have provided a statutory base for decentralised education planning. In fact, the 20th century has witnessed a global upsurge in UEE. Widespread ignorance, illiteracy and poverty often are stumbling blocks but still the mandate of alleviating poverty through HRD has initiated a change that now characterises every process of growth and development.

Prior to Independence, the system of education had limited access and denied mass education. Greater emphasis was laid on confirmism to the prevailing socio-political and economic system. Macaulay's objective of education system was to create a new breed of Indians similar to Europeans. However, this approach was dismissed by the national movement leaders, which expressed global sentiments of education for all. Gokhale's Compulsory Education Bill reflected the spirit of India's freedom movement.

The first major education policy formulation was spelled out by the Kothari Commission Report (1964-66) in the year 1968. It led to restructuring of school education system in 10+2+3 pattern. A major attempt at transforming the structure and content of education in the country was taken in 1986. with the announcement of National Policy on Education (NPE). The intervening period between 1968 and 1986 was marked by considerable education expansion in educational facilities, which has reached more than 90 per cent of the country's area and habitations having a learning centre within 1 km. In 1988, National Literacy Mission was launched. The year 1990 was celebrated as International Literacy Year reiterating the message of education for all.

The Government of India has made efforts to eradicate poverty in the country over the past decades. These efforts have met with considerable success. India's past strategies for poverty alleviation has included strong policy and financial support from the government, economic and education reforms and increased community participation. The past experiments have brought home a point that a successful HRD approach through education is the only basis for alleviating poverty. This has been the experience of other developed and populous countries like China too.

Zimbabwe achieved universal primary education in three years by taking measures to increase enrolments and cut down costs of UPE. In Vietnam, poverty incidence in households headed by those with no education is 68 per cent. It decreases to 54 per cent for those with primary education and 41 per cent for those with secondary education. In Niger, the incidence of poverty is 70 per cent in households headed by an adult with no education, compared to 56 per cent for those who have attended primary school. In Bangladesh, the average salary of secondary educated woman is seven times that of a woman with no primary education. In India, one year increase in average number of years of primary schooling of the workforce would raise outputs by 23 per cent.

India has undoubtedly been successful in evolving a national structure for elementary education in the last 50 years. National literacy rates have improved from 15 per cent in 1951 to 52 per cent in 1991 to 65.38 per cent in 2001. Rajasthan's literacy levels increased from 38.55 per cent in 1991 to 61.03 per cent in 2001. While doubling the female literacy rates, during this decade, the male literacy rates touched the 75.49 per cent mark. The sprawling academic support system has been built up at national and state level through NCERT, NIEPA, NCTE, SCERTs, CIEMATs, DIETs, BRCS and CRCs to provide technical support and guidance to the elementary education system. The initiation of market mechanism in economic and adoption of an integrated approach by the government to poverty alleviation has been some of the key reasons for growth. Though literacy has enabled rural poor to acquaint themselves with technical skills necessary for increasing their income and thus, reducing the incidence of poverty.

Decentralised education planning, improving the quality of basic education and adjusting the structure of education system to local needs has had a positive impact on poverty situation in the country. Further, community participation and mobilising the communities to take responsibility for ensuring quality education for every child is the core strategy of new initiatives like DPEP, LJP, SKP, and BEB. Many of the state and local governments have taken up elementary education programmes vigorously. Kerala's success in alleviating absolute poverty has been well recognised.

Poverty and deprivation indication such as HDI when taken in the national context, have been at par with most industrialised countries of South East Asia and far higher than those at the national levels. While noting the substantial contribution of the Kerala Government in absorbing household consumption of the poor, through direct subsidies and indirect income transfers, a key explanation of the relatively low level of poverty has been the popular demand for literacy and education in the state. The Rajasthan government has launched recently in November, 2001, "Shiksha Aap Ke Dwar" with the objective of bringing all the children (10.65 lakh) of 32 districts in age group of 6-14 in the fold of education and considerable success (70 per cent) has been achieved so far.

The plan allocations for elementary education has increased steadily and the Central Government increased its allocations for elementary education after 1976 when education became a concurrent subject. Plan expenditure on elementary education has increased to nearly 50 per cent of the central expenditure on education. The external assistance and internationally assisted projects too have given priority to low literacy areas, girls and disadvantaged sections, with a view to their capacity building in making them productive and useful members of society. Though many factors have contributed in changing the country from "poor house to powerhouse", investment in education and more education is probably the most important of all. The enhanced budget allocations have resulted in an amazing picture of access to learners at all levels. The implicit social and personal benefits to individuals also should be reckoned with, as even the modest level of education is most effective contraceptive and passport to better health and a road to empowerment.

The future strategies for poverty alleviation need to take care of practical skill training reforms in the education system, popularisation of science and technology and its application in vocational and technical education, gender awareness, women's needs and linked issues, environmental education, entrepreneurship development, NGOs and community participation and participatory approaches on a continuous basis to combat and contain the tentacles of poverty. Education and HRD alone are the key for India becoming a super power in this century.

In India, Universalisation of Elementary Education (UEE) has been recognised as a crucial input for nation building since independence. The founding fathers of our Constitution had given a prominent place to educational endeavours when they made a provision for free and compulsory education for children up to 14 years of age within a period of 10 years in the Directive principles of State Policy. However, this goal has proved elusive so far. Our inability to achieve this goal 36 years after the target date has been a cause for serious concern within the country and in international fora. Our failure to achieve UEE has resulted in a number of interconnected problems like the population explosion, prevalence of unacceptable levels of poverty, unemployment and disease, one of the largest adult illiterate populations in the world; and lack of adequate skilled manpower to achieve our economic goals.

According to the Department of Education, the proposal to amend the Constitution to make the right to free education, a Fundamental Right and provision of opportunities for education for children up to 14 years of age a fundamental duty of the citizens of India, is expected to provide the desired momentum to the efforts being made in the country to achieve UEE by 2000 AD. It is expected to stimulate Central and State Governments to meet the special needs of under-served and unserved populations and regions.

The Department of Education have stated that the thrust of the Central and State Governments in Universalisation of Elementary Education (UEE) has been on Universal access, universal participation, universal retention and universal achievement. The Committee is, however, constrained to note that notwithstanding these achievements, the task of UEE is far from complete. There are several gender, regional, sectional and caste disparities in provision of elementary education. Even after 50 years of Independence, a very large segment of children of school-going age still remains out of school. It is a tragic state of affairs that only two-third of those who join school complete primary schooling and only half complete upper primary schooling.

A significant proportion of children drop-out from school before completing their studies due to socio-economic and cultural factors. Lack of basic amenities, shortage and absenteeism of teachers, non-availability of teaching learning materials and a curriculum which is not fully related to local needs are equally responsible for the ever increasing drop-out problem. Not only this, studies have revealed low achievement levels in primary school even in States which are considered educationally advanced.

The Department in the written note stated that the Supreme Court in its judgement in Unni Krishnan J.P. Vs. Andhra Pradesh, 1993, has held that children of this country have a Fundamental Right to free education until they complete the age of 14 years. According to the Supreme Court, this right flows from Article 21 relating to protection of life and personal liberty and its contents and parameters have to be determined in the light of Article 41 which provides for right to work, to education and to public assistance in certain cases and Article 45 which provides for free and compulsory education to children up to the age of 14 years. The apex court has observed that the obligation created by these Articles of the Constitution can be discharged by the State either by establishing institutions of its own or by aiding, recognising and granting affiliation to educational institutions. It was further stated that the Saikia Committee recommended that the Constitution of India should be amended to make the right to free elementary education up to 14 years of age a fundamental right.

Many people expert in education who have submitted a written memoranda to the Committee, have welcomed the proposal of the Government. They are, however, against deletion of Article 45. They felt that there could be a simple fundamental right in the proposed Article 21 (A) and Article 45 can be retained. On these doubts expressed by several educational experts as to whether it is wise to delete Article 45, the Secretary, Education stated that the Law Ministry advised that after it is converted into Fundamental Right, Article 45 becomes redundant, and they went by the advice of the Law Ministry.

Article 45, lays down that every child up to the age of 14 years shall receive free and compulsory education. The proposed article 21 (A) lays down that the State shall provide free and compulsory education to all citizens of the age of 6-14 years. Many people in the written memoranda have opposed the proposal of restricting the age limit for providing free compulsory education between 6 to 14 years of age. According to them Article 45 which is sought to be deleted, was framed by the founding fathers to provide education to children up to the age of 14 years without mention of lower limit and deletion of article 45 without simultaneously making a provision for the education of children under 6 years will be tantamount to taking away the rights sought to be given to this age group by the founding fathers.

As regards limiting the age at 14 year also, many representationists expressed the view that it should be increased from 14 to either 16 or 18. The general feeling was that at the time of framing of article 45, the formal certification of school education was at standard 7th and the founding fathers had set the limits of free and compulsory education for the child one year beyond the age at which standard 7th could be completed. However in the present scenario, a child can finish education up to standard 8th within the age of 6 - 14 years and no more. The current educational pattern have no formal certification of completion of school studies until the successful completion of standard 10th. This means that the child who cannot afford education except when it is free will have to discontinue her/his education before formal certification. This closes further avenues of learning or employment. It was, therefore, prayed that the age limit should be increased up to 16 years.

On this the Secretary, Education stated that the Department, after agonising over this issue for a very long time, thought that though this issue could not be ignored, but while coming to a situation where it becomes as justiciable fundamental right, what is possibly enforceable is the age-group i.e. after 6 years when one enters into a formal system. Prior to that, it is very essential, very necessary, but it is entirely a different exercise and a big problem as to how it can be converted into a structure, pattern under which it can be enforced as a fundamental right.

It was informed by the Department of Education to the Committee that the Constitutional amendments to make elementary education a Fundamental Right enforceable against the State and a Fundamental Duty of parents would need to be backed by suitable statutory measures for making elementary education compulsory. At present there is no Central Legislation, making elementary education compulsory. About having a Central Legislation, the Secretary stated that the question was debated extensively by the Committee of Ministers. The Committee of Ministers, after some discussions, came to the conclusion that in this land of enormous diversity, it would be, perhaps, undesirable to go in for a Central Legislation which may not be able to take care of the requirements and specific needs of the State. The consensus was clearly in favour of State legislation, he added.

Most of the experts were of the view that the term 'free' needs to be clearly defined. They felt that it should not mean a mere non-payment of fees but should also include one meal, books notebooks/Slates, medical assistance, transport where needed and above all guaranteed presence of teacher and a school. The Committee was given to understand that free education, so far, has been equated with the exemption of tuition fees which is negligible in the case of students in primary and upper primary schools run by Government and local bodies, the consensus which emerged was that there should be, at least, free tuition up to the primary stage, for both boys and girls. If certain States are in a position to provide additional incentives, they can do it. But in so far as the common understanding is concerned, the minimum is, up to the primary level, free tuition and free books, he added. As regards the question of providing free stationery, he clarified that there was no clear consensus.

One of the main apprehensions voiced by the eminent educationists was that the State cannot provide a fundamental right to compulsory education. Only a right to education can be provided. The Secretary Education clarified that the compulsion more or less, is being looked at as compulsion of the State Government to provide basic facilities which the Government must provide.

Clause (3) of the proposed Article 21 provides that the State shall not make any law for free and compulsory education under clause (2), in relation to the educational institutions not maintained by the State or not receiving aid out of State funds. However, strong apprehensions were voiced about clause (3) of the proposed new Article 21 A. Many of the people in the written memoranda and also educational experts in the oral evidence have expressed displeasure over keeping the private educational institutions outside the purview of the fundamental right to be given to the children.

The Secretary, stated that the Supreme Court in the Unni Krishnan judgement said that wherever the State is not providing any aid to any institution, such as institution need not provide free education. The Department took into account the Supreme Court judgement in the Unni Krishnan case which laid down that no private institution, can be compelled to provide free services. Therefore, they provided in the Constitutional amendment that this concept of free education need not be extended to schools or institutions which are not aided by the

Government, the Secretary added. He, however, stated that there was no intention, to exclude them from the overall responsibility to provide education.

The total additional financial requirement estimated to be incurred to Rs. 7,200.00 crore per annum in case the fundamental right to elementary education is operationalised. Some educationists felt that the amount may increase. But they suggested that if all irrelevant and non-priority wasteful expenditure on elementary education can be done away with, it will be possible to fulfil the commitment.

The eminent Educationists felt that the bill is silent on the Quality of Education. They suggested that there should be a reference to quality of education in the Bill. The Secretary, Education agreed that the quality aspect also has to be seen. Education definitely must mean quality education and anything less than that should not be called education. Therefore, the emphasis would be through strengthening the teacher education content, the Secretary stated.

The proposed insertion of Article 51 A, provides for a fundamental duty of every citizen who is a parent or guardian to provide opportunities for education to all children upto 14 years of age. Apprehensions have been expressed by the educationists that compulsion on parents as a result of this Article would pose major problem, particularly for those parents who ostensibly cannot afford to send their children to school. Defaulting parents would be subject to considerable harassment resulting in widespread resentment among the general population.

The Secretary, Education, on being asked to comment on this, informed the Committee that the Constitutional amendment as such is not talking about penalising the parents. But there are already certain existing State legislations in different States which do have penal provision. When this issue came up before the Saikia Committee, they took the view that the emphasis should be on the motivation of parents. But, in an extreme case, where there are aberrations, a penalty should be resorted to as a last resort. But, there again, the Saikia Committee felt that instead of bringing it under the provisions of the Indian Penal Code, it should be taken to the court of society, the Secretary added.

PARLIAMENTARY STANDAING COMMITTEE REPORT ON COMPULSORY ELEMENTARY EDUCATION

XV OBSERVATIONS AND RECOMMENDATIONS

The Committee welcomes the initiative of the Government to make the right to free elementary education a Fundamental Right. It is indeed a welcome step. In spite of a large number of schemes taken up for universalisation of elementary education since independence, it is unfortunate that the country is still languishing with a sizeable number of illiterates. The high drop-out rate has resulted in total disarray in the implementation of the education programmes. Reasons for high drop-out rates are varied-social, economic, quality, lack of interest and lack of attraction can be cited as a few examples. It is unfortunate that the drop-our rate in 1996-97 in class I to V was as high as 39.37%. This explains the state of affairs obtaining in the country. The committee hopes that the amendment of the constitution to provide free education to children as a fundamental right would motivate both Governmental as well as non-Governmental sectors to take necessary measures so as to achieve universalisation of elementary education, the ultimate goal of the country. The committee welcomes the spirit behind the amendment and welcomes it in principle.

However, the committee feels that in the enthusiasm to provide this fundamental right, the quality of education should not be ignored. The education that is provided should be able to create attraction and interest among the children. The Committee understands that the National Policy on Education makes a reference to 'education of satisfactory quality' Quality is the most important aspect of education which should not be ignored. The Committee strongly feels that quality aspect has been totally forgotten and children who can afford are compelled to go to private institutions for better and quality education. There is, therefore, a necessity of improving the quality. For this, there is an urgent necessity to improve teacher training. In regard to the point as to whether there should be a reference to 'Quality' in the proposed amendment, the committee feels it appropriate to leave it to the Government to either make a reference to quality aspect in the proposed amendment or not. The committee, however, strongly recommends that all efforts should be directed towards providing quality education. Teacher training programmes are not very much oriented for effective utilisation of human resources. They do not give stress on techniques and activities that make learning joyful for students. Lack of follow up measures make them forget and not utilise whatever they had learnt during their pre-service training programmes. Without primary level teaching or research experience, particularly on rural schools, teacher educators are poorly prepared to educate. Most of the teacher educators imparting training in elementary teacher training institutions do not have primary level teaching/research experience. This affects the quality of training imparted by them. The methods of transaction of theory classes of these teacher educators are generally devoid of active teaching learning approaches. There is no specific teacher educator preparation programmes. Teacher educators also need continued assistance for their professional development. The UGC provides assistance for professional development of teacher educators in teacher training colleges and departments of education of universities. But such facilities are at present not available for elementary level teachers educators. The committee accordingly recommends that teacher training should be given sufficient importance and emphasis should be laid on improving the training component.

The committee takes note of the fact that the words compulsion and enforcement as proposed in Article 21 A do not go with the theme and spirit of the Fundamental Right. A right is not given in a spirit of enforcement. The Secretary's clarification that the compulsion is being looked at as compulsion on the part of the State Government, is an acceptable proposition. But it should be made amply clear in the proposed amendment to clear all doubts.

The Committee understands it well that with elementary education becoming a justiciable Fundamental Right, the possibility of increased litigation cannot be denied. The citizens would have every right to go the courts of law if their fundamental right is violated. The committee, therefore, urges upon the Government to find out ways and means to face this challenge.

The current education pattern has formal certification after the successful completion of standard 10th only. This, therefore, means that the children who cannot get education except when it is free, will have to discontinue their studies before formal certification, thus closing their further avenues of earning and employment. Thus, suggestions received by committee were either to extend the age-limit up to 16 years or certification may be issued at the end of Eighth standard. The committee, however, feels that increasing the age limit may not be a viable proposition because of enormous resources that are required and due to other compulsions of the Government. The Members discussed this at length. Many Members were of the opinion that it would not be appropriate to put such a heavy burden on the Government.

However, a child should be able to receive some sort of certificate so as to easily get a gainful employment. The committee, therefore, feels that the Government may introduce formal certification at the end of standard 8th to enable the children who come out of the school after 8th to join some gainful employment or pursue some technical vocational courses with the help of the certificate. Several Members, however, felt that it may not be advisable to introduce another Public examination.

As regards follow-up legislation, there are divergent views. Some Members of the Committee felt that there should be a separate central legislation providing for the basic structure and the details could be made out by the respective states. Whereas the others did not feel the necessity of a central legislation. The Secretary, stated that the central legislation may not be able to take care of the requirements and specific needs of the states. After a thorough discussion in this matter, the Committee feels that the Centre should not leave everything to the states. The Centre could make one simple legislation with some skeletal framework which may also indicate the Central share in the financial burden. The details can be formulated by the respective states according to their requirements. The Central Government may, therefore, consider working out the necessary legislation.

Imposition of penalties on parents is one aspect which has agitated the minds of the Members. The Committee agrees that the penal provision would lead to harassment of the parents. It is true that the proposed amendment does not talk of any penalty, but many states in their existing legislations have made penal provisions. Accordingly, the new follow up legislations may also have similar provisions. After considering the pros and cons of this, the committee strongly desires that such penal provisions on the parents should be avoided in the follow up legislation to be made. The Centre may make necessary provision to this effect either in the follow-up legislation or in the guidelines that may be issued to the States. The Committee feels that compulsion should be on State Governments to provide for essential facilities for UEE rather than on the parents, majority of whom are struggling for their survival.

Providing free education is another important aspect in the proposed Article 21 A (1). On this, the Committee takes note of the fact that the bill does not define free education. The Committee understands that there is confusion over the provision of free education. Many states are already providing free education, but the components vary from state to state. The Committee has noted that there is a general feeling that free education means exemption from payment of fees. The Members were, however, unanimous that free education should not confine just to exemption from payment of fees. The Committee desires that free education should also include various other components such as text-books, stationery, uniform, one meal and transportation wherever necessary etc. The Government may consider including all these components in the free education.

Financial implications is another important aspect of the Bill. In the Financial memorandum, the Committee has noted that the estimated financial expenditure to implement the obligation is forty thousand crores rupees every year. The Committee is constrained to note that the allocations, made to education every year have so far been very insufficient. From such a situation to go up to Rs. 40,000 crores, in the Ninth Plan is a gigantic task. The Committees strongly recommends that the required amount should be allocated to achieve the goal. Unless this is done, a mere constitutional amendment and providing a fundamental right is not going to serve the purpose. Besides increasing the allocation, Government may also take steps to reduce unnecessary expenditure to reduce unnecessary burden on the State's exchequer.

The Committee feels that financial burden may be shared by both the Centre and the States. Administrative responsibility should be left to states for implementation according to their convenience.

The proposed Article 21 A (1) provides that the State shall provide free and compulsory education to all citizens of the age of six to fourteen years. The Committee understands that there is a lot of controversy over the restriction of age limit of the children between 6 - 14 years of age. It is true that this provision seeks to take away the rights of children in the age group 0 - 6 years. The Committee is, however, aware that an infant's education in the age group 0-6 is an enormously complicated one. Much of the education imparted in this age group is non-formal through the mother and it is difficult to standardise it. It is all the more difficult to make a justiciable Fundamental Right.

The Committee is also aware that the Departments of Women & Child Development and Family Welfare are already working to take care of the requirements of the children in this age group. The controversy in this regard has arisen because Article 45 does not make any mention of age restriction whereas Article 21 A (1) seeks to restrict the age to 6-14 years. The proposal also includes deletion of article 45. As regards deletion of Article 45, the Committee deals with it in the succeeding paragraph. Due to various practical difficulties, the provision in the present Article may be allowed, providing for free education to children of 6 to 14 years in the fundamental right. But Directive Principles should be followed wherever possible.

Now, the Committee will deal with the proposal to delete Article 45. The Committee is not convinced by the reply of the Secretary, Education, that this has been done on the advice of the Law Ministry that after it is made a fundamental right, article 45 becomes redundant. The Directive Principles, of which Article 45 is a part, were incorporated in the Constitution with an objective of seeking to achieve the ideal of a democratic welfare state set out in the preamble. This also embodies of the State. They are directed towards the ideals of building a true welfare state.

Therefore, the Committee feels that by providing a fundamental right, the very philosophy of the Constitution which is embodied in the Directive Principle (Article 45) should not be removed. The purpose of a fundamental right is different from that of the Directive Principle. The Directive Principle is not merely a moral precept but is a positive mandate to the State. Article 45 provides a directive on the State to endeavour to provide free and compulsory education. No conflict should be seen between the Fundamental Right and Directive Principle. Both are complementary to each other.

Similarly, proposed Article 21 A seeks to provide Fundamental right to free and compulsory education to the citizens in the age group 6-14 at present. However, Article 45 seeks to provide free education to all up to the age of 14 years without any age restriction. Therefore, Article 45, besides, giving a directive on the state to provide free education and explain the object and philosophy of the Constitution, also takes care of the children in the age group 0-6 as well. In view of the forgoing conclusions, the Committee feels that Article 45 is required to be retained in the Constitution. The Government may, therefore, reconsider its proposal to delete Article 45.

Clause (3) of the proposed Article 21 (A) prohibits the State from making any law for free and compulsory education in relation to educational institutions not maintained by the State or not receiving aid out of state funds. This issue was discussed by the Members of the Committee at length. The Members were in agreement that even though the so called private institutions do not receive any financial aid, the children studying in those institutions should not be deprived of their fundamental right. As regards the interpretation as to whether the private institutions should provide free education or not, the Committee is aware of the Supreme Court Judgement given in the Unni Krishnan case. This judgement provides the rule for application and interpretation.

In view of the judgement, it is not necessary to make a clause in the Constitution. It would be appropriate to leave the interpretation to the courts instead of making a specific provision in black and white. Some Members, however, felt that the private institutions which do not get any financial aid, provide quality education. Therefore, it would be inappropriate to bring such institutions under the purview of free education. Those members, accordingly, felt that Clause (3) should not be deleted. The Committee, however, after a thorough discussion feels that this provision need not be there. The Committee recommends that clause (3) of the proposed Articles 21 (A) may be deleted

3

Expansion of Elementary Education

Since independence, the central and state governments have been expanding the provision of primary formal and non-formal education to realise the goal of Universilisation of Elementary Education (UEE). The challenge now is to sustain and deepen current reforms in education and encourage local planning and management of strategies for expanding and improving primary education. With a view to cushioning the impact of rising costs of text books and exercise books, the government has exempted writing and printing paper supplied to all State Text Book Corporations from excise duty. It is expected that this would make school text books more affordable for students from weaker sections of society.

Removal of systemic deficiencies in the implementation of UEE and forging ahead necessitates the creation of informed public opinion and a facilitative environment akin to that of the Total Literacy Campaign. This has to be achieved through effective and sustained advocacy, massive community mobilisation and consciousness building. With this perspective, a national programme of media publicity and advocacy has been planned. The programme will target:

i) teachers and all those involved in education of children;

ii) students and parents of students, particularly non-literate parents; and

iii) community opinion leaders.

The Kasturba Gandhi Shiksha Yojana, a programme to establish residential schools for girls in all the districts which have a particularly low female literacy rate has been announced. A sum of Rs. 2500 million has been provided in this year's budget. The central government has also decided to grant financial incentives and scholarships for the girl child born in families living below the poverty line.

Several central and state level initiatives have been in operation from the early 1980s. While the design of these projects vary substantially, all of them address the objectives and strategies of the National Policy on Education 1986. They pay special attention to increasing girls' enrolment, improving educational outcomes, strengthening community involvement, improving teaching and learning materials and providing in-service teacher training. The status of some of these initiatives are discussed below.

OPERATION BLACKBOARD

This scheme launched in 1987, is aimed at improving the school environment and enhancing retention and learning achievement of children by providing minimum essential facilities in all primary schools. The scheme has brought about a remarkable quantitative and qualitative improvement in primary education. In all, 523,000 primary schools have been covered as originally envisaged. These schools have been provided with central assistance

DECENTRALISATION

Decentralised planning and management of elementary education is a goal set by the National Policy on Education, 1986. The Policy visualises direct community involvement in the form of Village Education Committees (VECs) for management of elementary education. The POA, 1992, emphasised micro planning as a process of designing a family-wise and child-wise plan of action by which every child regularly attends school or NFE centre, continues his or her education at the place suitable to him/her and completes at least eight years of schooling or its equivalent at the NFE centre.

The 73rd and 74th constitutional amendments provide for decentralisation of the activities and facilitate transfer of power and participation of the local self-government institutions or the Panchayati Raj Institutions. It has created a congenial ambience for the PRIs to play a more dynamic and proactive role. States are expected to evolve institutional arrangements both in rural and urban areas for undertaking these activities. These structures have been providing voice to women, Scheduled Castes and Tribes, minorities, parents and educational functionaries. They have also, been delegated with responsibilities with regard to location and relocation of existing primary and upper schools on the basis of micro planning and school mapping. In this regard, decentralisation of school management to grassroots level bodies is an important policy initiative.

During the 8th plan period several innovative efforts hove been made under the ongoing projects to establish decentralisation. For instance, the District Primary Education Programme has shifted the planning mechanism from the state to the district level, and Lok Jumbish has gone one step further by assigning decision making processes to a block level committee. At the village level, a VEC has the main responsibility for community mobilisation, school mapping, micro planning, renovation and construction of school buildings and improvement of pedagogical curriculum. In fact, the VECs of Shiksha Karmi schools have been activated as a result of the Lok Jumbish programme.

Since 1993-94, the scheme has been expanded to cover upper primary schools. More then 47,000 upper primary schools have been granted central assistance of Rs. 40,000 each for purchase of teaching- learning materials. Also, primary schools with enrolment exceeding 100 have been augmented with a third teacher. A Special Orientation Programme for Primary Teachers (SOPT) to facilitate optimum utilisation of materials supplied has also been launched to cover all primary school teachers in the country. The total expenditure under the scheme from 1992-93 to 1995-96 has been Rs. 8,163 million. The outlay for 1996-97 is Rs. 2,910 million.

NATIONAL PROGRAMME OF NUTRITIONAL SUPPORT TO PRIMARY EDUCATION (SCHOOL MEAL PROGRAMME)

This scheme was launched on 15 August, 1995 to give a boost to UEE in terms of increasing enrolment, retention and attendance in primary classes by supplementing nutritional requirements of children attending primary schools. It is an ambitious scheme that has been operationalised throughout the country in a very short period. The programme envisages provision of nutritious and wholesome cooked meal of 100 gms of food grains per school day, free of cost, to all children in classes I-V by 1997-98.

During 1995-96, 378 districts, 225,000 schools and 33.5 million children have been covered with an expenditure of Rs. 4,412 million. In 1996-97, the scheme was extended to cover 55.4 million children with an expenditure of Rs. 8,110 million. The scheme has become fully operational in 1997-98 covering nearly 110 million children in primary classes. A positive impact on school enrolment and retention has been reported.

District Primary Education Programme

The DPEP launched in November, 1994 is conceived as a beachhead for overhauling the primary education system in India. The programme aims at operationalising the strategies for achieving UEE through district specific planning and disaggregated target setting. It draws upon the accumulated national experience of several state level initiatives that were started earlier. It moves away from the schematic piecemeal approach of the earlier programmes and takes a holistic view of primary education with emphasis on decentralised management, community mobilisation and district specific planning based on contextually and research based inputs.

The basic objectives of DPEP are:

— To provide all children with access to primary education either in the formal system or through the non-formal education (NFE) programme.

— To reduce differences in enrolment, dropout rates and learning achievement among gender and social groups to less than 5%.

— To reduce overall primary dropout rates for all students to less than 10%.

— To raise average achievement levels by at least 25% over measured base line levels and ensuring achievements of basic literacy and numeracy competencies and a minimum of 40% achievement levels in other competencies by all primary school children.

The Government of India finances 85 % of the project cost as a grant to the DPEP State Implementation Societies and the concerned state government provides the rest. The central government's share is resourced by external funding. As of now, IDA has approved credit amounting to $260 million and $425 million under Phase-I and Phase-II respectively. The European Union (EU) is providing a grant of 150 million ECU. The ODA (UK) is extending a grant of $80.21 million. The grant from the Netherlands amounts to $25.8 million.

The first phase of the programme was launched in 42 districts in the states of Assam, Haryana, Karnataka, Kerala, Maharashtra, Tamilnadu and Madhya Pradesh. In the second phase, the programme has been launched in 80 districts of Orissa, Himachal Pradesh, Andhra Pradesh, West Bengal, Uttar Pradesh and Gujarat and in Phase I States.

DPEP has been able to set up project management structures at district, state and national levels, create the environment and capacity for micro planning, take up the challenge of pedagogical innovation, create a responsive institutional base which includes both government and non-government institutions, enhance community participation and strengthen the process of catering to special focus groups such as tribals, scheduled castes, women and other marginalised sections.

The first phase of the programme is under evaluation. The initial trends of impact studies are very positive. DPEP has made a decisive impact on increasing enrolment, reducing repetition rates and improving class room processes.

While the DPEP has been targeting backward districts with female literacy below the national average and where TLCs have stirred up a demand for elementary education, several state level initiatives have shown tremendous potential. These are directed at improving literacy levels in the five low literacy states of Andhra Pradesh, Bihar, Uttar Pradesh, Madhya Pradesh and Rajasthan.

Bihar Education Project

Bihar Education Project (BEP) was launched in 1991 with the express purpose of bringing about quantitative and qualitative improvement in the elementary system in Bihar. The project lays emphasis on the education of deprived sections of society, such as SCs, STs and women. Participatory planning and implementation are crucial ingredients of the project.

A midterm review highlighted certain major achievements such as: a) a strong Mahila Samakhya component; b) organisation of VECs and community involvement in programme implementation at grassroots level; and c) non-formal education through NGOs. The review suggested:

— consolidation of the programme in the existing seven districts,

— establishing strong linkages between BEP and the education system in Bihar,

— giving greater focus to the primary stage of classes I-V,

— building better linkages with the activities in other states under DPEP and other programmes,

— providing more emphasis to MLLs and teacher training, and conducting periodic base line studies.

It has now been decided to extend the project to the second phase of two years duration. The total outlay for the second phase (1996-98) is estimated to be Rs. 613 million to be shared between UNICEF, Government of India and Government of Bihar as per the existing funding formula of 3:2:1. The total project outlay for BEP is Rs. 3600 million. It is proposed to merge the project with DPEP during the next five years.

Uttar Pradesh Basic Education Programme

A project "Education for All" prepared by the Government of Uttar Pradesh was approved by The World Bank in June, 1993. The project is currently in operation in 12 districts. It is planned to expand the coverage to 15 districts under DPEP-II. It has an outlay of Rs. 7,288 million spread over seven years. International Development Agency (IDA), the soft loan window of The World Bank, would provide a credit of US$163.1 million and the state government's share would be approximately 13 per cent of the total project cost.

The progress of implementation of the project so far has been satisfactory. The construction work of schools and Block Resource Centres is being completed as per schedule. Training materials for teacher trainers on DIETs have been prepared. The first cycle of in- service teacher training was completed in October, 1995. About 40,000 teachers have been trained.

Community Mobilisation and Participation

Many educational innovations of recent years are based on the strong foundation of community support and participation. When progress is discussed and analysed of different levels within the project, "people's acceptance and participation" is used as an indicator.

Mobilising the village community to take responsibility to ensure quality education for every child, is the core strategy of both Lok Jumbish (LJ) and Shikhsa Karmi Project (SKP) in their efforts to universalise primary education and deliver quality education. It would not be far removed from truth if we say that community involvement has been the key factor for the success of the two projects.

LJ has had a positive effect on the empowerment of locally elected people, especially on female representatives at village level, who are often active members of the LJ core teams or women's groups. The Village Education Committees (VECs), carefully formed and trained though environmental building activities in the LJ programme, are actively involved in school matters.

SKP has constituted VECs in 2000 villages to promote community involvement in primary education and encourage village level planning. The role of the VEC is to mobilise resources for maintenance, repair and construction of school infrastructure. The VEC also helps in determining the school calendar and school timings in consultation with the local community and Shiksha Karmis (educational workers).

The positive impact of the LJ and SKP, focusing on supporting the teachers and the students by involving, the village community in taking responsibility for all educational activities of the village school, is serving as a demonstration of how deeply rooted problems of education in India can be addressed. Wide dissemination of these innovative approaches could inspire other educational programmes all over India and the world.

Andhra Pradesh Primary Education Project

The Andhra Pradesh Primary Education Project (APPEP), practised in the south central state of Andhra Pradesh, with a female literacy of just 34 %, adopts a two-pronged strategy of improving classroom transaction by training teachers and giving a fillip to school construction activities. The project has trained an estimated 80,000 teachers in 23 districts and more than 3,000 teaching centres have become operational. The project is assisted by the ODA with an estimated outlay of Rs. 1,000 million in the 8th Plan.

Shiksha Karmi Project

The Shiksha Karmi Project (SKP) is being implemented since 1987, with assistance from the Swedish International Development Cooperation Agency (SIDA). The project aims at universalisation and qualitative improvement of primary education in the remote and socio-economically backward villages of Rajasthan, with primary focus on girls. Since teacher absenteeism has been found to be a major obstacle in achieving the objective of UEE, the project uses the novel approach of substituting teachers in dysfunctional schools with local youth known as Shiksha Karmis who are provided with rigorous training and supervisory support. An important feature of this innovative project is the mobilisation and participation of the community in improving the functioning of primary schools.

The project is being implemented as an externally aided scheme with reimbursement of 90 % in Phase I and 50 % in Phase II, from SIDA. The project, with an outlay of around Rs.212 million in Phase I and Rs.490 million in Phase II, places strong emphasis on vigorous and continuous in-service training.

The SKP also runs non-formal classes called Prehar Pathshalas-schools of convenient timings. For girls' education, Angan Pathshalas are being run in three blocks. The programme at present covers over 150,000 students in 1,785 schools and 3,520 Prehar Pathshalas, involving over 4,271 Shiksha Karmis.

The project is known for its open participative style and continuous experimentation to achieve its objectives. The approach, strategies and achievements of the SKP have attracted national and international recognition. The project is slated for a major expansion with SIDA assistance in the 9th Plan. The total projections for the 9th Plan are estimated to be Rs. 4260 million.

Lok Jumbish Project

Barely five years old, Lok Jumbish (LJ) has made an indelible impression in the primary education landscape of Rajasthan. The coverage of the project has extended to 75 blocks, covering a population of approximately 12 million. Significantly, it has also achieved a major breakthrough in welding together government agencies, teachers, NGOs, elected representatives and the people into an interactive group effort to promote universalisation of primary education.

The seven guiding principles of Lok Jumbish are:

— a process rather than a product approach;

— partnerships;

— decentralised functioning;

— participatory learning;

— integration with the mainstream education system;

— flexibility of management; and

— creating multiple levels of leadership committed to quality and mission mode.

Special focus has been given to environment building in all training programmes under LJ. This helps in the development of an understanding about issues involved in people's mobilisation, use of different media forms and clarity about the messages to be given to the people.

The first phase of the project was for a period of two years from 1992-94, with the expenditure shared between SIDA, Government of India and Government of Rajasthan in the ratio 3:2:1. The second phase stretches up to 1998, with the sharing modality remaining the same. The allocation for LJP is Rs.1100 million for Phases I and II and Rs.4000 million for Phase III. A Norwegian grant of Rs. 200 million is also available.

Literacy

About 4.5 crore learners have acquired the threshold level of literacy under various Total Literacy Campaigns. The literacy rate today is 52.19% as against 18.33 % in 1951. Elementary education has been made a fundamental right in order to deal with the root cause of illiteracy. Female illiteracy continues to be a problem. To deal with this a special programme set up schools in areas with very low literacy has been launched. The Government has decided to increase the allocation to Education to 6% of the GOP as against 3.7% at present.

One of the directive principles of State Policy as enunciated in the Constitution of India is to promote the welfare of the people and to achieve this, the State Government have to undertake planned development in the State through the various Five Year Plans and Annual Plans. To help the Government to implement its policies effectively by more efficient utilization of the material, capital and human resources within the State and outside, the State Planning Commission was first constituted in Tamil Nadu on 25th May 1971, with the Chief Minister as Chairman, and a senior Government official as Deputy Chairman, an Economist as a Full Time Member and a few Experts/industrialists as Part Time Members. The State Planning Commission is an Advisory Body and make its recommendations to the Cabinet. The responsibility for taking and implementing policy decisions will rest with the Government.

Education in Ninth Five Year Plan (1997-2002)

Human Development will receive priority attention in the Plan. Focus will be on universal, qualitative and free primary education. Education will be made available in all hamlets for a population of 500 and above and within a distance of one Km. State will have 100 percent literacy coverage by end of the Plan. Ninth Plan will lay emphasis on qualitative multi-skill education system in general and universal education upto 14 years of age in particular. The users of technical and higher education viz., Industry, Trade, Commerce and Agriculture will be involved in the expansion of such educational facilities.

4

NATIONAL POLICY ON EDUCATION (NPE), 1986

PART I

INTRODUCTORY

1.1 Education has continued to evolve, diversify and extend its reach and coverage since the dawn of human history. Every country develops its system of education to express and promote its unique sociocultural identity and also to meet the challenges of the times. There are moments in history when a new direction has to be given to an age-old process. That moment is today.

1.2 The country has reached a stage in its economic and technical development when a major effort must be made to derive the maximum benefit from the assets already created and to ensure that the fruits of change reach all sections. Education is the highway to that goal.

1.3 With this aim ill view, the Government of India announced in January 1985 that a new Education Policy would be formulated for the country. A comprehensive appraisal of the existing educational scene was made, followed by a countrywide debate. The views and suggestions received from different quarters were carefully studied.

The 1968 Education Policy and After

1.4 The National Policy of 1968 marked a significant step in the history of' education In post-independence India. It aimed to promote national progress, a sense, a sense of common citizenship and culture, and to strengthen national integration. It laid stress on the need for a radical reconstruction of the education system, to improve its quality at all stages, and gave much greater attention to science and technology, the cultivation of moral values and a closer relation between education and the life of the people.

1.5 Since the adoption of the 1968 policy, there has been considerable expansion in educational facilities all over the country at all levels. More than 90 per cent of the country's rural habitations now have schooling facilities within a radius of one kilometer. There has been sizable augmentation of facilities at other stages also.

1.6 Perhaps the most notable development has been the acceptance of a common structure of education throughout the country and the introduction on the 10 + 2 + 3 system by most States. In the school curricula, in addition to laying down a common scheme of studies for boys and girls, science and mathematics were incorporated as compulsory subjects and work experience assigned a place of importance.

1.7 A beginning was also made in restructuring of courses at the undergraduate level. Centres of Advanced Studies were set up for post-graduate education and research. And we have been able to meet our requirements of educated manpower.

1.8 While these achievements are impressive by themselves, the general formulations incorporated in the 1968 Policy did not, however, get translated into a detailed strategy of implementation, accompanied by the assignment of specific responsibilities and financial and organisational support. As a result, pro͡blems of access, quality, quantity, utility and financial outlay, accumulated over the years, have now assumed such massive proportions that they must be tackled with the utmost urgency.

1.9 Education in India stands at the cross roads today. Neither normal linear expansion nor the existing pace and nature of improvement can meet the needs of the situation.

1.10 In the Indian way of thinking, a human being is a positive asset and precious national resource which needs to he cherished, nurtured and developed with tenderness and care, coupled with dynamism. Each individual's growth presents a different range of problems and requirements, at every stage from the womb to the tomb. The catalytic action of education in this complex and dynamic growth process needs to be planned meticulously and executed with great sensitivity.

1.11 India's political and social life is passing through a phase which poses the danger of erosion to long-accepted values. The goals of secularism, socialism, democracy and professional ethics are coming under increasing strain.

1.12 The rural areas, with poor infrastructure and social services, will not get the benefit of trained and educated youth, unless rural-urban disparities are reduced and determined measures are taken to promote diversification and dispersal of employment opportunities.

1.13 The growth of our population needs to be brought down significantly order the coming decades. The largest single factor that could help to achieve this is the spread of literacy and education among women.

1.14 Life in the coming decades is likely to bring new tensions together with unprecedented opportunities. To enable the people to benefit in the new environment will require new designs of human resource development. The coming generations should have the ability to internalise new ideas constantly and creatively. They have to be imbued with a strong commitment to humane values and to social justice. All this implies better education.

1.15 Besides, a variety of new challenges and social needs make it imperative for the Government to formulate and implement a new Education Policy for the country. Nothing short of this will meet the situation.

PART II

THE ESSENCE AND ROLE OF EDUCATION

2.1 In our national perception education is essentially for all. This is fundamental to our all-round development, material and spiritual.

2.2 Education has an acculturating role. It refines sensitivities and perceptions that contribute to national cohesion, a scientific temper and independence of mind and spirit-thus furthering the goals of socialism, secularism and democracy enshrined in our Constitution.

2.3 Education develops manpower for different levels of the economy. It is also the substrata on which research and development flourish, being the ultimate guarantee of national self-reliance.

2.4 In sum, education is a unique investment in the present and file future. This cardinal principle is the key to the National Policy on Education.

PART III

NATIONAL SYSTEM OF EDUCATION

3.1 The Constitution embodies the principles on which the National System of Education is conceived of.

3.2 The concept of a National System of Education implies that, tip to a given level, all students, irrespective of caste, creed, location or sex, have access to education of a comparable quality. To achieve this, the Government will initiate appropriately funded programmes. Effective measures will be taken in the direction of the Common School System recommended in the 1968 policy.

3.3 The National System of Education envisages a common educational structure. The 10+2+3 structure has now been accepted in all parts of the country. Regarding the further break-up of the first 10 years efforts will be made to move towards an elementary system comprising 5 years of primary education and 3 years of upper primary, followed by 2 years of high school.

3.4 The National System of Education will be based on a national curricular framework which contains a common core along with other components that are flexible. The common core will include the history of India's freedom movement, the constitutional obligations and other content essential to nurture national identity. These elements will cut across subject areas and will be designed to promote values such as India's common Cultural heritage, egalitarianism, democracy and secularism, equality of the sexes, protection of the environment, removal of social barriers, observance of the small family norm and inculcation of the scientific temper. All educational programmes will be carried on in strict conformity with secular values.

3.5 India has always worked for peace and understanding between nations, treating the whole world as one family. True to this hoary tradition, Education has to strengthen this world view and motivate the younger generations for international cooperation and peaceful coexistence. This aspect cannot be neglected.

3.6 To promote equality, it will be necessary to provide for equal opportunity to all not only in access, but also in the conditions for success. Besides, awareness of the inherent equality of all will be created through the core curriculum.

The purpose is to remove prejudices and complexes transmitted through the social environment and the accident of birth.

3.7 Minimum levels of learning will be laid down for each stage of education. Steps will also be taken to foster among students an understanding of the diverse cultural and social systems of the people living in different parts of the country. Besides the promotion of the link language, programmes will also be launched to increase substantially the translation of books from one language to another and to publish multilingual dictionaries and glossaries. The young will be encouraged to undertake the rediscovery of India, each in his own image and perception.

3.8 In higher education in general, and technical education in particular, steps will be taken to facilitate inter-regional mobility by providing equal access to every Indian of requisite merit, regardless of his origins. The universal character of universities and other institutions of higher education is to be underscored.

3.9 In the areas of research and development, and education in science and technology, special measures will be taken to establish network arrangements between different institutions in the country to pool their resources and participate in projects of national importance.

3.10 The Nation as a whole will assume the responsibility of providing resource support for implementing programmes of educational transformation, reducing disparities, universalisation of elementary education, adult literacy, scientific and technological research, etc.

3.11 Life-long education is a cherished goal of the educational process. This presupposes universal literacy. Opportunities will be provided to the youth, house-wives, agricultural and industrial workers and professionals to continue the education of their choice, at the pace suited to them. The future thrust will be in the direction of open and distance learning.

3.12 The institutions which will be strengthened to play an important role in giving shape to the National System of Education are the University Grants Commission, the All India Council of Technical Education, the Indian Council of Agricultural Research and the Indian Medical Council. Integrated planning will be instituted among all these bodies so as to establish functional linkages and reinforce programmes of research and postgraduate education. These, together with the National Council of Educational Research and Training, the National Institute of Educational Planning and Administration and the International Institute of Science and Technology Education will be involved in implementing the Education Policy.

A Meaningful Partnership

3.13 The Constitutional Amendment of 1976, which includes Education in the Concurrent List, was a far-reaching step whose implications—substantive, financial and administrative—require a new sharing of responsibility between the Union Government and the State in respect of this vital area of national life. While the role and responsibility of the States in regard to education will remain essentially unchanged, the Union Government would accept a larger responsibility to reinforce the national and integrative character of education, to maintain quality and standards (including those of the teaching profession at all levels), to study and monitor the educational requirements of the country, as a whole in regard to manpower for development, to cater to the needs of research and advanced study, to look after the international aspects of' education, culture and Human Resource Development and, in general, to promote excellence at all levels of the educational pyramid throughout the country. Concurrency signifies a partnership which is at once meaningful and challenging; the National Policy will be oriented towards giving effect to it in letter and spirit.

PART IV

EDUCATION FOR EQUALITY

Disparities

4.1 The new policy will lay special emphasis on the removal of disparities and to equalise educational opportunity by attending to the specific needs of those who have been denied equality so far.

Education For Women's Equality

4.2 Education will be used as an agent of basic change in the status of women. In order to neutralise the accumulated distortions of the past, there will be a well-conceived edge in favour of women. The National Education System will play a positive, interventionist role in the empowerment of women. It will foster the development of new values through redesigned curricula, textbooks, the training and orientation of teachers, decision-makers and administrators, and the active involvement of educational institutions. This will be an act of faith and social engineering. Women's studies will be promoted as a part of various courses and educational institutions encouraged to take up active programmes to further women's development.

4.3 The removal of women's illiteracy and obstacles inhibiting their access to, and retention in, elementary education will receive overriding priority, through provision of special support services, setting of time targets, and effective monitoring. Major emphasis will be laid on women's participation in vocational, technical and professional education at different levels. The policy of non-discrimination will be pursued vigorously to eliminate sex stereotyping in vocational and professional courses and to promote women's participation in non-traditional occupations, as well as in existing and emergent technologies.

The Education of Scheduled Castes

4.4 The central focus in the SCs' educational development is their equalisation with the non-SC population at all stages and levels of education, in all areas and in all the four dimensions—rural male, rural female, urban male and urban females.

4.5 The measures contemplated for this purpose include:

i) Incentives to indigent families to send their children to school regularly till they reach the age of 14;

ii) Pre-matric scholarship scheme for children of families engaged in occupations such as scavenging, flaying and tanning to be made applicable from Class I onwards. All children of such families, regardless of incomes, will be covered by this scheme and time-bound programmes targeted on them will be undertaken;

iii) Constant micro-planning and verification to ensure that the enrolment, retention and successful completion of courses by SC students do not fall at any stage, and provision of remedial courses to improve their prospects for further education and employment.

iv) Recruitment of teachers from Scheduled Castes;

v) Provision of facilities for SC students in students' hostels at district headquarters, according to a pha ?d programme;

vi) Location of school buildings, Balwadis and Adult Education Centres in such a way as to facilitate full participation of the Scheduled Castes;

vii) The utilisation of NREP and RLEGP resources so as to make substantial educational facilities available to the Scheduled Castes; and

viii) Constant innovation in finding new methods to increase the participation of the Scheduled Castes in the educational process.

The Education of Scheduled Tribes

4.6 The following measures will be taken urgently to bring the Scheduled Tribes on par with others:

i) Priority will be accorded to opening primary schools in tribal areas. The construction of school building will be undertaken in these areas on a priority basis under the normal funds for education, as well as under the NEEP, RLEGP, Tribal Welfare Schemes, etc.

ii) The socio-cultural milieu of the STs has its distinctive characteristics including, in many cases, their own spoken languages. This underlines the need to develop the curricula and devise instructional materials in tribal languages at the initial stages, with arrangements for switching over to the regional language.

iii) Educated and promising Scheduled Tribe youths will be encouraged and trained to take up teaching in tribal areas.

iv) Residential schools, including Ashram Schools, will be established on a large scale.

v) Incentive schemes will be formulated for the Scheduled Tribes, keeping in view their special needs and life styles. Scholarships for higher education will emphasise technical, professional and para-professional courses. Special remedial courses and other programmes to remove psycho-social impediments will be provided to improve their performances in various courses.

vi) Anganwadis, Non-formal and Adult Education Centres will be opened on a priority basis in areas predominantly inhabited by the Scheduled Tribes.

vii) The curriculum at all stages of education will be designed to create an awareness of the rich cultural identity of the tribal people as also of their enormous creative talent.

Other Educationally Backward Sections and Areas

4.7 Suitable incentives will be provided to all educationally backward sections of society, particularly in the rural areas. Hill and desert districts, remote and inaccessible areas and islands will be provided adequate institutional infrastructure.

Minorities

4.8 Some minority groups are educationally deprived or backward. Greater attention will be paid to the education of these groups in the interests of equality and social justice. This will naturally include the Constitutional guarantees given to them to establish and administer their own educational institutions, and protection to their languages and culture. Simultaneously, objectivity will be reflected in the, preparation of textbooks and in all school activities, and all possible measures will be taken to promote an integration based on appreciation of common national goals and ideals, in conformity with the core curriculum.

The Handicapped

4.9 The objective should be to integrate the physically and mentally handicapped with the general community as equal partners, to prepare them for normal growth and to enable them to face life with courage and confidence. The following measures will be taken in this regard:

i) Wherever it is feasible, the education of children with motor handicaps and other mild handicaps will be common with that of others.

ii) Special schools with hostels will be provided, as far as possible at district headquarters, for the severely handicapped children.

iii) Adequate arrangements will be made to give vocational training to the disabled.

iv) Teacher's training programme will be re-oriented, in particular for teachers of primary classes, to deal with the special difficulties of the handicapped children; and

v) Voluntary effort for the education of the disabled will be encouraged in every possible manner.

Adult Education

4.10 Our ancient scriptures define education as that which liberates i.e., provides the instruments for liberation from ignorance and oppression. In the modern world, it would naturally include the ability to read and write, since that is the main instrument of learning. Hence the crucial importance of adult education, including adult literacy.

4.11 The critical development issue today is the continuous upgradation of skills so as to produce manpower resources of the kind and the number required by the society. Since participation by beneficiaries in the development programmes is of crucial importance, systematic programmes of adult education linked with national goals such as alleviation of poverty, national integration, environmental conservation, energisation of the cultural creativity of the people, observance of small family norm, promotion of women's equality, etc. will be organised and the existing programmes reviewed and strengthened.

4.12 The whole nation must pledge itself to the eradication of illiteracy, particularly in the 15-35 age group. The Central and State Governments, political parties and their mass organisations, the mass media and educational institutions must commit themselves to mass literacy programmes of diverse nature. It will also have to involve on a large scale teachers, students, youth, voluntary agencies, employers, etc. Concerted efforts will be made to harness various research agencies to improve the pedagogical aspects of adult literacy. The mass literacy programme would include, in addition to literacy, functional knowledge and skills, and also awareness among learners about the socio-economic reality and the possibility to change it.

4.13 A vast programme of adult and continuing education will be implemented through various ways and channels, including:

a) establishment of centres in rural areas for continuing education;

b) workers' education through the employers, trade unions and concerned agencies of government;

c) post-secondary education institutions;

d) wider promotion of books, libraries and reading rooms;

e) use of radio, TV and films, as mass and group learning media;

f) creation of learners' groups and organisations;

g) programmes of distance learning;

h) organising assistance in self-learning; and

i) organising need and interest-based vocational training programmes.

PART V

REORGANISATION OF EDUCATION AT DIFFERENT STAGES

Early Childhood Care and Education

5.1 The National Policy on Children specially emphasises investment in the development of the young child, particularly children from sections of the population in which first generation learners predominate.

5.2 Recognising the holistic nature of child development, viz., nutrition, health and social, mental, physical, moral and emotional development, Early Childhood Care and Education (ECCE) will receive high priority and be suitably integrated with the Integrated Child Development Services Programme, wherever possible. Day-care centres will be provided as a support service for universalisation of primary education, to enable girls engaged in taking care of siblings to attend school and as a support service for working women belonging to poorer sections.

5.3 Programmes of ECCE will be child-oriented, focused around play and the individuality of the child. Formal methods and introduction of the 3R's will be discouraged at this stage. The local community will be fully involved in these programmes.

5.4 A full integration of child care and pre-primary education will be brought about, both as a feeder and a strengthening factor for primary education and for human resource development in general. In continuation of this stage, the School Health Programme will be strengthened.

Elementary Education

5.5 The new thrust in elementary education will emphasise two aspects: (i) universal enrolment and universal retention of children up to 14 years of age, and (ii) a substantial improvement in the quality of education.

Child-Centred Approach

5.6 A warm, welcoming and encouraging approach, in which all concerned share a solicitude for the needs of the child, is the best motivation for the child to attend school and learn. A child-centred and activity-based process of learning should be adopted at the primary stage. First generation allowed to set their own pace and be given supplementary remedial instruction. As the child grows, the component of cognitive learning will be increased and skills organised through practice. The policy of non-detention at the primary stage will be retained, making evaluation as disaggregated as feasible. Corporal punishment will be firmly excluded from the educational system and school timings as well as vacations adjusted to the convenience of children.

School Facilities

5.7 Provision will be made of essential facilities in primary schools, including at least two reasonably large rooms that are usable in all weather, and the necessary toys, blackboards, maps, charts, and other learning material. At least two teachers, one of whom a woman, should work in every school, the number increasing as early as possible to one teacher per class. A phased drive, symbolically called Operation Blackboard will be undertaken with immediate effect to improve primary schools all over the country. Government, local bodies, voluntary agencies and individuals will be fully involved. Construction of school buildings will be the first charge on NREP and RLEGP funds.

Non-Formal Education

5.8 A large and systematic programme of non-formal education will be launched for school drop-outs, for children from habitations without schools, working children and girls who cannot attend whole-day schools.

5.9 Modern technological aids will be used to improve the learning environment of NFE centres. Talented and dedicated young men and women from the local community will be chosen to serve as instructors, and particular attention paid to their training. Steps will be taken to facilitate their entry into the formal system in deserving cases. All necessary measures will be taken to ensure that the quality of non-formal education is comparable with formal education.

5.10 Effective steps will be taken to provide a framework for the curriculum on the lines of the national core curriculum, but based on the needs of the learners and related to the local environment. Learning material of high quality will be developed and provided free of charge to all pupils. NFE programmes will provide participatory learning environment, and activities such as games and sports, cultural programmes, excursions, etc.

5.11 Much of the work of running NFE centres will be done through voluntary agencies and panchayati raj institutions. The provision of funds to these agencies will be adequate and timely. The Government will take over-all responsibility for this vital sector.

A Resolve

5.12 The new education policy will give the highest priority to solving the problem of' children dropping out of school and will adopt an array of meticulously formulated strategies based on micro-planning, and applied at the grass-roots level all over the country, to ensure children's retention at school. This effort will be fully coordinated with the network of non-formal education. It shall be ensured that all children who attain the age of about 11 years by 1990 will have had five years of schooling, or its equivalent through the non-formal stream. Likewise, by 1995 all children will be provided free and compulsory education upto 14 years of age.

Secondary Education

5.13 Secondary education begins to expose students to the differentiated roles of science, the humanities and social sciences. This is also an appropriate stage to provide children with a sense of history and national perspective and give them opportunities to understand their constitutional duties and rights as citizens. Conscious internalisation of a healthy work ethos and of the values of a humane and composite culture will be brought about through appropriately formulated curricula. Vocationalisation through specialised institutions or through the refashioning of secondary education can, at this stage, provide valuable manpower for economic growth. Access to secondary education will be widened to cover areas unserved by it at present. In other areas, the main emphasis will be on consolidation.

5.14 It is universally accepted that children with special talent or aptitude should be provided opportunities to proceed at a faster pace, by making good quality education available to them, irrespective of their capacity to pay for it.

5.15 Pace-setting schools intended to serve this purpose will be established in various parts of the country on a given pattern, but with full scope for innovation and experimentation. Their broad aims will be to serve the objective of excellence, coupled with equity and social justice (with reservation for SCs and STs), to promote national integration by providing opportunities to talented children largely rural, from different parts of the country to live and learn together, to develop their full potential, and, most importantly, to become catalysts of a nation-wide programme of school improvement. The schools will be residential and free of charge.

Vocationalisation

5.16 The introduction of systematic, well-planned and rigorously implemented programmes of vocational education is crucial in the proposed educational reorganisation. These elements are meant to enhance individual employability, to reduce the mismatch between the demand and supply of skilled manpower, and to provide an alternative for those pursuing higher education without particular interest or purpose.

5.17 Vocational education will be a distinct stream, intended to prepare students for identified occupations spanning several areas of activity. These courses will ordinarily be provided after the secondary stage, but keeping the scheme flexible, they may also be made available after Class VIII. In the interests of integrating vocational education better with their facilities the Industrial Training Institutes will also conform to the larger vocational pattern.

5.18 Health planning and health service management should optimally interlock with the education and training of appropriate categories of health manpower through health-related vocational courses. Health education at the primary and middle levels will ensure the commitment of the individual to family and community health, and lead to health-related vocational courses at the +2 stage of higher secondary education. Efforts will be made to devise similar vocational courses based on agriculture, marketing, social services etc. An emphasis in vocational education will also be on development of attitudes, knowledge, and skills for entrepreneurship and sell-employment.

5.19 The establishment of vocational courses or institutions will be the responsibility of the Government as well as employers in the public and private sectors; the Government will, however, take special steps to cater to the needs of women, rural and tribal students and the deprived sections of society. Appropriate programmes will also be started for the handicapped.

5.20 Graduates of vocational courses will be given opportunities, under predetermined conditions, for professional growth, career improvement and lateral entry into courses of general, technical and professional education through appropriate bridge courses.

5.21 Non-formal, flexible and need-based vocational programmes will also be made available to neoliterates, youth who have completed primary education, school drop-outs, persons engaged in work and unemployed or partially employed persons. Special attention in this regard will be given to women.

5.22 Tertiary level courses will be organised for the young who graduate from the higher secondary courses of the academic stream and may also require vocational courses.

5.23 It is proposed that vocational courses cover 10 per cent of higher secondary students by 1990 and 25 per cent by 1995. Steps will be taken to see that a substantial majority of the products of vocational courses are employed or become self-employed. Review of the courses offered would be regularly undertaken. Government will also review its recruitment policy to encourage diversifications at the secondary level.

Higher Education

5.24 Higher education provides people with an opportunity to reflect on the critical social, economic, cultural, moral and spiritual issues facing humanity. It contributes to national development through dissemination of specialised knowledge and skills. It is therefore a crucial factor for survival. Being at the apex of the educational pyramid, it has also a key role in producing teachers for the education system.

5.25 In the context of the unprecedented explosion of knowledge, higher education has to become dynamic as never before, constantly entering uncharted areas.

5.26 There are around 150 universities and about 5,000 colleges in India today. In view of the need to effect an all round improvement in these institutions, it is proposed that, in the near future, the main emphasis will be on the consolidation of, and expansion of facilities in, the existing institutions.

5.27 Urgent steps will be taken to protect the system from degradation.

5.28 In view of mixed experiences with the system of affiliation autonomous colleges will be helped to develop in large numbers until the affiliating system is replaced by a freer and more creative association of universities with colleges. Similarly, the creation of autonomous departments within universities on a selective basis will be encouraged. Autonomy and freedom will be accompanied by accountability.

5.29 Course and programmes will be redesigned to meet the demands of specialisation better. Special emphasis will be laid on linguistic competence. There will be increasing flexibility in the combination of courses.

5.30 State level planning and coordination of higher education will be done through Councils of Higher Education. The UGC and these Councils will develop coordinative methods to keep a watch on standards.

5.31 Provision will be made for minimum facilities and admission will be regulated according to capacity. A major effort will be directed towards the transformation of' teaching methods. Audio-visual aids and electronic equipment will be introduced; development of science and technology curricula and material, research, and teacher orientation will receive attention. This will require preparation of teachers at the beginning of the service as well as continuing education thereafter. Teacher's performance will be systematically assessed. All posts will be filled on the basis of merit.

5.32 Research in the universities will be provided enhanced support and steps will be taken to ensure its high quality. Suitable mechanisms will be set up by the UGC for coordinating research in the universities, particularly in thrust areas of science and technology, with research undertaken by other agencies. An effort will be made to encourage the setting up of national research facilities within the university system, with proper forms of autonomous management.

5.33 Research in Indology, the humanities and social sciences will receive adequate support. To fulfil the need for the synthesis of knowledge, inter-disciplinary research will be encouraged. Efforts will be made to delve into India's ancient fund of knowledge and to relate it to contemporary reality. This effort will imply the development of facilities for the intensive study of Sanskrit and other classical language.

5.40 De-linking will be applied in services university degree need not be a necessary qualification. Its implementation will lead to a re-fashioning of job-specific courses and afford greater justice to those candidates who, despite being equipped for a given job, are unable to get it because of it is unnecessary for graduate candidates.

5.41 Concomitant with de-linking, an appropriate machinery, such as a National Testing Service, will be established, in appropriate phases, to conduct tests on a voluntary basis to determine the suitability of candidates for specified jobs and to pave the way for the emergence of norms of comparable competence across the nation.

PART VI

TECHNICAL AND MANAGEMENT EDUCATION

6.3 In order to improve the situation regarding manpower information, the recently set up Technical Manpower Information System will be further developed and strengthened.

6.4 Continuing education, covering established as well as emerging technologies, will be promoted.

6.5 As computers have become important and ubiquitous tools, a minimal exposure to computers and a training in their use will form part of professional education. Programmes of computer literacy will be organised on wide scale from the school stage.

6.6 In view of the present rigid entry requirements to formal courses restricting the access of a large segment of people to technical and managerial education, programmes through a distance-learning process, including uses of the mass media, will be offered. Technical and management education programmes, including education in polytechnics, will also be on a flexible modular pattern based, on credits, with provision for multi-point entry. A strong guidance and counselling service will be provided.

6.7 In order to increase the relevance of management education, particularly in the non-corporate and under-managed sectors, the management education system will study and document the Indian experience and create a body of knowledge and specific educational programmes suited to these sectors.

6.8 Appropriate formal and non-formal programmes of technical education will be devised for the benefit of women, the economically and socially weaker sections, and the physically handicapped.

6.9 The emphasis on vocational education and its expansion will need a large number of teachers and professionals in vocational education, educational technology curriculum development, etc. Programmes will be started to meet this demand.

6.10 To encourage students to consider 'self-employment' as a career option, training in entrepreneurship will be provided through modular of optional courses, in degree or diploma programmes.

6.11 In order to meet the continuing needs of updating curriculum, renewal should systematically phase out obsolescence and introduce new technologies or disciplines.

Institutional Thrusts

6.12 Some polytechnics in the rural areas have started training weaker groups in those areas for productive occupations through a system of community polytechnics. The community polytechnic system will be appraised and appropriately strengthened to increase its quality and coverage.

Innovation, Research and Development

6.13 Research as a means of renovation and renewal of educational processes will be undertaken by all higher technical institutions. It will primarily aim at producing quality manpower capable of taking tip R&D functions. Research for development will focus on improving present technologies, developing new indigenous ones and enhancing production and productivity. A suitable system for watching and forecasting technology will be set up.

6.14 The scope for cooperation, collaboration and networking relationships between institutions at various levels and with the user systems will be utilised. Proper mainte-nance and an attitude of innovation and improvement will be promoted systematically.

Promoting Efficiency and Effectiveness at All Levels

6.15 As technical and management education is expensive, the following major steps will be taken for cost-effectiveness and to promote excellence:

i) High priority will be given to modernisation and removal of obsolescence. However, modernisation will be undertaken to enhance functional efficiency and not for its own sake or as a status symbol;

ii) Institutions will be encouraged to generate resources using their capacities to provide services to the community and industry. They will be equipped with up-to-date learning resources, library and computer facilities;

iii) Adequate hostel accommodation will be provided, specially for girls. Facilities for sports, creative work and cultural activities will be expanded;

iv) More effective procedures will be adopted in the recruitment of staff. Career opportunities, service conditions, consultancy norms and other perquisites will be improved.

v) Teachers will have multiple roles to perform: teaching, research, development of learning resource material, extension, and managing the institution. Initial and in-service training will be made mandatory for faculty members and adequate training reserves will be provided. Staff Development Programmes will be integrated at the State, and coordinated at regional and national levels.

vi) The curricula of technical and management programmes will be targeted on current as well as the projected needs of industry or user system. Active interaction between technical or management institutions and industry will be promoted in programme planning and implementation, exchange of personnel, training facilities and resources, research and consultancy and other areas of mutual interest.

vii) Excellence in performance of institutions and individuals will be recognised and rewarded. The emergence of substandard and institutions will be checked. A climate conducive to excellence and innovation will be promoted with full involvement of the faculty.

viii) Select institutions will be awarded academic administrative and financial autonomy of varying degrees, building in safeguards with respect to accountability.

ix) Networking systems will have to be established between technical education and industry, R&D organisations, programmes of rural and community development, and with other sectors of education with complementary characteristics.

Management Functions and Change

6.16 In view of the likely emergence of changes in management systems and the need to equip students with the ability to cope with them, effective mechanisms will be devised to understand the nature and direction of changes *per se* and to develop the important skill of managing change.

6.17 In view of the integrated nature of the task, the Ministry of Human Resource Development will coordinate the balanced development of engineering, vocational and management education as well as the education of technicians and craftsmen.

6.18 Professional societies will be encouraged and enabled to perform their due role in the advancement of technical and management education.

6.19 The All India Council for Technical Education will be vested with statutory authority for planning, formulation and the maintenance of norms and standards, accreditation, funding of priority areas, monitoring and evaluation, maintaining parity of certification and awards and ensuring the coordinated and integrated development of technical and management education. Mandatory periodic evaluation will be carried out by a duty constituted Accreditation Board.

6.20 In the interests of maintaining standards and for several other valid reasons, the commercialisation of technical and professional education will be curbed. An alternative system will be devised to involve private and voluntary effort in this sector of education, in conformity with accepted norms and goals.

PART VII

MAKING THE SYSTEM WORK

7.1 It is obvious that these and many other new tasks of education cannot be performed in a state of disorder. Education needs to be managed in an atmosphere of utmost intellectual rigour, seriousness of purpose and, at the same time, of freedom essential for innovation and creativity. While far-reaching change will have to be incorporated in the quality and range of education, the process of introducing discipline into the system will have to be started, here and now, in what exists.

7.2 The country has placed boundless trust in the educational system. The people have a right to expect concrete results. The first task is to make it work. All teachers should teach and all students study.

7.3 The strategy in this behalf will consist of:

a) a better deal to teachers with greater accountability;

b) provision of improved student's services and insistence on observance of acceptable norms of behaviour;

c) provision of better facilities to institutions; and

d) creation of a system of performance appraisals of institutions according to standards and norms set at the national or state levels.

PART VIII

REORIENTING THE CONTENT AND PROCESS OF EDUCTION

The Cultural Perspective

8.1 The existing schism between the formal system of education and the country's rich and varied cultural traditions needs to be bridged. The preoccupation with modern technologies cannot be allowed to sever out new generations from the roots in India's history and culture. De-culturisation, de-humanisation and alienation must be avoided at all costs. Education can and must bring about the fine synthesis between change-oriented technologies and the country's continuity of cultural tradition.

8.2 The curricula and processes of education will be enriched by cultural content in as many manifestations as possible. Children will be enabled to develop sensitivity to beauty, harmony and refinement. Resource persons in the community, irrespective of their formal educational qualifications, will be invited to contribute to the cultural enrichment of education, employing both the literate oral traditions of communication. To sustain and carry forward the cultural tradition, the role of old masters, who train pupils through traditional modes will be supported and recognised.

8.3 Linkages will be established between the university system and institutions of higher learning in art, archaeology, oriental studies etc. Due attention will also be paid to the specialised disciplines of fine arts, museology, folklore, etc. Teaching, training and research in these disciplines will be strengthened so as to replenish specialised manpower in them.

Value Education

8.4 The growing concern over the erosion of essential values and an increasing cynicism in society has brought to focus the need for readjustments in the curriculum in order to make education a forceful tool for the cultivation of social and moral values.

8.5 In our culturally plural society, education should foster universal and internal values oriented towards the unity and integration of our people. Such value education should help eliminate obscurantism, religious fanaticism, violence, superstition and fatalism.

8.6 Apart from this combative role, value education has a profound positive content, based on our heritage, national goals universal perceptions. It should lay primary emphasis on this aspect.

Languages

8.7 The education policy of 1968 had examined the question of the development of languages in great detail; its essential provisions can hardly be improved upon and are as relevant today as before. The implementation of this part of the 1968 policy has, however, been uneven. The policy will be implemented more energetically and purposefully.

Books and Libraries

8.8 The availability of books at low prices is indispensable for people's education. Effort will be made to secure easy accessibility to books for all segments of the population. Measures will be taken to improve the quality of books, promote the reading habit and encourage creative writing. Authors' interests will be protected. Good translations of foreign books into Indian languages will be supported. Special attention will be paid to the production of quality books for children, including text books and work books.

8.9 Together with the development of books, a nation-wide movement for the improvement of existing libraries and the establishment of new ones will be taken up. Provision will be made in all educational institutions for library facilities and the status of librarians improved.

Media and Educational Technology

8.10 Modern communication technologies have the potential to bypass several stages and sequences in the process of development encountered in earlier decades. Both the constraints of time and distance at once become manageable. In order to avoid structural dualism, modern educational technology must reach out to the most distant areas and the most deprived sections of beneficiaries simultaneously with the areas of comparative affluence and ready availability.

8.11 Educational technology will be employed in the spread of useful information, the training and re-training of teachers, to improve quality, sharpen awareness of art and culture, inculcate abiding values, etc., both in the formal and non-formal sectors. Maximum use will be made of the available infrastructure. In villages without electricity, batteries or solar packs will be used to run the programme.

8.12 The generation of relevant and culturally compatible educational programmes will form an important component of educational technology, and all available resources in the country will be utilised for this purpose.

8.13 The media have a profound influence on the minds of children as well as adults; some of them tend to encourage consumerism, violence, etc., and have a deleterious effect. Radio and TV programmes which clearly militate against proper educational objectives will be prevented. Steps will be taken to discourage such trends in films and other media also. An active movement will be started to promote the production of children's films of high quality and usefulness.

Work Experience

8.14 Work experience, viewed as purposive and meaningful manual work, organised as an integral part of the learning process and resulting in either goods or services useful to the community, is considered as an essential component at all stages of education, to be provided through well-structured and graded programmes. It would comprise activities in accord with the interests, abilities and needs of students, the level of skills and knowledge to be upgraded with the stages of education. This experience would be helpful on his entry into the workforce. Pre-vocational programmes provided at the lower secondary stage will also facilitate the choice of the vocational courses at the higher secondary stage.

Education and Environment

8.15 There is a paramount need to create a consciousness of the environment. It must permeate all ages and all sections of society, beginning with the child. Environmental consciousness should inform teaching in schools and colleges. This aspect will be integrated in the entire educational process.

Mathematics Teaching

8.16 Mathematics should be visualised as the vehicle to train a child to think, reason, analyse and to articulate logically. Apart from being a specific subject, it should be treated as a concomitant to any subject involving analysis and reasoning.

8.17 With the recent introduction of computers in schools, educational computing and the emergence of learning through the understanding of cause-effect relationships and the interplay of variables, the teaching of mathematics will be suitably redesigned to bring it in line with modern technological devices.

Science Education

8.18 Science education will be strengthened so as to develop in the child well defined abilities and values such as the spirit of inquiry, creativity, objectivity, the courage to question, and an aesthetic sensibility.

8.19 Science education programmes will be designed to enable the learner to acquire problem-solving and decision-making skills and to discover the relationship of science with health, agriculture, industry and other aspects of daily life. Every effort will be made to extend science education to the vast numbers who have remained outside the pale of formal education.

Sports and Physical Education

8.20 Sports and physical education are an integral part of the learning process, and will be included in the evaluation of performance. A nation-wide infrastructure for physical education, sports and games will be built into the educational edifice.

8.21 The infrastructure will consist of playfields, equipment, coaches and teachers of physical education as part of the school improvement programme. Available open spaces in urban areas will be reserved for playgrounds, if necessary by legislation. Efforts will be made to establish sports institutions and hostels where specialised attention will be given to sports activities and sports-related studies, along with normal education. Appropriate encouragement will be given to those talented in sport and games. Due stress will be laid on indigenous traditional games. As a system which promotes an integrated development of body and mind, yoga will receive special attention. Efforts will be made to introduce yoga in all schools; to this end, it will be introduced in teacher training courses.

The Role of Youth

8.22 Opportunities will be provided for the youth to involve themselves in national and social development through educational institutions and outside them. Students will be required to participate in one or the other of existing schemes, namely, the National Service Scheme, National Cadet Corps, etc. Outside the institutions, the youth will be encouraged to take up programmes of development, reform and extension. The National Service Volunteer Scheme will be strengthened.

The Evaluation Process and Examination Reform

8.23 Assessment of performance is an integral part of any process of learning and teaching. As part of sound educational strategy, examinations should be employed to bring about qualitative improvements in education.

8.24 The objective will be to re-cast the examination system so as to ensure a method of assessment that is a valid and reliable measure of student development and a powerful instrument for improving teaching and learning. In functional terms, this would mean:

- i) The elimination of excessive element of chance and subjectivity;
- ii) The de-emphasis of memorisation;
- iii) Continuous and comprehensive evaluation that incorporates both scholastic and non-scholastic aspects of education, spread over the total span of instructional time;
- iv) Effective use of the evaluation process by teachers, students and parents:
- v) Improvement in the conduct of examinations;
- vi) The introduction of concomitant changes in instructional materials and methodology;
- vii) Introduction of the semester system from the secondary stage in a phased manner; and
- viii) The use of grades in place of marks.

8.25 The above goals are relevant both for external examinations and evaluation within educational institutions. Evaluation at the institutional level will be streamlined and the predominance of external examinations reduced.

PART IX

THE TEACHER

9.1 The status of the teacher reflects the socio-cultural ethos of a society; it is said that no people can rise above the level of its teachers. The Government and the community should endeavour to create conditions which will help motivate and inspire teachers on constructive and creative lines. Teachers should have the freedom to innovate, to devise appropriate methods of communication and activities relevant to the needs and capabilities of and the concerns of the community.

9.2 The methods of recruiting teachers will be reorganised to ensure merit, objectivity and conformity with spatial and functional requirements. The pay and service conditions of teachers have to be commensurate with their social and professional responsibilities and with the need to attract talent to the profession. Efforts will be made to reach the desirable objective of uniform emoluments, service conditions and grievance-removal mechanisms for throughout the country. Guidelines will be formulated to ensure objectivity in the postings and transfers of teachers. A system of teacher evaluation—open, participative and data-based—will be created and reasonable opportunities of promotion to higher grades provided. Norms of accountability will be laid down with incentives for good performance and disincentives for non-performance. Teachers will continue to play a crucial role in the formulation and implementation of educational programmes.

9.3 Teachers' associations must play a significant role in upholding professional integrity, enhancing the dignity of the teacher and in curbing professional misconduct. National level associations of teachers, could prepare a Code of Professional Ethics for Teachers and see to its observance.

Teacher Education

9.4 Teacher education is a continuous process, and its pre-service and in-service components are inseparable. As the first step, the system of teacher education will be overhauled.

9.5 The new programmes of teacher-education will emphasise continuing education and the need for teachers to meet the thrusts envisaged in this policy.

9.6 District. Institutes of Education and Training (DIET) will be established with the capability to organise pre-service and in-service courses for elementary school teachers and for the personnel working in non-formal and adult education. As DIETs get established, substandard institutions will be phased out. Selected Secondary Teacher Training Colleges will be upgraded to complement the work of State Councils of Educational Research and Training. The National Council of Teacher Education will be provided the necessary resources and capability to accredit institutions of teacher-education and provide guidance regarding curricula and methods. Networking arrangements will be created between institutions of teacher education and university depart-ments of education.

PART X

THE MANAGEMENT OF EDUCATION

10.1 An overhaul of the system of planning and the management of education will receive high priority. The guiding considerations will be:

a) Evolving a long-term planning and management perspective of education and its integration with the country's developmental and manpower needs;

b) Decentralisation and the creation of a spirit of autonomy for educational institutions;

c) Giving pre-eminence to people's involvement, including association of non-governmental agencies and voluntary effort;

d) Inducting more women in the planning and manage-ment of education; and

e) Establishing the principle of accountability in relation to given objectives and norms.

National Level

10.2 The Central Advisory Board of Education will play a pivotal rote in reviewing educational development, determining the changes required to improve the system and monitoring implementation. It will function through appropriate committees and other mechanisms created to ensure contact with, and coordination among, the various areas of human resource development. The departments of education at the centre and in the states will be strengthened through the involvement of professionals.

Indian Education Service

10.3 A proper management structure in education will entail the establishment of the Indian Education Service as an All-India Service. It will bring a national perspective to this vital sector. The basic principles, functions and procedures of recruitment to this service will be decided in consultation with the State Governments.

State Level

10.4 State Governments may establish State Advisory Boards of Education on the lines of CABE. Effective measures should be taken to integrate mechanisms in the various State departments concerned with Human Resource Development.

10.5 Special attention will be paid to the training of educational planners, administrators and heads of institutions. Institutional arrangements for this purpose should be set up in stages.

District and Local Level

10.6 District Boards of Education will be created to manage education up to the higher secondary level. State Governments will attend to this aspect with all possible expedition. Within a multi-level framework of educat-ional development, central, state, district and local level agencies will participate in planning, coordination, monitoring and evaluation.

10.7 A very important role must be assigned to the head of an educational institution. Heads will be specially selected and trained. School complexes will be promoted on a flexible pattern so as to serve as networks of institutions and synergic alliances to encourage professionalism among teachers, to ensure observance of norms of conduct and to enable the sharing of experiences and facilities. It is expected that a developed system of school complexes will take much of the inspection functions in due course.

10.8 Local communities, through appropriate bodies, will be assigned a major role in programmes of school improvement.

Voluntary Agencies and Aided Institutions

10.9 Non-government and voluntary effort including social activist groups will be encouraged, subject to proper management, and financial assistance provided. At the same time, steps will be taken to prevent the establis-hment of institutions set up to commercialise education.

PART XI

RESOURCES AND REVIEW

11.1 The Education Commission of 1964-66, the National Education Policy of 1968 and practically all others concerned with education have stressed that the egalitarian goals and the practical, development-oriented objectives of Indian society can be realised only by making investments in education of an order comme-nsurate with the nature and dimensions of the task.

11.2 Resources, to the extent possible, will be raised by mobilising donations, asking the beneficiary communities to maintain school buildings and supplies of some consumables, raising fees at the higher levels of education and effecting some savings by the efficient use of facilities. Institutions involved with research and the development of technical and scientific manpower should also mobilise some funds by levying access or charge on the user agencies, including government departments, and entrepreneurs. All these measures will be taken not only to reduce the burden on State resources but also for creating a greater sense of responsibility within the educational system. However, such measures will contribute only marginally to the total funding. The government and the community in general will find funds for such programmes as: the universalisation of elementary education; liquidating illiteracy; equality of access to educational opportunities to all sections throughout the country; enhancing the social relevance, quality and functional effectiveness of educational programmes; generating knowledge and developing technologies in scientific fields crucial to self-sustaining economic development; and creating a critical consciousness of the values and imperatives of national survival.

11.3 The deleterious consequences of non-investment or inadequate investment in education are indeed very serious.

Similarly, the cost of neglecting vocational and technical education and of research is also unacceptable. Sub-optimal performance in these fields could cause irreparable damage to the Indian economy. The network of institutions set up from time to time since independence to facilitate the application of science and technology would need to be substantially and expeditiously updated, since they are fast becoming obsolete.

11.4 In view of these imperatives, education will be treated as a crucial area of investment for national development and survival. The National Policy on Education, 1968, had laid down that the investment on education be gradually increased to reach a level of expenditure of 6 per cent of the national income as early as possible. Since the actual level of investment has remained far short of that target, it is important that greater determination be shown now to find the funds for the programmes laid down in this policy. While the actual requirements will be computed from time to time on the basis of monitoring and review, the outlay on education will be shaped up to the extent essential for policy implementation in the Seventh Plan. It will be ensured that from the Eighth Five Year Plan onwards it will uniformly exceed to 6 per cent of the national income.

Review

11.5 The implementation of the various parameters of the new policy must be reviewed every five years. Appraisals at short intervals will also be made to ascertain the progress of implementation and the trends emerging from time to time.

PART XII

THE FUTURE

12.1 The future of education in India is too complex to envision with precision. Yet, given our tradition which has almost always put a high premium on intellectual and spiritual attainment, we are bound to succeed in achieving our objectives.

12.2 The main tasks is to strengthen the base of the pyramid, which might come close to a billion people at the turn of the century. Equally, it is important to ensure that those at the top of the pyramid are among the best in the world. Our cultural wellsprings had taken good care of both ends in the past; the skew set in with foreign domination and influence. It should now be possible to further intensify the nation-wide effort in Human Resource Development, with education playing its multifaceted role.

5

EARLY CHILDHOOD CARE AND EDUCATION

Pre-school teacher education prepares teachers for teaching pre-school classes, i.e. nursery and kindergarten. The minimum qualification for admission into the pre-school teachers' education programme is a secondary or a senior secondary examination i.e. ten or twelve years of schooling. The duration of the course varies from one to two years. Pre-school teacher training institutions are mostly unaided private institutions. In the case of course for nursery and primary teachers, State Education Departments prescribe a minimum percentage of marks in the qualifying examination as a requirement for admission.

ELEMENTARY STAGE

Elementary teacher education in for training teachers to teach primary classes (grades One to Five). The minimum qualification for admission to the elementary teachers' education programme is either ten or twelve years of schooling. Recently, most States have prescribed twelve years of schooling as the minimum requirement, though some of them still have a pass in the secondary school examination as the entry qualification. The duration of the programme is generally two years. Normally, the first year of training is devoted to the teaching of subject-matter or 'Content' and the second year to the 'methodology of teaching'. These programmes are given certificates such as the J.B.T. (Junior Basic Teachers' Training) or B.Ed (Diploma in Education) or T.D. (Teaching Diploma etc.).

Elementary teacher training institutions are of three types: government, private aided and private unaided. Recently, District Institutes of Education and Training (DIET) have been set up in all the states. An important features of the DIETs is that, besides providing pre-service teacher education, they conduct programmes of in-service education of teachers. As of date, the number of DIETs is 433 and these institutes are fully financed by the Central Government. The total number of elementary teachers' training institutions in India is 1,179.

SECONDARY STAGE

Secondary teacher education institutes prepare teachers for teaching at the upper primary and secondary levels (grades Six to Twelve). The minimum qualification required for admission into the secondary teachers' education programme is graduation in science, social sciences, humanities, commerce, agriculture etc. A large number of postgraduates also seek admission to these training institutions. Secondary teacher education is offered by secondary colleges of education, which are affiliated to different universities. Some university departments also offer a secondary teachers' education programme. The minimum qualification for admission to this programme is a graduation. These institutes are of three types-government, private aided and private unaided. There are around 600 secondary colleges of education.

Four Regional Institutes of Education (RIEs), constituent units of the NCERT, offer a four-year integrated course for secondary teachers. The minimum qualification for admission to this programme is a pass in senior secondary examination i.e. after twelve years of schooling. Recently, the University of Delhi, Delhi has started a four-year programme in elementary education in five colleges leading to the Bachelor's degree in Elementary Education (B.Ed.). The duration of the Delhi University programme is also four years. The products of the programme are qualified to teach classes I to VIII.

— *In-Service Training of Teachers*

In- service training of teachers is offered at the central, state, regional, district and sub-district levels. At the national level, in-service training programme are offered by institutions such as NCERT, the NIEPA, the Central Institute of Indian Languages (CIIL), Mysore, among many others. At the regional level the Regional Institutes of Education of the NCERT conduct inservice programmes for teachers of their region.

At the state level, programmes are mainly offered by the State Council of Educational Research and Training (SCERT), State Institute of Education (SIE), State Institute of Science Education (SISE), Institute of Advanced Study in Education (IASE), Colleges of Teacher Education (CTE) and State Institutes of Educational Technology (SIET). At the district level, District Institutes of Education and Training (DIET) conduct inservice training.

As follow up to the 1986 National Policy on Education (NPE), the Government of India financed a national scheme for in-service training of teachers (primary and secondary school teachers). The objectives of this scheme, known as the Programme of Mass Orientation of School Teachers (PMOST), were to sensitize teachers in the emerging concerns in education, the use of a learner-centered approach, as well as action research and enrichment of knowledge in curricular areas and the core components as given in the NPE. The duration of the PMOST training was ten days. The programme was implemented during 1986 to 1990. About 1.8 million teachers were given inservice education under the PMOST scheme. Video films relating to various modules of the PMOST training were telecast on the national network when training camps were held. The programme was implemented by the NCERT in collaboration with the SCERTs in different states.

After the PMOST, another programme known as the "Special Orientation Programme for Primary School Teachers" (SOPT) was launched in 1993-94 to improve the quality of the elementary education. The emphasis given in this programme is on training of teachers in pedagogy for developing the minimum levels of learning (MLLs) for the primary stage, training in the use of materials provided to primary school teachers under the scheme of Operation Blackboard and in child-centered approach to teaching-learning. Under this scheme 0.45 million teachers are to be provided inservice training each year. As in the case of PMOST, this programme too has been provided with media support.

— *Certification of Teachers*

- The certification of prospective teachers is done by the different examining bodies on successful completion by award of a professional degree/diploma.
- The certification at the elementary teacher preparation level (Junior Basic Teacher's Training/ Diploma in Teaching/Elementary Teacher Training/Diploma in Nursery Teacher Training) is done by the Directorates of Primary Education of the States.
- The certification in the form of an award of degrees, such as the Bachelor of Education (B.Ed.) is done by the universities.
- The teachers, who attend the inservice programmes are given the certificate of attendance.

Appointment of Teachers

States follow different recruitment procedures. In some States, the recruitment is made on the basis of candidates' performance in a competitive examination, whereas, in some other States, recruitment is made on the basis of the academic and professional background of candidates. The merit of each candidate is determined on the basis of his/ her score in the examinations he/she has passed in addition to previous teaching experience, if any. In some other states, a combination of the two procedures, i.e. performance in a competitive examination and academic achievement is suitably integrated. The performance of candidates in oral examinations through interview is also practiced.

Economic Status of Teachers

The pay scales of teachers are determined by States. Most states follow the national guidelines for salary scales of teachers working in state schools and private aided schools. In addition to the salary, a price-index linked "dearness allowance" is given to teachers. Various other allowances such as the city compensatory allowance, house rent allowance, hill allowance, winter allowance; backward, remote and tribal area allowance, island allowance etc. as applicable in different working conditions are added to the salary. These allowances differ from State to State and, within a State, from stages of education. Entry-level salaries for trained primary teachers are only slightly higher than those for untrained teachers. The maximum salary for a trained teacher is three to four times his/ her entry-salary, and it is usually reached after 16 to 20 years of service in most stages.

In addition, most States provide a fixed medical allowance or a reimbursement for medical expenses, advances for house building and for purchase of conveyance, free education for children of teachers, as well as retirement benefits, gratuity and group insurance. States also offer incentives to some special categories of teachers. For instance, in Assam, Bihar, Gujarat, Maharashtra and Tamil Nadu, female teachers working in rural and remote areas are given residential accommodation.

At the entry level, the annual income of teachers in India at different school levels such as Primary, Secondary and Senior Secondary are Rs.80,000/, Rs.1,00,000/ and Rs.1,20,000/, respectively. The average per capita gross domestic product (on current prices) was Rs.11,975/ in the year 1995-96*. The status of primary teachers is generally low.

N the light of the euphoria surrounding the Indian economy now, nobody likes to be reminded of the less flattering standards of living of a large section of the population. The country has always been a land of contrasts, which are at times too stark to be ignored. No wonder the Union Minister for Communications and Disinvestment, Mr Arun Shourie, took pride in highlighting through the newspaper he served years ago India's knowledge power and the supremacy it maintains in information technology and IT-enabled services.

The Finance Minister, Mr Jaswant Singh, waxes eloquent on the economy's sound fundamentals, exemplified in the remarkable rally in the stock market, the hefty foreign exchange reserves and a GDP target that may turn out to be even better than the 8.4 per cent for the second quarter of 2003-04 fiscal.

However, development also pertains to how well poverty is attacked, how educational opportunities are provided to the under-privileged, how social infrastructure is beefed up and physical infrastructure is improved. Unfortunately, the country's record is dismal in these areas. The media, which takes every opportunity to wax eloquent on economic performance, should not lose sight of the larger picture, particularly when the picture must capture the gross satisfaction quotient of the people and not just GDP.

Viewed against this backdrop, the Indian media missed the coverage of a crucial meeting held in the third week of December in Egypt, where Education Ministers from a group of nine highly populated countries (E-9) — Bangladesh, Brazil, China, Egypt, India, Indonesia, Mexico, Nigeria and Pakistan — assembled for three days under the Unesco umbrella to review the headway made in the goal of Education for All (EFA).

The EFA concept was unfurled in Delhi in 1993, but the progress towards its fulfilment is far from satisfactory. Though the nine countries account for more than 50 per cent of the world population and 53 per cent of the world's school-going children, the EFA is particularly for Egypt, India, Indonesia, Nigeria and Pakistan.

The Union Human Resource Development Minister, Dr Murli Manohar Joshi, and the Member, Planning Commission, Dr K. Venkatasubramanian, and other senior officials attended the Cairo conclave. The important outcome of the meeting was that India has accepted the Unesco model of beginning preparatory education at the age of three for a child. This path-breaking development is likely to usher in progress if substantial funds are found to take due care of all those left out of the system. This is because economists the world over have been highlighting the significance of education since the time of Adam Smith, who deemed acquisition of skills through education and study as a form of capital.

David Ricardo and Thomas Malthus considered education as a means to inculcate habits that would lead to slower population growth, while Alfred Marshall set store by education as a tool for enhancing industrial efficiency. Indubitably, the most tangible impact of education is to increase one's own income and productivity, and it is small wonder that classical economists celebrated education as a productivity-increasing mechanism. Today, India's supremacy in knowledge-intensive operations bears ample testimony to the success of adopting a science-based and technology-savvy syllabus at the tertiary level of education in the past when state-funding and relatively easy fee structures enabled many to graduate out of the portals of higher learning centres with skills.

Though India did produce a Nobel laureate like Prof Amartya Sen, who extols the virtues of primary education as the sure-fire route to progress, the state of primary schooling, leave alone preparatory schooling, today presents a pathetic picture.

While nursery and primary education have become centres for raking in the moolah with middle- and lower middle-class people spending their earnings on the so-called public schools, the state of the poor is quite unenviable. Governments, both at the Centre and in the States, particularly the latter, do not allocate sufficient funds to attract good talent and dedicated teaching staff to draw the poor. They also do not have enough provisions for mid-day meal schemes which at least encourage poor parents to send their children to spend time usefully. It is a cruel contrast that India boasts of cruising on the information super-highway, while the nation's poor children spend most of their time on the street, when they should be in schools for want of opportunities and lack of proper nourishment.

No doubt, Parliament ratified the Free and Compulsory Education for Children Bill last year, making education a fundamental right. But mere enshrining of rights alone will not bring in the desired results unless the authorities, particularly in the States, address the problem with earnestness. In India, primary education has, since Independence, meant the 6-14 age group and not below it. But the Unesco model addresses the crucial role of Early Childhood Care and Education (ECCE) in the 0-6 age group as a significant input, duly making up for early environmental deprivations at home by creating a stimulating milieu for the child.

According to Dr Venkatasubramanian, India's readiness to follow the Unesco model of ECCE is a significant step in improving the potential of the country's human resource. Besides facilitating the realisation of the goals of universal elementary education, Dr Venkatasubramanian is sure the ECCE will help prepare children for schooling in terms of getting them used to regularly attending a centre-based programme away from home and imparting to them "certain pre-reading, pre-writing, and pre-number skills concepts and vocabulary which can help them negotiate the primary curriculum better."

Moreover, the formative years of a child have always been singled out for habit formation and brain development. As the ECCE also addresses the health and nutritional requirements of children, it enables involvement of the girl child, who is often not able to attend school because of mundane chores, such as sibling care, through provision of substitute care for the sibling.

According to Dr Venkatasubramanian, only 19 per cent of children in the 3-6 age group are reported to be actually utilising the benefit of the available ECCE programme, while the proliferation of ECCE centres in the garb of nursery schools in the private sector run by untrained or ill-trained personnel with inadequate facilities and capabilities has kept the benefits beyond the reach of the poor. Though India has had such schemes as the Integrated Child Development Services (ICDS), a centrally-sponsored scheme begun in 1975, its implementation remained sectoral with education component being only one of the six addressed by it. That India is now advancing the cause of the ECCE should be welcomed.

Where funds are a constraint, public-private partnership can be attempted to see that India's teeming population, particularly the sections that deserve state support, get it in ample measure so that the dream of pitch-forking India into the developed nations' league by 2020 can be advanced. The sooner this is realised the better as it would speed up the moulding of the nation. With coalition governance becoming a reality, the constituent units of the alliance being forged for the forthcoming elections should also declare their unreserved support for the concept of ECCE so that, down the line, the States, which share the major responsibility for spread of primary and pre-school education, act in concert with the Centre in heralding a new development paradigm for India, based on the blend of technical skill, superior knowledge and a population of literate Indians.

India has 375 million children, more than any other country in the world. India has made some significant commitments towards ensuring the basic rights of children. There has been progress in overall indicators: infant mortality rates are down, child survival is up, literacy rates have improved and school dropout rates have fallen. But the issue of Child Rights in India is still caught between legal and policy commitments to children on the one hand, and the fallout of the process of globalisation on the other.

With State support to the social sector being systematically reduced, more than 360 million people, about 36 per cent of the population (1999-2000 statistics) are living below the poverty line, though the government's latest estimates put this figure at 26 per cent. It is estimated that women and children account for 73 per cent of those below the poverty line. The cuts in the social sector are, therefore, bound to have a direct impact on the lives of children. More than 75 million children continue to suffer from malnutrition, in spite of buffer food stocks, because of the abeyance of an equitable distribution system and the withdrawal of the public distribution system.

Socio-economic factors must also be taken into account. The girl-child has a lower status in India and enjoys fewer rights, opportunities and benefits of childhood as compared to the boy-child. The boy-child has first right on family and community resources. The girl-child is also neglected in matters of feeding and health care. The dietary consumption data of the National Nutrition Monitoring Bureau (NNMB) suggests that the girl in the age group 13-15 years consumes less than two-thirds of the recommended calorie intake. She remains intellectually underdeveloped, being denied the opportunity to attend school. Most tragically, the girl-child in India is unwanted and considered a liability by her own family. Marriage is considered a priority as soon as she attains puberty.

Children are also the main targets of the labour market. They can be hired at much lower wages than adults. Many of

India's children are forced into the labour market when they are only three years old!

The Convention on the Rights of the Child, which India has ratified, defines children as persons below the age of 18. However, in India there are several different definitions of the child. The Census of India defines children as those below the age of 14. But social scientists include females in the age group of 15-19 years in the girl-child demographic data.

According to the Constitution of India (Article 23), no child below the age of 14 must be employed in a factory or mine or engaged in any other hazardous employment. Article 45 says that the State will provide free and compulsory education to all children up to the age of 14. The legal conception of a child varies, however. The age of majority is 18 years for girls and 21 years for boys under the Indian Majority Act. On the other hand, under the Indian Penal Code, the age of sexual consent for girls is 16 years. These different age-specifics under different laws confound the very definition of a child.

The Committee on the Rights of the Child says in its Concluding Observations of January 2000: "In light of Article 1, the Committee is concerned that the various age limits set by the law are not in accordance with the general principles and other provisions of the Convention. Of particular concern to the Committee is the very low age of criminal responsibility under the Penal Code, which is set at seven years; and the possibility of trying boys between 16 and 18 years as adults. The Committee is concerned that there is no minimum age for sexual consent for boys. The Committee is further concerned that minimum-age standards are poorly enforced (e.g. the 1929 Child Marriages Restraint Act)."

Government Policy on Children

On November 20, 1989, the UN General Assembly adopted the Convention of the Rights of the Child (CRC). On January 26, 1990, the opening day of the session, 61 countries signed it. It came into force on September 2, 1990 with 20 ratifications. It covers all children under the age of 18 years, regardless of sex, colour, language, religion or race. India ratified the CRC in 1992.

Several constitutional provisions protect the children of India. Among them: Article 15 affirms the right of the State to make special provision for women and children; Article 24 provides that no child below the age of 14 shall be employed to work...in any hazardous employment; Article 39(e) of the Directive Principles of State Policy provides that children of tender age should not be abused and that they should not be forced by economic necessity to enter avocations unsuited to their age or strength; Article 39(f) requires children to be given opportunities and facilities to develop in a healthy manner and in conditions of freedom and dignity and that childhood and youth be protected against exploitation and moral and material abandonment; Article 45 of the Directive Principles of State Policy provides for free and compulsory education for all children until they complete the age of 14.

Prior to the Fifth Five Year Plan, the government's focus was on child welfare, through the promotion of basic minimum services for children. This culminated in the adoption of the National Policy for Children in 1974. The Fifth Five Year Plan (1974-79) saw a shift of focus from welfare to development, and the integration and co-ordination of services after the launch of the Integrated Child Development Services, 1975. The Sixth Five Year Plan was the period of strengthening child welfare and development. It led to the spatial expansion and enrichment of child development services through a variety of programmes. The focus of the Eighth Five Year Plan period (1992-97) shifted the focus to human development through advocacy, mobilisation and community empowerment.

The Government of India has declared its commitment to every child in the Ninth Five Year Plan (1997-2002). But despite these laws, policies and commitments, what is the actual situation of India's children vis-à-vis health, education, early childhood care and protection?

Resource Allocation for Children

Legal and programmatic commitments have to be matched by financial commitments, as reflected in the national and provincial budgets. The allocation and spending of adequate financial resources on children, although not the only indicator, is an important reflection of the government's commitment.

A HAQ-Centre for Child study indicates an increase in allocation and spending on children over the last decade. However, this rise is from 0.6 per cent at the beginning of the last decade to 1.2 per cent of the Union Budget in 1998-99. Thus, for every Rs 100 spent by the Union Government of India, only Rs 1.20 was, on an average, spent on children in the last decade! The highest percentage spent by the Government in a single year was Rs 1.80 in 1997-98. This declined to Rs 1.60 in 1998-99.

Survival and Healthcare

Article 24 of the Convention of the rights of the child requires the State partied to recognise the right of the child to the enjoyment of the highest attainable standard of health and to facilities for the treatment of illness and rehabilitation of health. It further directs the State Partied to strive to ensure that no child is deprived of his or her right to access to health care services. The convention also lays stress on development of primary health care, combating disease and malnutrition, appropriate pre-natal and post-natal care for mothers, and development of preventive health care.

Over the years, there has been some improvement in the health status of children in India. This is reflected in reduced mortality rates. Nevertheless, two million infants die each year, almost the same number as in 1960 (Directorate of Women and Child Development). The National Health Policy 1983 provides a comprehensive framework for planning, implementation and monitoring of health care services. Several committees have examined the health situation and recommended the need for improved access and quality of services to women and children.

Based on the National Health Policy, the National Plan of Action for children was drafted in 1992. Its major goals were the reduction of infant mortality rates to less than 50 per 1,000 live births and reduction of child mortality rate to less than 10 by the year 2002. It aimed to eradicate poliomyelitis by the year 2000; eliminate neo-natal tetanus by 1995; reduce measles deaths by 95 per cent by 1995 and measles cases by 90 per cent compared to pre-immunisation levels; achieve and maintain immunisation coverage at a level of 100 per cent for infants; reduce by 50 per cent deaths due to diarrhoea in children under the age of five and to reduce the incidence of diarrhoea by 25 per cent; and reduce mortality rates due to Acute Respiratory Infection (ARI) among children under five by 40 per cent by 2000 AD.

The government admits that the task of providing health care to 375 million children is an enormous challenge; especially since one-third of them live in conditions of abject poverty and neglect.

Nevertheless, several achievements have been made:

— Age-specific mortality rates have declined. The decline in the age group 0-4 years and 5-14 years is substantial.

— Infant mortality rates have decreased from 134 in 1946-50 to 72 in 1997.

— Under-five mortality rates declined from 177 in 1980 to 100 in 1993.

— Every girl-child born today can expect to live up to the age of 58 years, as against 41 years in 1951-60.

— Every boy-child can live to 58 years, as against 42 years in 1951-60.

— More deliveries take place in health facilities (33 per cent in 1992-93, compared to 25 per cent five years ago).

— More children receive the essential vaccines protecting them from tuberculosis, diphtheria, pertussis, tetanus, measles and polio (42 per cent, up from 36 per cent). The Universal Immunisation Programme aims at immunising all 25 million children born in the country each year against the six vaccine-preventable diseases.

And yet

— Of every 1,000 children born in a year, 48 die within 28 days of birth. The incidence is much higher in the rural areas: 52 child deaths at birth.

— There are not enough beds to accommodate the 25 million annual births.

— One in 13 infants dies before reaching the age of one year.

— One in nine children die before reaching the age of five. This figure corresponds to official figures for 1961.

— Approximately 70 per cent of infant deaths occur in the first week of life.

— Acute Lower Respiratory Infection (ALRI) continues to claim15-20 per cent of infant deaths, especially in the first three or four months of life.

— 380,000 deaths occur each year due to Vitamin A, iron and iodine deficiencies. And 210,000 children are born cretins, or turn blind at pre-school age.

— Every year 7 to 8 lakh (700,000-800,000) children die from a preventable disease, like diarrhoea.

— In a country that has buffer stocks of food grains, nearly 75 million children below the age of 5 years are malnourished.

— 45 per cent of children below three are severely and chronically malnourished.

— Only 44 per cent of children have completed the immunisation schedule. A massive 14 per cent have not received a single vaccine.

Early Childhood Care

Articles 3, 6 and 18 of the CRC require State agencies to: ensure to the maximum extent possible the survival and development of the child; render appropriate assistance to parents and legal guardians in performance of child-rearing responsibilities; ensure the development of institutions, facilities and services for the care of children. It also requires State agencies to ensure that children of working parents have the right to benefit from the child-rearing services and facilities for which they are eligible. There are 127.6 million children below the age of six in the country; 60 million of them below the poverty line.

The first six years in a child's life are crucial. It is in these years that the physical, cognitive, language and social development of the child is at its peak. Investment in early childhood care and education (ECCE) is essential. Recognising this, the government has launched several programmes, the most important being the Integrated Child Development Services programme. Investing in early childhood care and education means: comprehensive maternal care and entitlements; provision of crèches, child care, nutrition; immunisation and health care; pre-school education; protection and care to children; and creating child care services to release girls from sibling care responsibilities, so they can get an education.

The government has launched a number of schemes in these areas. These include: Crèches / Day Care scheme for Working and Ailing Mothers; National Fund for Child Care Services; Integrated Child Development Services (ICDS); Balwadi Nutrition Programme; Early Childhood Education through assistance to Voluntary Agencies.

Achievements:

— As against 18.9 million in 1997, the ICDS in 1999-2000 reached approximately 26.5 million children below the age of six. Of these, nearly 12.7 million children, between the ages of three and six, participate in centre-based pre-school educational activities.

And yet:

— "It is estimated that India today requires 800,000 crèches for its children. Against this, we have been able to set up only 14,925 crèches under these two schemes, leaving an enormous gap ..."

Education and Development

Articles 28 and 29 of the Convention on the Rights of the Child recognise the right of children to education. The development of children is integrally linked to their right to education. Article 28 makes it obligatory for State agencies to recognise the right of children to education. This is to be achieved on the basis of: equal opportunities; compulsory primary education freely available to all; secondary, higher education accessible to all children; educational and vocational information and guidance; measures to encourage regular attendance at schools and to reduce the drop out rates.

By virtue of Article 29, State agencies agree that the education of the child shall be directed to the development of the child's personality, talents, and mental and physical abilities, to their fullest potential. India's commitment to 'provide for and ensure Universal Elementary Education for all children' up to the age of 14 has been reiterated time and again. The Kothari Commission (1964-1966), the Acharya Ramamurthy Committee (1990), the Prof Yash Pal Committee (1993), the Saikia Committee (1997) have all reiterated the need for free and compulsory universal elementary education (UEE) and quality education.

In 1993, the Supreme Court clearly declared education a fundamental right, in the Unnikrishnan vs. State of Andhra Pradesh case and others. It said, "Though the right to education is not stated expressly as a fundamental right, it is implicit in and flows from the right to life guaranteed under Article 21."

The Saikia Committee reported an average expenditure per student in classes I-VIII in 1995-96 to be Rs 948 per annum. It recommended an additional investment of Rs 40,000 crores in the next five years to ensure education for all children out of school. In its report submitted to the Government of India, the Dr Tapas Majumdar Expert Committee estimated a requirement of additional Rs 1,36,000 crores over a period of 10 years ending 2007-2008.

Although literacy rates more than doubled from 24 per cent in 1961 to 52 per cent in 1991, there are 60 million more illiterate persons in the country than there were in 1961. Only 65 per cent of children reach Grade 5. Many of those 'completing primary school' cannot even read and write.

In the field of education we have achieved,

— Increase in literacy rates from 18.33 per cent in 1951, to 52.21 per cent in 1991

— Decrease in dropout rates from 62.7 per cent in 1977-78, to 39.37 per cent in 1995-96

— Increase in enrolment at primary school from 19.2 million in 1950-51, to 109.8 million in 1995-96

— Increase in primary schools from 209,671 in 1950-51, to 590,421 in 1995-96

And yet

— It is estimated that between 40-60 per cent of children in the 6-14 age group are out of school.

— About 40 per cent of children drop out of school before they reach Class V.

— Fifty-four per cent of children drop out of school before they complete their elementary education. Of them, 51 per cent are boys and 59 per cent girls.

— Enrolment rate at the primary level is 88 per cent: 98 per cent for boys and 81 per cent for girls. The enrolment rate at the middle level drops to 59 per cent -- 67 per cent for girls and 50 per cent for boys.

— As far back as 1962, the Kothari Commission had recommended a minimum of 6 per cent of the GNP as allocation for education. Four decades later, our allocation for education is a mere 3.5 per cent.

— Twelve per cent of primary schools have only one teacher, 58 per cent had only two rooms, 60 per cent had leaking roofs, and only 25 per cent of teachers were found teaching.

Protection and Rights

There are children who are particularly disadvantaged because of their social, economic, physical or mental condition. These children are placed under the category of children under special or difficult circumstances. The following groups of children have been included in this category by the Government of India:

— Children in labour

— Street children

— Children who are neglected or treated as juvenile offenders

— Children who are physically or mentally challenged

— Destitute children in need of adoption

— Drug addicts

— Children in prostitution

— Children of prostitutes

— Children of prisoners

— Refugee children

— Slum and migrant children

Convention on the rights of the child has provisions for all children who need protection.

Article 20 of the convention concerns children who are temporarily or permanently deprived of his/her family environment. Article 21 makes it obligatory for the State Parties to ensure that only component authorities authorize the adoption of a child.

Article 22 addresses the Right of refugee children to appropriate protection and humanitarian assistance, including tracing family members. Article 2 of the convention requires the States to ensure and respect all the rights set forth in the convention for the disabled children within their juridiction. Article 23 further provides guidance on realising the rights of the disabled child.

Article 32 recognise the right of the child to be protected from economic exploitation and from performing any work that is likely to be hazardous or interferes with the child's education or is harmful to the child's health or development.

Article 33 requires the ratifying states to take all appropriate measures to protect children from the illicit use of narcotic drugs and psychotropic substances and prevent the use of children in the production of trafficking of such drugs.

Articles 11, 21, 32, 33, 36 of the Convention protect children from sexual exploitation, abduction, sale and trafficking.

Articles 37 bars the death penalty and life imprisonment without possibility of release and insists that any restriction of liberty must be used as the last resort and for shortest possible time period. Article 39 requires measures to promote physical and psychological recovery, and social re-integration, of child victims. Article 40 details a list of minimum guarantees for the child and requires the State Parties to set a minimum age of criminal responsibility, to provide measures for dealing with children who may have infringed the penal law without resorting to judicial proceedings and to provide a variety of alternative dispositions to institutional care.

In spite of the achievements in health, nutrition and education, the government admits that the special needs and rights of children in difficult circumstances have remained "subdued" in the larger framework of meeting other basic needs of children. The National Plan of Action emphasises the need for tackling the root causes of such situations. The major constraint in providing services is the paucity of reliable data on children in difficult circumstances. Some of the data that is available is as follows, but it must be remembered that these data are guess-estimates and projections:

Child labour

India has the largest number of working children in the world. Estimates on the magnitude of child labour vary from approximately 11.28 million (Census of India. 1991) to 23.2 million estimated by the International Labour Organisation. The government admits that about 2 million children are employed in hazardous industries, occupations and processes. Other unofficial sources estimate 100 million working children in the country.

There are about 74.4 million children according to the National Labour Institute, who are neither enrolled in schools nor accountable for in the labour force. These are all potential child labourers. The 45 per cent of children who are out of school are also prospective child labourers. All child labour-related schemes and programmes of the ministry of labour fall under the broader scheme called 'Improvement in working conditions of women and children'. In 1998, because of the increasing magnitude of the problem, the ministry of labour set up a full-fledged Division on Child Labour headed by a joint secretary.

In August 1987, the National Child Labour Policy was adopted to deal with a situation where children work, or are compelled to work, on a regular or continuous basis, to earn a living for themselves or their families. The policy encourages voluntary organisations to take up non-formal education, vocational training, of health care, nutrition and education for working children. Based on the Policy, the National Child Labour Projects (NCLP) were launched for the first time in 1998 in areas of high concentration of child labour. In 1994-95 a high-powered body, the National Authority for the Elimination of Child Labour was constituted to withdraw child labour working in hazardous occupations, and for rehabilitating them through special schools. During 1999-2000, 91 child labour projects have been sanctioned in child labour endemic states.

Street children

India has the dubious distinction of having the largest population of street children. Street children suffer from destitution, neglect, abuse and exploitation. It is estimated that in urban areas alone there are 11 million children on the streets. Of them 420,000 street children live in the six metropolitan cities of the country. Under the Scheme for Welfare of Street Children, more than 24,000 street children are being benefited. The problem of destitution persists in the country in spite of a network of institutional and non-institutional programmes, and services being provided by the government and voluntary organisations.

Juvenile delinquency

India has a well-planned juvenile justice system, comprising the Juvenile Justice Board, Juvenile Courts, Juvenile Homes and After Care Organisations. With the Juvenile Justice Act 1986 in full force and a scheme for the prevention and control of Juvenile Social Maladjustment being implemented, juvenile crime in the country has declined over the years and accounts for 0.6 per cent of total crime. One of the most important objectives of the Juvenile Justice Act is to ensure that no child is lodged in jail or police lockup under any circumstances.

Children of migrant workers and construction labourers

Children of construction workers and migrant labourers are deprived of health, nutrition and education facilities. Day-care facilities for the children are negligible. The National Crèche Fund set up by the Department of Women and Child in 1994, gives assistance to voluntaty organisations to set up crèches for children of working mothers.

Child prostitutes

Over the years there has been an increase in the number of child prostitutes. Government of India estimates put the number at 400,000. According to UNICEF, almost 15 per cent of prostitutes enter the profession before the age of 15, and 25 per cent enter between 15-18. A number of children in prostitution are children of prostitutes. According to government estimates, at least 25,000 children are engaged in prostitution in the major metropolitan cities: Bangalore, Calcutta, Chennai, Delhi, Hyderabad and Mumbai. The Central Advisory Committee on Child Prostitution estimates this number at 100,000. Unofficial estimates say India has two million prostitutes, of whom 20 per cent are below 15. Almost all of them became victims of exploitation when they were children, i.e less than 15 years old.

The government has set up a Central Advisory Board to frame a plan of action for the rescue and rehabilitation of child prostitutes. Beside, three out of four rape victims are minors. In the last 10 years, rape of minors below 16 has accounted for more than 25 per cent of the total rape cases and rape of children below the age of 10 years increased by 10 per cent. Incestuous rape is the commonest form of sexual abuse. Delhi Police data shows there was a rise from 8 per cent in 1998 to 11 per cent in 1999.

Children with disabilities

According to government estimates, one in every 10 children is born with, or acquires, a physical, mental or sensory disability. So India could have 12 million disabled children.

It is estimated that 75 one per cent of the disabilities are preventable. Official agencies estimate that only one per cent of children with disability have access to education. The ministry of welfare is the nodal department for implementing schemes and programmes for the disabled. Article 45 under the Directive Principles of the Constitution of India reads as follows:

— 'The state shall provide within a period of ten years, free and compulsory education for all children up to the age of 14 years.' This goal was expected to be reached by 1960.

— The government's own data of 1990 shows that half the children and two-thirds of the girls are out of school. Child labour is reliably estimated to be around 20 million.

— It is against this backdrop that the Indian government policy shifts in education of the last 15 years and the various forces influencing these shifts need to be evaluated.

The National Policy on Education, 1986, heralds the beginning of a systematic and progressive dilution of the commitment to the constitutional obligation in ways hitherto not in evidence. The policy, for the first time, admitted to the enormity of the task of universalization of elementary education, and the actual number of children in school. In stark variation to Article 45, the policy admits that it cannot reach out to all the children through the formal system and proposes a parallel non-formal stream of education for those children who, due to their economic condition cannot go to school. This decision, far from mitigating the problem of child labour, actually condones it. The policy also bifurcates elementary education into primary (5 years) and upper primary (3 years).

Since the World Conference of Education for All (EFA) held in Jomtien, Thailand, in March 1990, these early indicators begin to take on a clearer focus. During the post-Jomtien phase, the commitment to ensure eight years of elementary education for all children has been reduced, for all practical purposes, to five years of primary education, delinking it from the upper primary stage to the extent that the term elementary is replaced with primary in virtually all programme documents.

India's ratification of the UN Convention of the Rights of the Child (CRC) in 1992 re-affirms the commitment to make primary (not elementary) education compulsory and available free for all. The District Primary Education Programme (DPEP), funded by the World Bank and a consortium of the European Community, restricted to five years of schooling, is being promoted as a dominant strategy for universalization of elementary education. In 1995, five leading agencies of the United Nations (UNICEF, UNDP, ILO, UNESCO and UNFPA) initiated a collabourative effort to provide programme support in a coordinated manner, to the on-going efforts of the government of India towards universalization of elementary education with $20 million aid. The programme, titled UNSCOPE will operate specially in areas with low female literacy, low female participation in school and high fertility areas.

In the wake of CRC, the National Literacy Mission has begun to include the out-of-school children in the 9-14 age group in its programmes. As a result of this, the state can claim fulfilment of educational responsibility of its children, if a child attends 2 years of an adult literacy class, without ever having stepped into school. This makes literacy, a dimension of education, a national goal synonymous with education itself. In 1990, the central government introduced the scheme of Minimum Levels of Learning (MLL) in the primary school programme. Some of the features of MLL are:

— division of primary education into 'cognitive' and 'non-cognitive' domains.

— defining MLL for environmental studies, language and mathematics for class I-V.

— vocabulary control and use of 'appropriate' language in formal and informal situations.

— subdivision of language skills leading to a labourious exercise of deciphering printed symbols for factual communication.

— acquisition of language competencies without any reference to mother tongue at the primary stage.

To seek answers, we need to look into not the policies themselves, but to related developments in the last 20 years in the areas of demographic control and the process of liberalization of the Indian economy. Since the failure of the draconian population control of the mid- seventies, the focus of family planning has shifted almost exclusively from men to women. That this is a regression in the process of equal responsibility of men and women is carefully avoided in any governmental discourse. The large-scale failure of the condom mode of contraceptive usage has been acknowledged by policy documents since the mid-eighties, when the government was obliged to explain how, if the contraceptive usage figures were true, could these figures explain the high crude birth rates being recorded at the same time?

Family planning policies since 1990, have begun to state that education (read literacy) of girls is the best 'contraceptive'. Kerala's high female literacy figure and low birth rates are co-related directly without any reference to Kerala's long history of socio-economic development and matrilinearity. This female literacy-birth rate connection appears even more credible to population policy makers when states such as Bihar, Uttar Pradesh, Madhya Pradesh, Uttar Pradesh, infamously called BIMARU or 'ill' by facetious writers, have not only low female literacy, but high birth rates. To those for whom being poor equals being ill, it is not hard to believe, ability to read and write will mean having less children. Thus, the case for substituting education with literacy is made. That is why rising female literacy levels, not education, is the much-treasured goal of policy makers. Is it a coincidence that the MLL competencies in environmental science has developed verbal and pictorial messages of 'small family, happy family', where the small family pictures depicts an affluent setting and the large family, a deprived one?

India was perhaps the only third world nation to have forbidden by law, injectible contraceptives such as Norplant, being much promoted by the west, thanks to the vigilance of a small band of women activists and the judiciary on the grounds that these devices have not been adequately tested and proven safe for the life conditions of poor women. Population growth of the third world countries is probably one of the most threatening aspects of the third world in the eyes of the 'developed' nations, and it should not come as a surprise that a major goal of all forms of aid is ultimately a decrease in population of the third world. Aid to India is no exception.

The relationship between the need for literate citizens and liberalization of economy and 'opening up' of markets is so obvious that those in the field of education appear to have entirely missed the connection. Now the policy shifts from elementary education to primary, from education to literacy, and, for those within the formal school system, from the curriculum designed to think critically to the curriculum designed to create receptors of messages, that the MLL has become clear. Who needs education for developing the critical faculty when multi-national markets have to function?

That these shifts affecting a nation of nearly 1 billion people have occurred with very little resistance must also be seen in conjunction with the fact that the external aid in the education sector is around 4.2% of the public expenditure on elementary education. Such is the power of the post-Jomtien phenomenon in Indian education.

6

MICRO-PLANNING IN EDUCATION

Budgets impact women's lives in several ways. They directly promote women's development through the allocation of budgetary funds for women's programmes and reduce opportunities for the empowerment of women through budgetary cuts. Structural adjustment programmes and globalisation policies have increased women's unpaid work burden, thereby increasing women-provided subsidies in the economy. Devaluation of incomes, as a result of new economic policies, price rises, incompetence of the Public Distribution System (PDS) and the reduction of services offered by the public healthcare system means that women bear a disproportionate share of the burden.

In patriarchal families it is the woman who has to shoulder the responsibility of providing meals and looking after sick family members. Hence women have a high stake in preventing increases in the proportion of indirect taxes on essential commodities and in budgetary provisions to guarantee food security and healthcare.

WOMEN'S COMPONENT PLAN AND GENDER BUDGETING

The Planning Commission of India has always focused on women's issues as per the perceptions of their members on the status of women in the economy. The First Five-Year Plan

(1951-1956) set up the Central Social Welfare Board in 1953 to promote welfare work through voluntary organisations, charitable trusts and philanthropic agencies. The Second Five-Year Plan (1956-1960) supported the development of mahila mandals to undertake work at the grassroots. The third, fourth and interim plans (1961-74) made provision for women's education, pre-natal and child health services, supplementary feeding for children, nursing and expectant mothers. The Fifth Five-Year Plan (1974-1978) marked a major shift in the approach towards women, from welfare to development.

The Sixth Five-Year Plan (1980-85) accepted women's development as a separate economic agenda. It took a multi-disciplinary approach with a three-pronged thrust on health, education and employment. The Seventh Five-Year Plan (1985-1990) declared as its objective bringing women into the mainstream of national development. The Eighth Five-Year Plan (1992-1997) projected a paradigm shift from development to empowerment and promised to ensure a flow of benefits to women in the core sectors of education, health and employment. The outlay for women rose from Rs 4 crore in the first plan to Rs 2,000 crore in the eighth plan. The Ninth Five-Year Plan (1997-2002) stated that empowerment of women was its strategic objective. It accepted the concept of a women's component plan to assure that at least 30% of funds/benefits from all development sectors flow to women. The Tenth Five-Year Plan (2002-2009) sugges^- specific strategies, policies and programmes for the empowerr.ient of women. They are:

"Measurement of development has to go beyond the achievement of GDP growth to indicators of distributive justice and their monitoring. Women-headed households have to be specifically targeted, identifying added disadvantages in the rural and urban locations with reference to different parameters of deprivation. Formulation of gender development indicators to measure human development and their use as a tool for monitoring development needs to be hastened.

"The component plan approach, which did not address compartmentalisation of government functioning, should be replaced by a mandated approach of convergence of services at all levels of governance, through inter-sectoral committees of all ministries/departments at the Centre and the states with specific responsibility given to the panchayats and municipalities to administer at the grassroots level."

The United Nations has suggested that,

> "To protect the gains of the past and ensure steady progress on indicators of social development and gender equality, and in order to give a fresh impetus to the process of women's empowerment, the Tenth Plan needs to take some bold policy initiatives. Earmarking of funds for women under all major poverty alleviation programmes and the maintenance of gender disaggregated records of implementation of all poverty alleviation programmes. Mandatory registration of all assets provided under government programmes (land, house, animals, production units) in the joint names of husband and wife. Intensified focus on rights education and capacity-building interventions for women in all strategic sectors, including health and reproductive health, agriculture, natural resource management, technology (including information technology) and legal awareness. Revision of regulatory framework to allow women's collectives to access institutional credit, obtain medium-term leases for cultivation on wastelands and common lands, bid for contracts for the collection and sale of minor forest produce and other collective activities that will ensure household food security while regenerating the natural resource base."

Women's groups have demanded allocations for women-specific programmes to achieve the desired goals in a shorter time span. They should target women of different age-groups in terms of strategic interventions to take specific notice of adolescent girls, older women and women in difficult circumstances. Strategic gender tools like gender audits, gender impact assessments, gender analysis and gender budgeting to monitor implementation and impacts must be developed. Gender audit of plans, policies and programmes of various ministries with pro-women allocations has to be part of the monitoring process.

There is a need for provisions in the composite programmes in the education, health and rural development sectors to target them specifically at girls/women as the principal beneficiaries and disaggregated within the total allocation. It may also be necessary to place restrictions on their re-appropriation for other purposes.

To effectively attain population stabilisation, policies and plans need to empower women, promote their reproductive rights and involve men in reproductive decision-making and household responsibilities. Particular attention should be given to improve women's access to quality reproductive health services, including adolescent girls, to counselling on reproductive health and sexuality issues.

The strategy of organising women into self-help groups in the Ninth Plan period has paid good dividends for expanding micro-credit. This should be extended not only to reach larger numbers of women but also increase awareness of and access to social development, apart from encouraging a process of convergence in the delivery of services in a decentralised setup. It is important to empower women's organisations and citizens groups to monitor the enforcement of equal and minimum wages legislation by state governments, and the adherence to norms in poverty alleviation programmes. Professional organisations including universities should be included to help undertake evaluation and research studies to identify issues requiring special attention. The National Institute of Public Finance and Policy has undertaken a gender audit of Budget 2002-03, in its publication, `Gender Budgeting in India'. According to this report, the budgetary allocation for women-specific schemes increased only in the area of family planning. Family planning schemes received an additional Rs 700 crore in the present budget.

For economic services concerning women, the present budget has made provision for only Rs 153.70 crore. For Rashtriya Mahila Kosh, the nodal agency for micro-credit schemes, the budgetary allocation was reduced from the earlier Rs 3 crore to Rs 1 crore. Budgetary allocation for providing drinking water and electricity connections to marginalised sections remain inadequate. Women's groups have criticised budgetary cuts on schemes to provide foodgrain to adolescent girls as well as pregnant women and nursing mothers. Per capita allocation funds for nutritional support for girl children, through mid-day meal schemes, declined from Rs 112 to Rs 70. Per capita allocation of budgetary provision for girls' education is only Rs 286.

There has to be coordination between the launching of new schemes and budgetary allocations. It does not serve women's interests if the funds are not available for already-launched schemes, or funds allocated for non-existing schemes as these funds will remain unutilised. In the absence of women-specific educational schemes, Rs 160 crore allocated for the national programme for women's education remained unutilised.

Women's groups have condemned the budgetary allocation for weapons of destruction and military expenditure as wasteful expenditure. Nearly half of the population of south Asia suffers as a result of pauperisation. Budget analyses from the gender perspective should be introduced and promoted in all women's groups, educational and research institutions. Public debate on gender sensitive budgets will help the country tilt the balance in favour of area development and the peaceful use of resources in the present atmosphere of jingoism.

Allocation and expenses of resources for women in panchayat budgets: To engender budgets at the panchayat level, we need to analyse budgets scheme-wise, sector-wise, category-wise and year-wise with their budget estimates, revised estimates and actual expenditure. It is also important to make a thorough study of the economic survey published by the Government of India and the state human development reports, state policies for women and the allocation of resources in the state plans published by state governments that guide programmes and budgetary allocations. Now, women's groups are demanding that each and every ministry allocate separate funds for women-specific needs.

Each state has a detailed list of programmes/schemes benefiting women under four categories:

— Women-specific schemes where 100% of the allocation is required to be spent on women.

— Pro-women schemes where at least 30% of the allocation and benefits flow to women.

— Gender-neutral schemes meant to benefit the community as a whole where both men and women avail of the benefits.

— Residual state-specific programmes that have a profound effect on women's position/condition.

The All India Institute of Local Self Government, Mumbai, provides details of all schemes under these four categories through its publications and through workshops and training programmes.

Problem of Utilisation of Funds Allocated for Area Development

Rs 2 crore is allocated to each MP for the development of the constituency as per the MP Local Area Development Scheme (MPLADS). Utilisation of government funding is maximum in the north-eastern states because of strong horizontal and vertical networking. The prosperous states depend more on private funding to avoid bureaucratic hassles. If poorer areas in the state don't have a highly motivated administration or an NGO network, then too funding remains unutilised. In areas dominated by the lower middle class and poorer groups, there are demands for more schools, libraries, bridges, toilets, drains, tubewells, community centres and crematoriums. In prosperous areas, the demands are for road repair and schools.

The private sector of the economy demands banks, hospitals and shopping plazas. Members of Parliament (MPs) and Members of the Legislative Assembly (MLAs) have to strike a balance by keeping in mind the immediate needs and long-term considerations of their constituencies. As much as Rs 312.51 lakh, out of a total of Rs 730 lakh allocated by the ministry of tribal affairs to the Tribal Cooperative Marketing Federation of India Limited (TRIFED), which markets minor forest produce, to set up 1,876 grain banks remained unutilised in 1999-2000, as per the 20th report of the parliamentary committee on the welfare of SCs and STs. It is ironic that even as an estimated 320 million people in India face starvation, close to 65 million tonnes of foodgrain lie rotting in government godowns.

In Maharashtra, only 66.5% of funds under MPLADS is utilised. While local bodies suffer a chronic shortage of funds, as little as one-third of the funds released by the Union government under MPLADS remained unutilised in the state. A report by the Comptroller and Auditor General (CAG) points out that the Union government released over Rs 214 crore under MPLADS for the period 1997-2000, but its utilisation was only around Rs 73 crore. In some cases MPs did not make even a single recommendation. For example, district collectors of Beed, Pune and Satara invested Rs 5.76 crore allotted to the MPs of their areas in small savings schemes to achieve their targets for 1999-2000.

The strategy of organising women into self-help groups in the Ninth Plan period has paid good dividends. This should be extended not only to reach larger numbers of women but also to increase awareness of and access to social development, apart from encouraging a process of convergence in the delivery of services in a decentralised setup. Technical workshops on allocation and expenditure of panchayat budgets should be organised in November for pre-budget inputs for advocacy and lobbying, and in March for a critical evaluation of budgetary allocations.

Financial matters and PRIs

A recent survey of panchayats working in 19 states, conducted by the National Institute of Rural Development, Hyderabad, suggested that panchayats remain toothless because functional and financial autonomy has not been granted to PRIs. The study by the Institute of Social Sciences shows that the extent of fiscal decentralisation through the empowerment of PRIs has been very limited. The report of the working group on decentralisation appointed by the Karnataka government has been criticised severely because, "it betrays utter lack of trust in the people, which is the keystone of decentralised democracy,".

Case studies of panchayat finances in the gram sabhas of Midnapur district in West Bengal have corroborated these facts in terms of lack of fiscal autonomy, neglect of girls' education and a resource crunch. But it has played a substantial role in the development of infrastructure, for example rural roads, drinking water, health, education, irrigation and power.

Elected representatives, district officials and NGOs working in the area should act as facilitators in preparation of plans for area development and social justice. The UN system has supported the allocation of resources for women in PRIs, right from the beginning. "The evidence on gender and decentralisation in India thus suggests that while women have played a positive role in addressing, or attempting to address, a range of practical gender needs1, their impact on strategic gender needs is not remarkable,".

STRENGTHENING OF COMMUNITY BASED MECHANISM FOR SCHOOL MANAGEMENT AND SUPPORT

Strengthening of community based mechanism for school management and support will involve in particular, establishing Village Education Committees (VECs), training them and other community-based organisations in micro-planning, conducting school mapping, community level monitoring system and establishing purposeful interaction between VECs and Zila Parishads, block panchayats and gram panchayats.

Developing government and local body schools as "empowered community schools". The aim is to work with government schools and through a process of change emanating from fostering ownership of the school by the community, turn them into "empowered community schools". Improving teaching methodology for multigrade classroom through pre and in-service teacher development programmes offered by district, block and cluster level institutions to make them more interactive child-centred and gender-sensitive.

Developing a teacher empowerment package for teachers of "empowered community schools", including motivational training and skill development, and strengthening local capacity to utilise community based teachers. Facilitating information exchange on best classroom practices, policy and community participation through interstate and intra state visits. Applying an integrated social development approach which converges activities and resource inputs by all agencies.

In line with these key elements the programme is envisaged to achieve the following outcomes in five years i.e. from 1998 to 2003. Institutional capacity building of key community institutions including VECs and panchayats, as well as Department of Education, NGOs, and skills of community institutions to sustain the process of community-based planning to improve quality of education. Better educational opportunity and improved learning processes for all eligible children and their protection from exploitation. Concomitant with this outcome shall be the increased community awareness and responsibility for respecting, protecting and fulfilling child rights. Educational needs of handicapped children specially the integration of partially disabled children into schools shall be one of the thrust areas.

A multigrade curriculum methodology based on the content of the official primary school curriculum for use in primary schools.

A capacity development programme for teachers to enable them to learn how to utilise the multigrade curriculum methodology.

An empowerment package for teachers, including refined community-based teachers' selection and placement mechanism, organisation of in-service teachers training programme and motivational initiatives.

Through regular interaction with State Progamme Coordinators (SPCs), another major thrust for the programme has been identified viz. the Janshala blocks must plan for achieving Universal Primary Education by the end of the programme period. This would imply universal enrollment, regular attendance, retention and appropriate achievement levels for all children. Thus issues of physical access and universal participation of children belonging to deprived groups has been stressed. For some of the most disadvantaged groups like urban deprived children, working children, migrant children and street children, diversified strategies for alternative schooling would need to be implemented.

Integrated Education for Disabled Children is another area for which a special emphasis is required. Each state programme should by now have developed a clear strategy for education of disabled children.

Thus the Review Team should study the programme keeping in mind the following points:

What has been the progress in Janshala states towards the outcomes as identified in para 3 & 4. In case concrete progress has not been made, the team should take note of the strategies/conceptualisation articulated by state/ district and block teams on these areas of work and understand the timeframes proposed by the state sub programme. All the programme states have adopted microplanning as an important strategy for decentralised need identification and involvement of community. The team should look at microplanning results and see how the sub programme proposes to address issues identified during microplanning.

How has the microplanning data been used in the formulation of strategies? What is the level of community involvement after about three years of programme implementation? Who are the volunteers/activists of the programme that keep regular contact with VECs/School Committees/women's groups to ensure that they function actively? What is the general assessment of the community involvement strategy of the programme? Involving the community in school management would require attitudinal change on part of teachers and educational administrators. How has this been addressed? How is the community involved in school management - please list concrete responsibilities being carried out by the community or community-based organisations like VECs? What has been the mechanism to respond to the issues raised by the community?

How does the community monitor enrolment, attendance and retention of children? Has there been any attempt in involving the community in the quality improvement effort and assessing learning of their children? Is the vision of a community empowered school widely shared by all programmes personnel? Is this vision (if evolved) also known/shared by teachers and community members? After several programme interventions, do teachers, educational administrators and project personnel share the vision of improved classroom teaching learning process? How effective is the regular academic support system for teachers and schools through block/cluster level resource persons and centres?

Have these centres become vibrant centres of academic activity? Are rich variety of curriculum related TLMs being prepared regularly at the cluster/block level and by teachers? How do the classrooms look? How do the basic minimum conditions in schools, as outlined in baseline surveys, at the beginning of the programme compare with their condition now? Is there a special thrust on understanding gender issues within the classroom? Have block and cluster personnel received adequate orientation/exposure to be able to guide teachers? Are they motivated? What is their acceptability in the field?

Has the programme utilised DIETs? Do BRCs/CRCs have linkages with Diets? Do the state team, district and block personnel have a clear focus on equity issues? Is there clear attention on the most disadvantaged groups? Achieving UPE in most states now means specific initiatives for specific disadvantaged groups. Is the understanding clear in the programme? How is it being operationalised?

The Janshala programme is also meant to promote decentralisation and community ownership. In view of this, the planning process and delegation of financial powers to the block education officers and other project personnel may be reviewed through discussion with state, district and block level officials.

Is the programme receiving active support of educational administrations at district, block and sub block levels? What are the indicators developed by the state to measure progress in achieving the programme objectives? How does the state collect information and measure the programme qualitatively? Does it include classroom observation? How is community empowerment measured? In which areas does the team think the state programme needs technical support/inputs, exposure or understanding of strategies being implemented elsewhere etc.? What is the state's own assessment of this requirement?

Review the achievements against the target proposed in the AWP&B, 2000-01 and activity-wise progress so far in implementation of the AWP 2001-02. The team could discuss the AWP 2001-02 with state sub programme and understand the priorities. What is the financial progress of the programme against -

a) Overall project cost

b) AWPs 2000-01 and 2001-02

What are the constraints of programme management in taking up a larger number of activities? The SPC and her team should be able to identify these constraints. How do they propose to address them, considering that the programme is left with only two years and there is still a wide gap between objective and achievement? Compared to last year's progress does the AWP 2001-02 appear to be feasible? How does the state/district/block teams justify such high allocations? How would the programme change gears for implementation this year?

The review team would undertake the following tasks:

Initial discussions with state team including discussion on strategies, Annual Work Plan, staffing, orientation and capacity building, strategies in different components, development of indicators, planning for UPE and out of school children etc. Field visits including discussion with district, block and sub block personnel, educational administrators, school teachers, parents, community members, panchayat representatives, DIET personnel etc. Also visits to schools, observation of classrooms, studying VEC records and registers. Discussion regarding training programmes and their impact, problems of specific disadvantaged groups, analysis of microplanning data etc.

Discussion with SPC and state team about field observation and finalising a list of observation and recommendations. Discussion with Education Secretary and briefing him/her about the programme achievements/ constraints and suggestions. Certain agreements may be arrived at with the Education Secretary and SPC about certain activities/tasks to be carried out within a certain timeframe.

7

INSTITUTIONAL PLANNING

India has steadily raised primary enrollment rates since independence and today has the world's second largest education system after China, with 108 million children aged 6-10 attending primary school. However, more than 25 million primary school-age children are not in school. Two out of five first-grade students will not complete the primary cycles of 4 to 5 years (depending on the state), and the learning achievement of those graduating is low.

Children from poorer families are at a greater disadvantage. The drop-out rate for the poorest households is about four times that of the richest ones. There are large gaps in access to education; quality of education; and learning according to gender, social class, and location.

The World Bank has been an active partner with the Government of India and state governments to respond to these and other education challenges. The World Bank's assistance to India's education sector began with an Agricultural Education Project in 1972 and was followed by a Vocational Training Project and Technician Education Projects 1 & 2 in the late 1980s.

The World Conference on Education, held in Jomtien, Thailand in 1990, highlighted the lack of access to and quality of India's basic education system. Issues raised at the conference resulted in an active collaboration between the Government of India and the World Bank in the field of basic education.

Bank assistance for basic education in India aims to expand enrollment levels and reduce drop out rates, while raising students' academic performance. Projects focus especially on girls, children from disadvantaged scheduled castes and scheduled tribes, working children, children with disabilities, and other children with limited opportunities to attend primary school.

The main project activities are working to increase access, improve classroom instruction, strengthen community participation in education, and build institutional and management capacity.

There are seven ongoing projects with the Ministry of Human Resource Development. Two more operations in Uttar Pradesh and Rajasthan are under preparation. These will be financed by the International Development Association (IDA), the World Bank's concessionary lending affiliate that provides interest-free credits to the poorest countries.

UTTAR PRADESH BASIC EDUCATION PROJECT I AND II

The Uttar Pradesh Basic Education Project (UPBEP I), the Bank's first investment in basic education in India, was approved in 1993. It is financed by a $165 million IDA credit. The unanticipated increase in enrollments resulting from the UPBEP I interventions led to the approval of the Second UP Basic Education Project (UPBEP II) approved in 1997 and financed by an IDA credit of $59.4 million.

The project complements ongoing state efforts by financing construction of new schools and additional classrooms, recruiting and training new teachers, establishing school improvement funds, and providing learning materials. UPBEP I and UPBEP II target both primary and upper-primary education.

The UPBEP I and II project interventions are showing remarkable results. Enrollment at the primary as well as upper-primary school levels in the UPBEP districts have shown a major increase. At the primary level enrollment has increased by 66.8 percent and at the upper-primary level by almost 64.07 percent. Comparing girls enrollment increase in project and non-project districts in Uttar Pradesh the increase reported is 66.79 percent and 33.11 percent, respectively.

Improvements have also been recorded in the mid-term learning assessment conducted in 1996 in which composite mean scores for grade 5 in language improved over the baseline from 34.18 to 37.30 and mean scores for mathematics were higher in project districts as compared to the non-project districts.

Classroom activities also reflect more variety and 60-90 percent of teachers report constructing and using teaching aids as compared to 25-60 percent in the baseline survey. The project has also built government capacity by supporting the establishment of the State Institute of Educational Management and Training, which will serve as a training and resource institution for the northern region.

DISTRICT PRIMARY EDUCATION PROJECT I, II AND III

The 7-year District Primary Education Project (DPEP), approved in November 1994, is financed by an IDA credit of $180 million. The project will create about 470,000 additional primary school places. A trend analysis between 1995 to 1998 on access and retention in DPEP I districts by the National Institute for Educational Planning and Administration (NIEPA) reports an average increase in enrollment in all districts (except Kerala) of 9.43 percent in 1995-96 and 6.48 percent increase in 1996-97.

District Primary Education Project (Andhra Pradesh)

The District Primary Education Project, which is part of the

Andhra Pradesh Economic Restructuring Project, was approved in 1998 and is financed by an IDA credit of $137.4 million. The project is being implemented in 15 districts with low female literacy levels within the framework of the centrally sponsored DPEP.

Rajasthan District Primary Education Project

Support for primary education in 10 educationally disadvantaged districts in Rajasthan was approved in 1999. The credit of $85.7 million is in line with other DPEP projects and focuses on expanding access for about 600,000 additional children and raising the quality of education provided.

VOCATIONALL/TECHINAL EDUCATION AND TRAINING

The Vocational Training Project provided assistance through a revised IDA credit of $138 million. The project, which closed in December 1998, aimed to improve the quality and efficiency of craftsman and apprenticeship training, expand the scope and relevance of advanced skills training programs, and strengthen the capacity for planning and management of vocational training at central and state levels. The project also aimed to increase modern sector training opportunities for women. About 550 industrial training institutes in 28 states/union territories and 20 centrally administered institutions were financed under the project.

The First Technician Education Project, which closed in September 1998, was financed by an IDA credit of $225 million. The project covered the states of Bihar, Goa, Gujarat, Karnataka, Kerala, Madhya Pradesh, Orissa, Rajasthan, and Uttar Pradesh and supported the Ten-Year Technician Education Investment Program (1990-99) by expanding capacity and improving quality and efficiency.

The project helped to provide India's industrial sector with qualified technicians in new areas of engineering and technology. Female enrollment in technician education increased from 11 percent to 30 percent. Some facilities were also created for technical training of the disabled.

A $255.7 million credit for the Technician Education II Project was approved in 1991 and extends the Technician Education I Project to the states of Andhra Pradesh, Assam, Haryana, Himachal Pradesh, Maharashtra, Punjab, Tamil Nadu, West Bengal, Pondicherry, and Delhi.

Elementary Education

The World Bank's involvement in basic education in India is grounded in a major study of primary education entitled Primary Education in India. The study explores issues surrounding access; learning achievement; and gaps in enrollment, retention, and achievement. It identifies essential actions to expand access and improve learning. The study was prepared in close collaboration with the Ministry of Human Resources Development and leading research institutions in India. It features pioneering efforts to survey learning achievements in India and in analyzing cost-effectiveness.

The work on primary education is currently being augmented by a study of the upper-primary stage of elementary education in close collaboration with the Ministry of Human Resource Development and Indian research institutions. As a result of the implementation of the District Primary Education Program and other initiatives to increase enrollment and retention in primary education, a surge in the demand for upper-primary schooling can be anticipated in the next few years.

In addition to the large amount of resources required to finance both initial investment costs and recurring liabilities, the intention to provide quality elementary education to every child raises many challenges associated with the management, structure, and delivery of upper-primary education. The overall objectives of the study are to provide a clearer understanding of enrollment patterns; the complexity of arrangements for delivering this type of schooling across and within states; curricular structure and teacher training; the constraints on its future development; and the basis for a strategy of intervention. The study uses enrollment projections to estimate the financial requirements of universalization.

Sector work has also begun in four other areas. First, in collaboration with the Bank's health and nutrition team, sector work is being initiated in the areas of early childhood development to assess the status of existing programs in this area from a holistic child development perspective and to identify possibilities for future cross-sector investment in early childhood development.

Second, in order to promote private initiative in education consistent with an envisaged realigned role of state involvement in elementary education, a status study focusing on the extent of demand for and provision of private elementary education is planned.

Third, in the area of student assessment, a survey of the system of student performance evaluation in India and ways in which evaluation influences educational policy, planning, and administration will be conducted.

The description and discussion of the existing mechanisms and strategies for evaluating student performance and its role in improving public elementary education would inform the establishment of an effective system of assessment that can influence policy and planning in elementary education.

Technical and Science Manpower Development

With the continuing liberalization of economy, industries and service sectors in India are facing a major challenge due to national and international competition. This is forcing rapid modernization and the introduction of new technologies and management approaches. High-quality technical and scientific manpower is critical for such developments.

The higher education system of India, responsible for developing such manpower, is facing major crises and is unable to meet the new expectations. This situation needs immediate attention if India is to stand against the challenges posed and fully benefit from its policy of liberalization.

The Sector Study on Technical and Scientific Manpower Development in India, which is almost completed, aims to understand critical issues in technical and scientific manpower development, and to identify strategies to improve the efficiency and responsiveness of educational institutions to the changing needs of the labor market.

THOUGH 50 years have passed ever since the Indian Constitution adopted the Universalisation of Elementary Education (UEE) under the Directive Principle of State Policy, it has eluded our grasp. It is now being debated whether adequate resources can be found if it is made a Fundamental Right, the bill for which has been passed only in the Rajya Sabha. The whole world is talking about education as a Human Right. In the meantime, a large number of interventions have been made in the elementary education sector since the 1986 National Policy on Education. Various schemes like Operation Blackboard, Teacher Education, Non-formal Education, Mahila Samakhya, National Programme for Nutritional Support for Primary Education, and other State Specific Education projects are undertaken in Bihar, Rajasthan, U.P. and A.P. A large number of these interventions have also been subjected to evaluation and impact studies.

Such Central Government interventions have taken the form of budgetary allocations in the Central budget. For example, the 1999-2000 budget allocations to education are viewed as the "National Human Development Initiative". Evaluation studies made have pointed to the need for effective decentralisation and with community ownership, sustainable financing, institutional capacity building at all levels and most of all effective educational administration system.

Also, a consensus emerged states that:

a) As far as possible, schools and teachers should be accountable to the community, and the curriculum should promote education for life rather than simply learning skills.

b) UEE of satisfactory quality would require more resources but it has to come with a larger community role in the management of the school. Such a role of the community will help the achievement of the goal of universalisation effectively with the mobilisation of community efforts in various forms like greater concern for quality and inputs.

c) Decentralisation down to the school level is the only long-term solution for excellence in schools.

The Sarva Siksha Abiyan is to examine whether the same is likely to succeed, especially because the country has been toying with decentralisation, and also in what manner the present exercise will be different. It will be argued that at present, with the three tiers of government, namely Central, State and Local bodies, there is a good scope for decentralisation to succeed, provided suitable planning and financial allocation procedures are adopted at all levels and hurdles to local level institutions to function removed. Planning with a clear-cut objective and community participation will be essential.

Despite all the previous Central Government interventions for effective universalisation of elementary education, it has not yet become a reality. According to the Government of India assessment 2000, enrolment of the 6-11 years at the primary level has been 90.3 per cent and 11 to 14 years has been 58.5 per cent in 1997, thereby showing the great leeway that is yet to be made for effective UAE. In addition, there are also out-of-school children whose number has become substantial which shows a regional variation. 1991 census revealed 7.55 crore children are out of school, out of which 4.194 were females and 3.36 crore, males. In the 6 to 14 age group, 45 per cent did not attend school.

A look at the expenditure trends on education shows that the goal of six per cent National Income as envisaged in National Policy on Education 1986-1992 is yet to be realised. In 1996-97 it was only 3.8 per cent of GNP. Even the share of elementary education, despite the constitutional obligation towards universalisation, has not been high, though it has increased from.48 per cent to 1.7 per cent of GNP during the last five decades. The central expenditure on education has increased substantially in the last decade.

Sarva Siksha Abiyan aimed at building a District Primary Educational Plan, taking into account the existing infrastructure in a district, the existing and projected gap and the resources available under the existing scheme supported by the Central and State governments. Habitation plans will be the basis for district plans so as to make it a demand-driven plan.

Sarva Siksha Abiyan is not to supplant any of the currently available resources, but just to supplement and cover the missing gaps. In fact it emphasises institutional reforms in States and districts in order to create a transparent and effective system for efficient use of resources and establishing a functional structure of decentralisation within the framework of the *panchayati raj* institutions. Many activities of an enabling nature will have to be provided for, and a sum of Rs. 50 lakhs has been allocated for this purpose.

The additional resource requirement, as worked out by the Department of Education, Government of India, amounted to an annual additional requirement of nearly 8,000 crores by the 10th year for both the Centre and the State. Over a 10-year period, projected additional resource is nearly 63,000 crores. *Sarva Siksha Abiyan* has been pleading for a long-term perspective on financial partnership between central and state governments, so that elementary education interventions by the Centre will be sustainable. At present more than 90 per cent of the expenditure on elementary education is borne by the States.

Sarva Siksha Abiyan programme provides for a 85-15 sharing between the Centre and the States till the 9th Plan and

75-25 sharing during the 10th Plan and a sustainable 50-50 sharing thereafter. Only such a long-term perspective will encourage the States to invest more on elementary education. In addition to a perspective plan, each district is expected to work out priorities in a particular financial year, based on the availability of resources. It is worth pointing out here that in planning of education, it is necessary to take into account class-wise and region-wise enrolment of boys, girls (SC-ST) rather than enrolment in 6 to11 or 11 to14 primary or elementary class students. Only when class-wise enrolment is considered and projected, an accurate resource requirement can be estimated.

For an assessment of the intervention, it is necessary to discuss the following inter-related issues: How will the convergent approach make the states invest more in elementary education and from where will they get resources needed. Of course, resources can be financial and others. Will the strategy for decentralisation proposed here in the *Sarva Siksha Abiyan* work? Decentralisation has been categorised into four —

(1) degrees of transfer of authority,

(2) deconcentration

(3) delegation and

(4) revolution and privatisation.

We might consider each of them in turn. Obviously the transfer of authority to the district level cannot be full or in toto, a certain amount of authority will have to be retained by the State level mission. Of course in certain matters there has to be a full degree of transfer of authority. With regard to the other three, there is delegation and devolution to the village education committee and the school committee. But with privatisation, there has to be a favour of the community owned school. *Sarva Siksha Abiyan* has conceived the decentralisation on all the four and it will have to vary presumably from one village to the other depending on the extent of initiative by the community.

What are the pre-conditions needed for the success of inducing States to make more investment for education as well as decentralisation. We may consider each of the above in the following paragraphs.

Full convergence is a method of making the resources as effective as possible by avoiding overlapping in objectives and coverage of the schemes. In essence, it will call for necessary modifications not only in the implementation of elementary education schemes, but of other ministries and departments like labour, social justice and empowerment of women, child, health, urban development, youth affairs and sports. In every department it has to be seen that some amount is allocated for elementary education and literacy increase so that the overall objective of UEE can be achieved in a complementary fashion with the help of other departments also. If necessary, this consideration has to be taken into account at higher levels also.

The convergence cannot be limited to the district level to be reflected in the district elementary educational plan, there has to be convergence of all the existing schemes, right from the national to the district. Also, to help the process of decentralisation, it is necessary to remove the hurdles for raising resources for local body institutions such as the *panchayati raj.* In fact these bodies should be encouraged to become self-governing institutions rather than be mere agents for the government, and they should be held accountable to the village education committee and school management committee on the basis of intensive community mobilisation and processes. There has to be rethinking of the whole process to ensure that additional resources are obtained from other departments and ministries and from the community in the surrounding areas.

Local school committees will have to play a prominent role in deciding school priorities. For this purpose, there has to be a generation of political support from the proposed changes in the school habitation and districts as well as the community at large and also increase the capability to persons who can be involved in decision-making. They can be divided into three groups — the producers of education, distributors of education and users of education.

The reaction of all the three categories will have to be obtained in all the district level education plans, taking into account the State and National priorities in matters such as girl's education, education of SC and ST as well as removal of regional backwardness.

There has to be appropriate grants for the Centre and States to the field level missions, which will have people's representatives. But at the same time, these institutions should be encouraged to mobilise local resources. As the Santhanam Committee reported in 1963, no self-governing institution will he happy to either depend entirely on government grants or be able to raise all the resources locally. The spirit of self-governing institutions must permeate all along the line, right from the state up to the bottom layer.

It is suffice to say that the Centre has burdened itself with many of the activities which are really in the concurrent list of the Constitution of India, such as education, health, rural development and nutrition, which are best left to the local level organisations with appropriate financial transfers from the Centre and State level government. Whether there should be adhoc one time grant, regular grants or specific grants are matters to be decided, taking into account the level of educational development, and the backlog of infrastructure in every area and this will have to be monitored from time to time.

PLANNING, MANAGEMENT AND MONITORING

National Policy On Education (NPE)

National Policy on Education (NPE), 1986 and Programme of Action (POA), 1992 continued to be implemented with vigour. The States/UTs of Andhra Pradesh, Haryana, Kerala, Maharashtra, Meghalaya, Tamil Nadu, Tripura and UT of Chandigarh and Lakshadweep have formulated their State POAs while Arunachal Pradesh and Mizoram have completed its draft State POA. Besides, Orissa, Punjab, Uttar Pradesh and West Bengal have prepared State POAs in certain sectors like Elementary Education, School Education, Higher and Technical Education.

Indian Education on Internet

For wider dissemination of knowledge and information relating to the Indian Education System in general and policies and programmes of the Union Education Department in particular, a worldwide Website site has been created with the help of National Informatics Centre (NIC) which can be accessed from any part of the world through a computer linked to internet. In fact, this information could be also be accessed from all the districts headquarters of the country through NICNET.

Conference of State Education Ministers

A conference of State Education Ministers and State Education Secretaries was held on August 9-10, 1996 under the chairmanship of Minister Of Hum. an Resource Development (HRM) to review the status of the programmes in the areas of elementary, adult and secondary education and the measures needed to expedite achievement of national goals in these areas. The Conference decided to constitute a Committee of State Education Ministers of Andhra Pradesh, Bihar, Kerala, Karnataka, Haryana, Madhya Pradesh, Maharashtra, Manipur, Orissa, Rajasthan, Tamil Nadu, West Bengal and Member, Planning Commission and the advisers to State for Education to work out the modalities of the proposal for making the right to free and compulsory elementary education a Fundamental Right and to identify resources required to achieve universalisation of elementary education. It also decided that three major Centrally Sponsored Schemes viz. Computer Literacy and Studies in Schools (CLASS), Vocationalisation of Secondary Education and Promotion of Yoga would be transferred to the State Sector. The Committee submitted its report in January, 1997.

National Conference of Educational Experts

HRM had convened a National Conference of Education Experts on August 16, 1996 to discuss on certain key issues such as review of the progress of National Policy on Education (NPE), 1986, financial allocation for education in the Ninth Plan, the Common Minimum Programme of the Government etc. The Conference was attended by 37 Educational Experts in various fields of education and Heads of Statutory Bodies/Resource organisations.

Educational Statistics

Efforts have been made to reduce the time-lag in collection, compilation and publication of various Educational Statistics. For this purpose, a conference of Directors of Education/DPIs and Statistical Officers of States and Union Territories was convened on 9-10 April, 1996 to discuss the problems being faced by States/UTs Education Directorates for timely collection of Educational Statistics improving its quality, etc., A revised time schedule was convened to the Director of Education/ Statistical Officers of the States/UTs within which the States are required to submit the statistics to the Ministry. The progress made so far is being reviewed.

The Central Plan Scheme of Computerisation of Educational Statistics in States/UTs was reviewed in the Conference and a revised scheme was submitted to the Ministry. This revised scheme is under approval of the Government. Collection of numerical and financial data in respect of Universities, Degree Colleges and other colleges of Higher Education have started but the flow of data from the States has not yet picked up. States/UTs are being pursued for expediting submission of the Educational Statistics in respect of Higher Education.

Two Regional Training Programmes on Educational Statistics were organised in collaboration with respective States/ UT Govts at Bhubaneshwar (20-22 Nov. 1995) and at Pondicherry (26-28 Feb. 1996) for the benefit of Statistical Personnel engaged in the collection and compilation of Educational data at Block, District and State Directorates levels. Similar programmes shall continue.

National Institute of Educational Planning and Administration

The National Institute of Educational Planning and Administration (NIEPA) is an autonomous body set up by the Government of India as the national apex institution in the field of educational planning and administration. The Institute's main areas of activities include training of educational planners and Administrators, research, diffusion of innovations and consultancy services. During the Year under report the institute continued to undertake activities in respect of training of educational planners and administrators, research, diffusion of innovations and consultancy services. Training Activities

NIEPA organises a large number of seminars, workshops and training programmes each year for various categories of educational functionaries with a view to increasing their awareness about new educational developments, acquainting them with modern techniques of educational management and enhancing their capability for educational planning and administration. During 1996-97, the institute organised 28 programmes (upto November 1996), another 15 programmes will be held during December-March 1997.

Research Activities

One of the main activities of the institute is to undertake, aid, promote and coordinate research in various fields of educational planning and administration. During the Year, 10 research studies/projects have been completed whereas, 10 research studies/projects are in progress, out of these, one is a sponsored study.

Consultancy and Professional Support

The faculty members of the Institute provided consultancy and professional support to national, state and institutional level bodies as well as International organisations. Among the agencies which were given consultancy and professional support included the Ministry of Human Resource Development, University Grants Commission, State Education Departments, SIEMTs, SCERTs and other institutions within the country. Consultancy services were also provided to international agencies such as UNESCO, UNICEF, World Bank, Asian Development Bank and SIDA.

District Primary Education Programme(DPEP)

The Institute faculty is deeply involved in the DPEP projects by way of providing professional support in the formulation of district plans and appraisal of the projects to be submitted for external assistance and implementation of the same in the selected states. A DPEP Cell has also been created in the Institute. Several training programmes were conducted and the proposals for initiating researches are on the anvil. Exercises in order to develop training modules are underway.

Scheme of Assistance for Studies, Seminars, Evaluation etc. for Implementation of Education Policy

The Scheme of Studies, Seminars, Evaluation etc, for the implementation of Education Policy is intended to provide financial assistance to deserving institutions and organisations, for conduct of seminars, workshops, impact and evaluation Studies etc. on such issues that have relevance to the Education Policy, its management, implementation and related issues.

During 1996-97, financial assistance has been provided for organisation of one workshop, two seminars, five conferences and one study (until December, 1996).

Computer based Management Information Systems developed by NIC for Department of Education

National Informatics Centre (NIC) continued to provide software, hardware and consultancy support to Department of Education in developing computer based Management Information Systems. NIC has established a computer Centre in the Department of Education and has installed a Pentium Processor based Computer system and a DCM COSMOS 486 system and has established a Local Area Network (LAN) of 40 terminals. A team of officers of NIC is working in close coordination with the officials of the Department. Highlights of the year 1996-97 are as follows:

a) Sixth All India Educational Survey

1. National level tables based on data of Village Information Form (VIF) and School Information Form (SIF-1) of Sixth All India Educational Survey have been generated in order to provide quick estimates for the formulation of 9th plan proposals.

b) Department of Education

1. A Home Page has been created for Department of Education to be put on World Wide Web.
2. CD-ROM cutting of various publications brought out by Department of Education has been taken up. Limited tender has been floated, bids have been evaluated and job order has been placed for OCR scanning of documents, conversion to ASCII, editing and HTML coding of information for retrieval by a standard web browser software.
3. In connection with establishment of Local Area, Network (LAN) under WINDOWS environment with

CLIENT-SERVER architecture for Department of Education, a meeting of NIC-Ministry coordination committee has been organised and implementation of decisions taken in the meeting is in progress.

4. Parliament Questions Information System has been implemented under both DOS and UNIX environments and entire data for one year (1995) has been got entered by hiring data entry operators from a private agency.

5. Designed input/output proformae and developed software for scholarships information system.

6. Management Information System for National Programme of Nutritional Support to Primary Education (Mid Day Meal Programme)has been developed and software alongwith operation manual sent to all state centres of NIC in connection with the implementation of the system.

7. Publication based on data of budgeted expenditure on education for the period 1993-96 brought out.

8. Publication entitled 'Budget Resources for Education' has been brought out by updating data.

9. Arranged a demonstration of Public Utility databases under GIST and Power Builder software to senior officers of Department of Education.

10. Provided INTERNET connectivity and imparted necessary training on the usage of the same for exchange of electronic mail and accessing of information to some of the senior officers of the Department.

11. A presentation on the facilities like Video Conferencing, Multimedia, CD-ROM cutting, MEDLARS, Teletext, etc. available at NIC Hq., CGO Complex has been made to some of the senior officers of the Department.

12. A report has been brought out highlighting the impact of vocationalisation based on data collected from schools through survey.

13. Software has been developed for culling out information from the data of Sixth All India Educational Survey for bringing out the publication 'Education in India's for the year 1993-94 and software distributed to states by conducting a workshop.

14. Necessary support in the computerisation and generation of various reports has been provided to Non-formal Education Division in connection with Grant-in-aid committee meeting and various other requirements.

15. Presentation charts and graphs have been produced from time to time in connection with various studies.

16. Payroll system has been implemented and operationalised in Kendriya Vidyalaya Sangathan (KVS).

17. GPF/CPF information system has been developed and implemented and the package made operational by imparting training to concerned officials of KVS.

18. Construction activities information system has been developed and implemented at KVS. Necessary training has been imparted to concerned officials of KVS in connection with operationalisation of the package.

19. Development of software in respect of Pension Information System and Personnel Information System has been taken up and is in progress.

20. Software maintenance support has been provided in respect of

    i) Grant-in-aid to voluntary agencies of Adult Education Bureau.

    ii) Parliament assurances for generating weekly reports.

iii) Monitoring of ACC appointments.

iv) Copyright office for generating discrepancy letters, register of copyrights and index cards.

v) Monitoring the progress of Total Literacy campaigns of National Literacy Mission.

Computerised Management Information System (CMIS)

Department of Education has established a unit called "Computer Management Information System (CMIS)" to meet the day-to-day needs of its computerisation work. The main objectives of this Unit are the following :-

a) Identify areas for computerisation and conduct feasibility studies for the development of computer based management information system.

b) analysis, design and development of software for the implementation of the management information system.

c) Maintenance of software packages as per varying needs of the users in the Ministry.

d) Act as a resource unit and provide training to the officials of the Ministry to develop local know-how for day to day processing of information.

e) Design and develop database methodologies and build an effective educational information system, and

f) Liaison with the National Informatics Centre.

The major achievements of the Unit during the year 1996-97 are as follows:-

— This Unit provided assistance for the implementation of the scheme on the National Programme on Nutritional Support to Primary Education by providing various information on state-wise, district- wise and block-wise enrolment of children, foodgrain requirements. supply of foodgrains to State Governments, lifting of foodgrains etc. for the implementation of the Programme.

— Assisted the Planning, Monitoring and Statistics Division in bringing out the following publication :-

  — Selected Educational Statistics 1995-96

  — Education in India Vol.I (S)

  — Education in India Vol.II (S)

  — Education in India Vol.I (C)

  — Education in India Vol.II (C)

  — Selected Information on School Education

— Database on Education Ministers, Chief Secretaries, Education Secretaries, DPIs of all States/UTs.

— Pay-billing and pay-slip system of the Deptt.

— Miscellaneous recovery schedules of the officers to the various Department, Organisation etc.

— Telephone Directory of the Department

— Retrieval of information on Parliament Questions

— Administrative Annual Report 1995-96 of the Department

— A compilation of Scholarship Schemes

— Software and Hardware assistance to FIRM, MOS and senior executives of the Department.

Miscellaneous

The Unit has provided consultancy in finalising the hardware requirements for the officers of the Department. This Unit also presented charts, slides and graphs for various studies on education from time to time. Maintained the softwares and hardwares installed in the Department and provided all assistance on computers to various Bureaus of the Department. Training was also organised on usage of application packages for the officers of the Department.

not the best agency to promote education. He believed that education is a process of empowerment. It integrates physical, mental and emotional development. He stressed that education must promote respect for manual labour rather than abhorrence for it.

Fresh Approach

The fervour for freedom and patriotism to achieve "swawalamban", made our leaders search for an alternative approach to elementary education. Article 41 and 45 of the Constitution enunciating the Directive Principles of State Policy on education provided the basis for the new approach. 14 States and 4 Union Territories enacted Legislation for free and compulsory primary education. All States have exempted children from tuition fee up to upper primary classes. However, compulsion has not been enforced due to socio-economic and political considerations.

Expansion and Growth

The thrust of the Central and State Governments in universalising elementary education so far has been on three aspects namely, universal access, universal retention and universal achievement. Concerted efforts made in these areas have resulted in significant expansion of elementary education in the country. The number of primary schools has increased from 2.10 lakh in 1950-51 to 5.90 lakh and number of upper primary schools from 13,000 to 1.71 lakh respectively in 1995-96. During this period, Gross Enrolment Ratio (GER) at primary levels has increased from 43% in 1950-51 to 104.% in 1995-96. 95% of the rural population in the country have a primary school within 1 kilometre and 85% an upper primary school within a distance of 3 kilometres. With 15 Crore children enrolled and 3o lakh teachers, we have one of the largest elementary education systems in the world. The proportion of girls in classes I-VIII as also women teachers has increased steadily.

Table 1. Results of efforts towardsUEE

	No. of Institutions (in lakhs)	
	1950-51	1995-96
Primary Schools: Classes I-V	2.10	5.90
Upper Primary Schools: Classes VI-VIII	0.13	1.71
Total	2.23	7.61
	No. of Teachers (in lakhs)	
Primary Schools: Classes I-V	5.38	17.40
Upper Primary Schools:Classes VI-VIII	0.36	11.65
Total	6.24	29.05
	Gross Enrolment	
	1950-51	1995-96
Primary Stage		
Total Enrolment (in million)	19.2	109.73
Gross Enrolment Ratio percentage	43.1	104.30
Upper Primary Stage		
Total Enrolment (in million)	3.1	41.01
Gross Enrolment Ratio percentage	12.0	67.20

Quality Improvement

The quality of elementary education has been one of the major concerns right from 1950s. The National Policy on Education, 1986 brought to the forefront the need for quality improvement in terms of learning achievement of children. As a result, greater efforts have been made to impart competency based learning, particularly from 1990 when the Minimum Levels of Learning (MLLs) were introduced. A clear shift from teacher dominated teaching to a child centred approach has been observed in most states. Integrated Textbooks which include workbooks are replacing traditional books. A large number of teaching, learning and reading materials have been developed, with active participation of teachers and NGOs. Efforts are continuing to promote competency based learning both at primary and upper primary levels by re-orienting and training teachers. Results so far have been encouraging.

Policy and Planning

The period after Independence saw a linear expansion of the elementary education system through allocation of additional resources. It was in 1964 that the Central Government recognised the need to take a holistic view of education and appointed the Education Commission(1964-66). The Commission was entrusted with the task of evolving a national system of education. It recommended a radical transformation in the prevailing education system and highlighted the need for the "common school approach" to promote equity and social justice. The first National Policy on Education, 1968 recommended free and compulsory elementary education and equalisation of educational opportunities especially for girls and children belonging to SCs and STs. The National Policy on Education 1986 and its Programme of Action, (1992) was enunciated on the basis of a detailed review of the country's educational performance. The policy resolves to achieve UEE by 2000 AD.

The plan allocations for elementary education have increased steadily, though still not adequate to fulfil the constitutional commitments. Fifty years of freedom have seen higher levels of spending by the Central and State Governments to provide quality of education for all. Better school infrastructure, more and better-paid school teachers, timely availability of subsidised or free text books in regional languages, provision of scholarships, uniforms and mid day meals have all received attention of state governments who are the main providers of elementary education. The Central Government increased its allocations for elementary education after 1976 when education became a concurrent subject. These allocations were aimed at providing additional funds to resource poor states on the basis of the principle of equalisation and for quality improvement.

The period following the adoption of National Policy on Education (NPE), 1986 saw the introduction of a number of centrally sponsored schemes to cater to the specific needs of the elementary education sector. These included Operation Blackboard (1987) to improve school environment, enhance retention and learning achievement of children by providing minimum essential facilities in all primary schools; restructuring and strengthening of Teacher Education (1987) to upgrade pedagogical skills of teachers through establishment of dedicated teacher training institutes at District level (DIETS); Non-formal Education Programme (1987) to provide alternative education facilities for girls, working children and children in far flung areas; Minimum Levels of Learning (1990) to improve learning achievements of children; and the National Programme -of Nutritional Support to Primary Education, commonly known as Mid-day Meal Scheme, to provide nutritional support to children in primary classes. Plan expenditure on elementary education has increased to nearly 50% of Central expenditure on Education. States continue to discharge the main responsibility for management, expansion and maintenance of schools. Since there is considerable variation in their fiscal capacity to do so, there is need for targeted interventions to improve primary education in such states.

External Assistance

Following the World Conference for Education for All (EFA) in Jomtien (Thailand) in March 1990 there is a greater commitment and willingness on the part of multilateral and bilateral aid agencies to invest in primary education in developing countries. A major internationally assisted programme namely District Primary Education Programme (DPEP) was launched in 1992 with assistance from World Bank and European Union. The programme adopts a holistic approach to promote primary education through decentralized planning and integrated programming at district level. The programme has been extended to 149 districts in 14 States in 1997. The Lok Jumbish and Shiksha Karmi Projects are two other successful internationally assisted projects. Lok Jumbish, meaning a people's movement for UEE, has a holistic understanding about the problem of UEE and is implemented by establishing an interface between the local community, the teaching profession, the educational administration and the learners. The Shiksha Karmi Project envisages a paradigm shift in delivery of primary education. Inspired by the concept of barefoot teachers, the project has effectively responded to the problem of teacher absenteeism in the remote and inaccessible areas of Rajasthan.

Internationally assisted projects for basic education have focussed attention on decentralisation, people's participation, construction of school buildings, development of innovative teaching learning materials, participative teacher training, enhancement of institutional capacities and improvement in learning levels. The overall strategy and approach of these projects gives priority to low literacy areas, girls and disadvantaged sections of society.

Decentralisation and Community Mobilisation

The process of decentralisation has been an encouraging feature of our efforts to universalise elementary education. NPE, 1986 visualises direct community involvement in the form of Village Education Committees (VECs) for management of elementary education. The POA, 1992 emphasised micro-planning as a process of designing a family-wise and child-wise plan of education by which every child regularly attends a school or a NFE centre, continues his or her education at a place suitable to him/her and completes at least eight years of schooling or its equivalent at the NFE centre.

The Seventy-third and Seventy-fourth Constitutional Amendments have hastened the process of community management of elementary schools. These amendments have created a congenial ambience for the Panchayat Raj Institutions (PRIs) to play a more dynamic role. These institutions now provide a greater voice to women, scheduled castes and scheduled tribes. Increasingly PRIs and VECs are becoming involved in social mobilisation, planning and supervision for UEE. The introduction of micro-planning and school mapping have brought the school closer to the community while sensitising people to issues and problems in their local schools.

Recent trends in community participation indicate a greater thrust on empowerment of communities. Mobilising the communities to take responsibility to ensure quality education for every child is the core strategy of several innovative initiatives in elementary education including DPEP, LJP, SKP and BEP. Genuine community involvement is the key factor for the success of LJP and SKP in Rajasthan. LJP has had a positive effect on the empowerment of locally elected people, especially women at village level who are often active members of the LJ core teams and Mahila Samoohs. The VECs, carefully formed and trained through environmental building activities in the LJ, are actively involved in school matters. SKP has constituted VECs in 2000 villages to promote community involvement in primary education and encourage village level planning. DPEP is making useful investments in orientation and training of VEC members. An important role of the VEC is to mobilise resources for maintenance, repair and construction of school buildings. The VECs also help in determining the school calendar and school timings in consultation with the local community.

Partnership with NGOs

NGOs are emerging as important partners in efforts of the Central and State Governments towards UEE. They have been instrumental in mobilising social support for UEE, development of socially relevant curriculum, contextual teaching learning materials, innovative teacher training, pedagogic renewal, review and evaluation of educational experiments, action research for UEE, and designing of alternative education programmes. The participation of NGOs together with community support has helped to improve the physical conditions and environment of elementary schools as well as promotion of education for girls and children belonging to SCs and STs and working children. As of now, nearly 750 NGOs are supplementing the Governmental efforts towards UEE by rendering cooperation and resource support to Non-formal Education with assistance from the Government.

Future Challenges

The country has undoubtedly been successful in evolving a national structure for elementary education in the last fifty years. Primary education is now provided in the mother tongue or regional language in all the States and UTs. There has been substantial increase in access to elementary education, with reduced class, caste and sectional disparities. First generation learners, girls and the under privileged sections of society have been provided with unique opportunities for vertical mobility. Literacy standards have substantially improved across all the States and UTs. National Literacy rate has increased from 15.% in 1951 to 52.% in 1991. An impressive academic support system has been built up at national and state level through NCERT, NIEPA, NCTE, SCERTs, CIEMATs, DIETs, BRCs, and CRCs to provide technical support and guidance to the elementary education system.

Despite substantial achievements, the task of UEE is far from complete. Schools and enrolments have certainly increased but so have the number of out of school children. The country today has one of the largest illiterate populations in the world. Caste, gender, class and regional disparities in UEE though reduced, are still glaring and persistent. While the demand for quality education is showing perceptible increase because of improved awareness and social mobilisation through organised efforts such as TLCs and PLCs, supply is generally inadequate. The educational administration in most states and UTs is yet to effectively tackle endemic problems concerning shortage of teachers, teacher absenteeism, inadequate and improperly designed school buildings, lack of teaching learning equipment, need based teacher training, and a curriculum related to real life requirements. Teachers' esteem in a society that worshipped Gurus is low. They are called upon to do variety of non-teaching jobs, leaving little time for teacher-pupil interaction. Teacher education, considered crucial to improve quality of education, has not made the vital difference in the classroom.

A traditional style of administration and the tendency for centralisation is impeding genuine people's participation and effective partnership with NGOs. Lack of transparency and rigid procedures have not facilitated confidence building measures necessary for empowerment of women and the poor. Imperative in these shortfalls is the need to consolidate the gains, design specifically targeted programmes to reach the unreached, improve quality of education making it contextually relevant and related to real life, and make UEE a social movement. We need to redouble our efforts in promoting education for girls, SCs and STs and minorities.

The recent measures initiated by the Government, namely DPEP, Mid–day Meal Programme and the proposal for NEEM, the National Programme Media advocacy and Publicity for UEE and the Joint GOI-UN System Education Programme are expected to address some of these challenges more effectively. The proposed National Elementary Education Mission should evolve strategies for reaching the unreached and achieving the goal of UEE within a given time-frame in a systematic, sustained and integrated manner by involving all segments of civil society in this national endeavour. The resolve of the Government to make elementary education a fundamental right of all children of 6-14 years is expected to spur the government and non-government sectors to take necessary measures to achieve UEE. It is a demonstration of political will and administrative resolve to achieve UEE and eradicate illiteracy. Efforts of the Government to mobilise resources for education to the extent of 6% of GDP will also help in hastening the process of universalising elementary education.

8

EDUCATIONAL PLANNING AT THE DISTRICT LEVEL

District Primary Education Programme (DPEP), launched in India in 1994, is one of the largest education projects of its kind in the world. The Programme aims to achieve the long cherished goal of Universalisation of Elementary Education (UEE) in the country through district-specific planning with emphasis on decentralised management, participatory processes, empowerment and capacity building at all levels.

The objectives of District Primary Education Programme are to:-

— Provide all children with access to primary education (class I to V)

— Reduce primary dropout rates for all students to less than 10 percent.

— Reduce differences in enrolment, dropout rates, and learning achievement among gender and social groups to less than 5 percent.

— Raise the average achievement levels of students by at least 25 per cent in language and mathematics and at least 40 percent achievement levels in other subjects.

— DPEP also seeks to strengthen the capacity of national, state and district institutions and organisations for planning, management and evaluation of primary education.

The criteria for selection of districts under DPEP are:

— Educationally backward districts with female literacy below the national average (39.29 percent) and

— Districts where Total Literacy Campaign (TLC) have generated demand for elementary education.

DPEP is different from other schemes in several ways.

a. *Holistic View*: DPEP adopts holistic approach, from the schematic to the integrated, with emphasis on convergence of existing programmes and resources.

b. *District Specific*: It adopts area - specific approach with district as the unit of planning and implementation. The key strategies of this district-specific planing have been to retain the contextuality and sensitivity to local conditions. This means plans are tailored to the specific needs of the districts.

c. *Decentralized Planning:* Corollary to the area - specific approach is the local area planning or decentralized planning with disaggregated target setting.

d. *Participatory Process*: Consistent with the philosophy of decentralisation, plans are prepared at districts through participatory process involving district and sub-district functionaries, teachers, parents and community members.

e. *Sustainability*: DPEP has a marked focus on sustainability, sustaining the benefits beyond the project period.

f. *Equity*: Equity is a major concern in DPEP. All plans strategies and intervention are tailored to address the specific needs of the disadvantaged groups such as Scheduled Caste (SC), Scheduled Tribe (ST), minorities, girls and the disabled.

g. *Community Ownership*: The Programme stresses on community participation and community ownership.

h. *Home grown Idea*: DPEP, which has adopted innovative practices and approaches, is a home grown idea.

i. *Additionality*: DPEP is an additionality to the existing resources for education. A basic requirement of DPEP is that at least 1991-92 levels of expenditure on elementary education should be maintained in real term.

j. *Convergence:* The programme encourages convergence of services in education, health, NFE, ECCE etc. rather than replicating them.

PROJECT PERIOD

The period of the project varies from 5 to 7 years.

Project Expenditure

Upto a maximum amount of Rs. 40 crore is provided for implementation of the Programme in each district. Out of the total project cost, about 70% of funds is spent on improving quality of education. Expenditure on civil works is limited to 24% and management cost to 6%.

Funding

The project is a Centrally sponsored scheme with 85 per cent of the project cost shared by the Government of India and the remaining 15 per cent by the State Government concerned. Both the Central share and State share are passed on to the State Implementation Societies directly as grant.

PROGRAMME MANAGEMENT STRUCTURE

DPEP has evolved a management structure from the Centre right upto the village level with substantial autonomy, high degree of flexibility, and above all, space to experiment with different methods and models. The Programme is working towards institutionalization of an appropriate management culture across the primary education system in the country. The management structure of the Programme has several levels-national, state, district, block, cluster and village. Details of these structures are given below.

— *National Level*: The role of National Level Structure (NLS) of DPEP is in facilitation, capacity building, appraisal, co-ordination and overall direction of the programme. Till adequate capacity is built in states, it would also assist in planning and implementation.

— *State Level*: At the state level, the Programme is implemented in a mission mode through a registered autonomous society, which has two organs.

  — General Council (GC) with Chief Minister as ex-officio president and

  — Executive Committee (EC) headed by the Chief Secretary/Education Secretary of the State.

— *District Level*: District and sub-district level programme planning and management are carried out by the District Project Committee headed by the District Collector or the Chief Executive Officer of the Zilla Parishad.

— *Sub-District Level*: Some of the Project districts also have Block Project Implementation Committees. Block Resource Centre lends academic support, so also Cluster Resource Centre at cluster level (group of villages).

— *Village Level:* At village level, there are Village Education Committee (VEC), Mother - Teacher Association (MTA) and Parent - Teacher Association (PTA) to oversee implementation of the Project.

Structure at the National Level

1. The Centre-State relation must be given due consideration.

Good management on this) account has become particularly important in View of the 42nd amendment of the Constitution.

2. The University Grants Commission may exercise the authority used by the Medical Council of India to review the functioning of the Universities and de-recognising degrees where default and deficiency persist.

3. The UGC Act requires to be amended as to give it powers to derecognize certain degrees as and when necessary subject of course to suitable safe-guards. Furthermore the UFC should develop effective monitoring mechanisms of a kind which would help the universities to remain ever vigilant as far as high maintenance of performance is concerned.

4. In the establishment of new Institutions of National or Statewide importance, a deliberate effort should be made to set them up in cities and towns other than the major metropolitan. centres where such centres are now concentrated.

5. Linkages between various agencies like UGC, NCERT, NIEPA, CSIR, Planning Commission, Industry, Services etc. must be effective. To this end, a model coordinating agency may be set up covering the entire higher education field.

6. There is a need for the Boards role to clearly emphasize the total dimension of promoting both quality of education and developmental education of the total personality of the child. This, exercise would need to be given practical shape in terms of formulation of modified curriculum, re-orientation of teachers and head of institutions, preparation of both textual and support materials, and adoption of improved methods of evaluation.

7. The Board, as presently constituted, face many difficulties in fulfilling even the minimum role assigned to them. Hence it is urgent to revise existing constitution and powers and functions of the Boards to make them more effective

instrument to carry out its aims and objects. To begin with, it was felt that the Boards should enjoy real functional autonomy. While they should be linked with the State or Centre and be accountable through them to the State Assembly/Parliament specific revisions must be made in the boards constitutions to safeguard and promote their authonomy, particularly in matters of internal administration, curriculum formulation, determination of courses and syllabi, preparation and development of textual materials, affiliation and recognition of schools, in the conduct of examinations. in laying down conditions for teachers qualifications and. teachers certification.

8. The women's cells in the ICSSR and NCERT ought to be revised. New ones should be set up in the U.G.C. and in the Ministries and Departments of Education at the Centres and in the States. These will help clear administrative bottlenecks and give a boost to women's education. however, it should be ensured that the higher position in these cells/units are held by women.

9. A Central nodal agency designated as the National Council of TechnicaL Education may be created to ensure coordination in matters of policy, planning, financing, and monitoring OF Engineering education. This council may be composed of representatives from state governments, industry (private and public sector), professional society and academia.

10. The council should have a, small Executive Committee for the purpose of issuing necessary directives to the Secretariat of the Council.

11. Necessary Advisory boards concerning UG & PG, Engineering education., technician education and management education will assist the Council in policy formulation and implementation at the national level in their respective spheres. The Boards in turn may form subject panels dealing with individual specialisations.

12. A Technical Education Committee to the Union Cabinet may be set up to promote various technology endeavours in the nation.
13. A National System for Accreditation of Programmes and institutions be established having linkages with regional. and state level agencies and with industry.
14. The Technical Education Bureau of the National Level, the Regional Offices, The Technical Teachers Training Institutes, The State Directorates and Boards be appropriately strengthened in terms of infrastructures and expertise for improving their current functions and performing additional functions related to the development and installation of management information systems maintenance of prescribed norms and standards and national accreditation.
15. Planning, coordination, optimisation of resources and coordination of courses and programmes offered by vocational schools, ITIs and Polytechnics be brought within the purview of the Ministry of human Resources Development acting at the Nodal Ministry. The same concept should apply at the state level also.
16. A National council for technician education be set up as a statutory body having responsibilities for policy formulation and review, norms for award of autonomy, National accreditation certification and awards and periodic review of norms and standards. The national council will have a permanent secretariat and linkages with regional and state agencies for effective function.
17. At the National Level there should be an all India Advisory and coordinating body and accrediting body which can be called as NCVE. At the state level there should be Managerial and Executive body (in some of the States the existing Director of Vocational Education could play the role) at the District level there shall be monitoring wings.
18. Rational Testing Service: The present system of State boards working in isolation and independent of each other

has led to the present situation of a large number of Boards examining the students in their respective areas with no way of comparing the result of one with the other. This has also led to loss of national character in evaluation and proliferation of testing examinations by many major employers or higher academic bodies. The result is a lot of avoidable expenditure and effort in the nation and means an unfair burden on the student.

The Seminar is therefore of the firm view that the examination system should be urgently rational and a predominantly local evaluation supplemented by a national testing service should be brought about. The Seminar realises that a variety in medium of instruction and difference in standards prevailing in different boards, would pose many problems for evolving an equitable national testing service, but the dysfunctionality of the present system is so patent and benefits accruing from the proposed restructuring are so obviously substantial that this reform should no longer be postponed.

Structure at the State and District Levels

1. Multi-Level System of Educational Planning and Administration : There is at present a great degree of disparity in the system of planning and management among different States in respect of different levels/spheres of the educational systems. For efficiency, effectiveness and efficacy of system of educational planning and administration, it is essential that there should be functional linkages between spatial levels as identified for general planning and administration with levels of planning and administration of various sectors of education. Therefore, levels of educational planning and administration below the state level should be co-terminus with the units of developmental planning and revenue administration. For elementary education, the block should be the primary unit of planning and administration, district for secondary and

higher secondary education and state for higher and professional education. It would help to develop a multi-level system of educational planning and administration and to develop structural linkages with other sectors of development.

2. Strengthening of Professional Support: The various organisations/agencies providing professional support like SCERT, etc. should also follow integrated approach to avoid duplication of efforts in research and training functions. The SCERT must be an apex resource centre at the state level with its counterparts at district level for strengthening academic and training aspects of education. However, conduct of public examinations and printing and distribution of text books should be locked after by separate autonomous bodies.

3. Advisory committees consisting of experts in the field of Secondary Education should be formed at the district level, so that, they would advise the department of education in terms of inservice training of teachers, preparation of learning aids and other educational activities at the district level.

4. Since disaggregation of the levels of planning and management of education in respect of different stages has been considered essential, it is that the existing pattern of strong head-quarter and weak grass-root level planning and administration structures and processes should be reversed.

The group feels that in view the new dimensions of education envisaged. It has become imperative to debureaucratise the system and involve the community in planning and management processes of the education system at various levels, i.e. at the village, block and the district levels. The establishment of district education boards with elected representatives from Panchayats, officials and professionals is indicated under the circumstances. Appropriate delegation of administrative and financial powers will make the boards effective in their operation.

This board, for its proper functioning, will need the support of professional advice and for that purpose, the establishment of District Resource Centre is recommended. This centre, in addition to the jobs specified above, will also perform the functions of the SCERT at the District level, like collection and analysis of data, monitoring and evaluation of ongoing programmes, project experimentation, etc.

5. The District Resource Centre should have a representative from Technical Teacher Training Institutes, and there should be a close collaboration between the two as far as vocational education is concerned.

6. A possible alternative could be to decentralise the examination system and place requisite trust on teachers for evaluation of their pupils. The practice of ungraded system as adopted for classes I and II can be extended to Classes III to IX and there can be a continuous internal assessment where teacher may play a key role. Even if the concept of terminal examination at grade V, VIII and X are envisaged some affective decentralised system of evaluation for a cluster of 10 to 15 schools may be established. This while also enhance the Teachers' participation, give them a sense of belongingness and competitiveness. The State level examination at the school stage have little significance, particularly, when the emphasis is being laid on decentralised, need-based, local specific curriculum geared to vocational development. In view of this even the public examination at grade XII could be held at the district level only. The State level examination system is not likely to meet this challenge. This may eventually facilitate delinking of degrees with jobs.

7. At the Secondary Level: Development of curriculum, teaching aids, evaluation procedures should be decentralised at the district level.

   How can State Resource Centres be made more effective and decentralised? 1. Resource support may be decentralised 2. District Resource Units may be set up Details of the scheme to be worked out and agency to be made responsible for this work will need to be identified.

8. The terminal examinations at the end of the 10th Standard, which are by and large, conducted at the State level, should be so decentralised that they should be done at the district level keeping in view the enormous expansion of secondary education. More autonomy should be given for the internalisation of the examinations and continuous assessment of the students.

9. In order to enable that Boards to perform all its functions, the Boards should be sufficiently strengthened and where necessary expanded through recruitment of competent and experienced academicians, which will form a core academic team within the Board. However, they should fully use real resources available in many institution both national and regional.

10. The Council of Boards of Secondary Education in India(CBSE)has a critical, catalytic and coordinating role to play. Apart from critical studies of the functioning Boards, so as to help them their strengths and weaknesses and take suitable remedial measures.

11. For promoting quality of education and enabling institutions to perform at higher levels, selected institutions should be granted necessary freedom and autonomy for experimentation and innovation. They should be selected from all categories of schools, namely government, government aided as well as unaided, so as to affect educational renewal. Since this is not envisaged as a means to provide further privilege to the already privileged, while granting experimental status of institutions, it must be ensured that such institutions have a designated number of other schools of the area working with them closely, so that in all the schools educational renewal takes place.

12. The group felt that the guidelines developed by the Working Group of experts for such experimental schools

and contained in the booklet 'Freedom To Learn' should provide the boards a practical direction for implementing the programme on a pilot level.

13. A National Commission in the case of Central Universities and State level commissions in the case of State Universities should be instituted as statutory bodies, to set guide lines, select and appoint vice-chancellors all develop performance appraisal systems for the University Administrators to perform the line functions in the Universities.

14. State council for higher education shall be established in each state which will set broad policies for education. The Council will consist entirely of academics of high stature. The council will be reasonable for obtaining and disbursing the requisite funds from the State Government.

15. A State level nodal agency designated as State Council for Technical and Vocational Education may be created with suitable linkages with institutions in the State and the National Council of Technical Education. This State Council shall also provide linkages at the State level between vocational education, technician educaiion and engineering education.

16. The AICTE and the State Boards of Technical Education be made Statutory Bodies.

17. There is no escape from having educational technology for promoting education for development of human resources as the pressure of expanding knowledge, explosion of, numbers and the requirements of special regions were grounding, vary fast. It was necessary to have a system approach to exploit this new potential by setting up State Institute of Educational Technology, Media Resource Centres, at district level, opening training institutions, providing graduate and post-graduate courses in educational technology and decentralising area specific need-based educational technology. A proper system for maintenance of hardware' and development of local specific softwares was necessary.

18. There should be an integrated system of educational management at the state level, with the, DPI at there appex, coordinating the activities of the Directors of Elementary, Non-Formal, Adult, Secondary and Higher Education. (2)

19. The SCERTs, which work in collaboration with the state authorities and similarly, the District Resource Centres which work, in collaboration with the district authorities, should be vested with the task of monitoring the development plans and projects in education at their respective levels.

SOCIAL SUPPORT FOR EDUCATIONAL PLANNING

1. Community Participation

   i) Community involvement on a systematic basis not only enhances social relevance of education but also improve delivery mechanism and facilitate realisation of targets.

   ii) A comprehensive act should be passed validating and recognising community involvement, through education committees right from institutions, village to the district levels. These committees should be associated closely in the planning and implementation of educational programmes of different sectors of education at their respective levels.

   iii) A duly constituted committee at the institutional level should ensure the extension of participatory planning to grass-root level and prepare detailed perspective plan including enrolment, curriculum, infrastructure, staff development, reduction of wastage etc.

2. Educational Institution and Eoluntary Agencies

   i) Stepping up of further involvement of educational institutions and voluntary organisations for undertaking adult literacy/adult education programmes.

ii) Providing larger sizes of the projects to voluntary organisations and the flow of funds speedily to these agencies so that funds reach them at the most within 6 weeks through the State Governments.

3. In the district level planning process, the participation of blocks, and village panchayats should be integral parts.

4. The task of managing and monitoring the educational system at the local level should be in collaborations with village level committee at the grass-roots level.

5. At the primary level more community participation should be ensured. For this, it was suggested that parent-teacher associations have to be formed at the school level. and develop such programmes which would rake them active and participatory.

6. Decentralised Planning and Implementation : The Role of Panchayats

   Participants representing village Panchayats and Panchayat Samiti strongly put forward the point that non-formal education should be treated by Government on par with activities of other development departments for decentralised implementation. full financial assistance should be given to a Panchayats, as in the case of social forestry or other subsided programmes of development, to conduct Non-formal primary education centres. For instance for developing social forestry in. a Panchayat area an amount of Rs.15,000 per year is given to the Panchayat concerned. Similarly, the amount required for conducting nonformal primary education centres, according to the needs of a given Panchayat area, should be fully provided.

7. Management of education should be taken over from the Local Boards and entrusted to Education Authorities, basic Shiksha Parishads, with corresponding Zilla, Shiksha Samitis and block shikhsa Samitis, with power to levy Education Cess of enhance tuition fees.

8. Proper legislation for the implementation of the State Directive should be prepared by experts in consultation with specialised Institutes at the capital administrative as well as Legal.

9. In the deliberations of the group, there was a difference of opinion regarding the role of private agencies and voluntary organisations. On the one hand, it was suggested that all possible encouragement should be given to the private and voluntary organisations in establishing and managing institutions with due security provisions for service and payment of salary to the teachers and admission of the wards of deprived sections, at par with the state policy. In all these institutions, however, the course of studies should be at par with the state/CBSE with suitable provisions for staff development. However, some of the delegates felt that there should not be any such of state patronage for private organisations for establishment schools. They favoured nationalisation of education at school level. with an inbuilt provision for accountability and performance. This plea was based on the rationale that the ultimate aim should be the development of common school system, eliminating the segregative system of education.

LINKAGES

Linkages with Various Systems

1. Regional networks between institutes and industry, with apex institutes in the region serving as a focus, should be formed to develop peaks of excellence in selected colleges departments. For any meaningful implementation of such programmes massive financial inputs would be necessary.

2. Industry Institute interaction programmes at institutional levels should be strengthened through appropriate Advisory Committee or Liaison boards. Such linkages will lead to feedback in curricula design, promote technological projects in Institutes to develop indigenous technology, provide

finances for infrastructure and generally improve quality of instruction and research.

3. Industrial training, of engineering students through meaningful cooperative programmes may be considered as a means of reducing the "indoctrination" time in industry.

4. Industry and Institutes should jointly promote the development and spread of a technological culture in society at large through modern media, exhibitions, popular lectures and other programmes designed to create an awareness and aptitude for technology.

5. Coordination-and Linkages

   i) There should be conceptional and functional link- apes among the different national level government and non-government institutions and organisations concerned with different levels and spheres of educational system. Similarly, their regional/state level counterparts should follow an integrated approach.

   ii) Education is an instrument as well a beneficiary of development. It promotes and at the same time draws its substance from development. Coordination and linkages between education and development is possible only through system of decentralised planning not only in education but also in other sectors of the economy. The development agencies should also build an educational component in their own plans and implementation strategies. It will also be desirable, to give representation to education in the District Rural Development Authority (DRDA).

   iii) The greater use of mass media for teaching- learning purposes and linkages with various development departments should be ensured for effective functioning of Non-formal. Education Programme and Open Learning Systems.

Inter-Institutional Linkages

1. Institutional networking, both horizontal and vertical, wherever feasible, should be tried out and eventually adopted, essentially for the purpose of academic improvement of the constituent institutions in collaboration with District Resource Centres. As such, it will take up subjects like supervision, monitoring and evaluation of the performance of the constituent schools. The functions of the networks and clusters will be mainly academic and less administrative; whereby the networking and cluster system can become a complementary factor to the existing educational administrative and management structures without necessarily destabilising the latter. In fact, the network system should be seen as supportive to the existing administrative structure.

   Considering the ways and means to develop and operetionalise the institutional networking, the group suggested the, following

   a) acceptance of institutional networking as a matter of policy, at the national level, (b) identification of the nature of networking horizontal or vertical, and (c) harnessing the willingness and cooperation of the constituent institutions. As retards, the role and function of the network and cluster of institutions, the group suggested that (i) delegation of academic leadership as well as the coordination and evaluation functions to the network and retention of personnel and financial management with the existing district block education officers is one way of functionalising the networking and (ii) instituting a common development committee between the institutional network and the district-block educational authorities and also representatives from the community.

2. School Complexes

   i) The large number of schools that have come up over the years have been getting superimposed on the existing district administration system. Each State has now a large number of schools administered and provided centrally with a separate supervisory arrangement. The academic supervision is in frequent and inadequate and in the state cadre teachers and schools are treated and provided as faceless members in the larger group rather than as individuals with specific needs and capabilities. This arrangement has come to mean a loss of individuality to the teacher and the school and being part of the remote and faceless State system the link between the school and community has not developed.

Since individuality of the students derives from the individuality of teacher and the school and since the basic aim of education is to develop the potential of the individual student, the seminar strongly feels that the present system should immediately give way to the school complex system in which one or more higher secondary schools along with feeder middle and primary/elementary schools form the unit for administrative, financial and academic management.

This would give individuality to the school allowing it to develop optimally, bring it closer to the community and so make education more locally relevant, allow for better supervision of attached schools and provide them regular academic guidance and provide framework for autonomy to schools with sufficient resources and resilience capable of innovating with and developing educational programmes and credibly conducting examinations locally which would come about in coming years.

3. Effort should be made to share limited resources like library, laboratory and other facilities.

4. Strengthening System of Inspection and Supervision

The existing system of inspection and supervision which work in isolation should be strengthened and made functional by networking of institutions and organisations. These institutional Complexes should be vested with all academic, administrative and financial powers within the complex. Role of the supervisory staff should be limited to coordination among institutional complexes. It would not only bring almost greater social equity but also facilitate more effective management and ensure multilevel involvement in the educational endeavour.

5. Inspection and Supervision

   Head of the Institution will have to take the major responsibility for supervision for school. He should be given necessary authority and orientation for supervising the work of his staff in the school. For inspection, a panel should be prepared at each district consisting of retired teachers end headmasters who may be invited for panel inspection in various schools. This would ensure utilization of available resources, possibility of frequent inspection, and saving of administrator's time., for inspection of schools.

PLANNING PROCESS

1. There is need to adopt a comprehensive view of investments in education. The existing investment (non-plan) should be taken in view while making new investments. Given the resource position, while allocating grants to education, the sectoral allocations should be made clear.

2. Highly centralised and non-participatory planning should be substituted by multi-level or area planning on participative basis.

   This will require strengthening of machinery at the Regional, block and District level, establishment of District Resource Centres for date analysis, monitoring, evaluation, project experimentation, research development etc. There will also be the need to give orientation and training to field level officers. For this purpose district level instituter, will have to be established.

3. Instead of highly aggregated and undifferentiated and based on global targets and programmes, the plan should be built

on the basis of programmes and projects drawn up from below.

4. The planning of academic aspects should be integrated with overall educational planning. Educational planning should take into account not only the quantitative aspects but also qualitative aspects of education.
5. Socio-economic variables effecting educational outcome should be taken into account.
6. In the planning process an integrated view of adult education, non-formal education, technical education etc., should be taken into account. Planning for vocationalisation has to be given equal importance as planning for literacy. For this institutional planning for true coordination and motivation so that self-employment opportunities can be maximised.
7. Long term or perspective planning should be undertaken and adequate research studies for the purpose should be undertaken. These programmes, particularly need to be linked with the developmental thrusts and in case of non-responsive groups, even entry point, can be awareness and functionality so as to generate urge for literacy.
8. Improving Educational Planning Process
   i) As the existing system of educational planning neither sufficiently takes notice of the micro-level and area level needs, it is essential that educational planning. should be made development oriented and multilevel in character.
   ii) Long-term perspective plans based on different futuristic scenarios should be prepared for educational development at district, state and national levels. These plans should form basis for mid-term and short- term plans.
   iii) Educational mapping should be done for P-11 parts of the country for expansion and rationalisation of

educational facilities. These plans should be based on well defined norms and standards. It would also help to decentralise the educational planning process and restrict interference of non-academic and political nature.

iv) Adequate professionally competent support should be provided to undertake above functions at different levels of educational administration.

v) The educational planning at present is largely preoccupied with plan programmes and neglects attention to non-plan or committed expenditures and tasks. This artificial distinction should be removed and planning, should undertake as integrated approach both to plan and non-plan expenditure and activities.

9. Strengthening and Integrating Process and Structures of Educational Planning and Management

i) There should be, an integrated system of planning and management within various sectors of education at different levels. District level education officers should be the 'king-pin' of all types of formal send non-formal education utp higher secondary level including adult education. Similarly, at the state level, all directorates of education and academic bodies should be under,the overall charge of a very senior seasoned educational administrator of the rank of a Commissioner.

ii) There is also an urgent need for strengthening and reinforcing the existing structures as well as creating new ones wherever needed. Adequate additional inputs, both financial and professionals should be provided for the same.

iii) As a matter of principle, at least 10% of the budget of new educational programmes should be earmarked for their planning and management. Similarly, at least 5% of existing educational budget should be earmarked for planning and administration for continuing programmes.

10. Project Management Approach

The plan implementation is as important as planning itself. Programming, project formulation and modern management processes should be followed in implementation of various educational programmes and schemes for optimal results and effective control.

MONITORING AND EVALUATION AND MIS

— *Monitoring and Evaluation*: The system of continuous monitoring and evaluation which at present are in name only, should become an integral component of all important educational programmes and schemes as a part of their control mechanism. System should be introduced at all levels of educational administration with short follow-up mechanism. For continuous,evaluation of important programmes an autonomous national level professional evaluation organisation should be set up either as an independent organisation or as a part of some professional competent organisation.

— *Monitoring*: Keeping in view that 'exclusively quantitative' monitoring by government of the various programmes has done an incalculable damage to the country's development process, it is essential that in NFE there should be an inbuilt system of monitoring. Some of the features of such monitoring could include:

— Peer monitoring, by NFE "instructors" during their monthly or quarterly meetings..

— Promotion of a joint group by the panchayat to undertake monitoring based on the report of the instructors', perceptions of, the parents, and observation of the local community.

- Monitoring based on the progress of the learners according to a set of 'criteria' which characterize successful learning

— Is selective intensive programme based or, project approach in fast developing areas preferably?

i) It would be necessary in case of SC/ST and women. However,

ii) for involving, voluntary agencies, formal education system, employers, trade unions, development departments and all those who have a stake in Adult Education Programme.

— Adequate monitoring and control systems should be developed for on-going institutions as well as new projects/ programmes.

— *Integrated Management Information System and Educational Surveys:* Integrated management information system should be introduced to meet requirements of educational administration, planning, statistics, monitoring and evaluation at all levels of educational planning and administration. Net work of Computer-based data banks containing information or, educational and related development areas should be set up at different levels. To provide bench mark data for planning and management, comprehensive educational surveys should be regularly conducted once in five year. Such a system would help to eliminate existing time-lag in finalisation of information, avoid duplication, remove data-gaps and improve quality of information.

— A computerised management information system for technical education be set up linking national, regional, state and institutional levels for planning, monitoring and decision making.

— Planning of new institutions, distribution of resources, allocation of priority etc. should be based or regional planning process supported by proper information on the present information on the present and future, societal needs.

— A framework has to be developed in order to have a system of continuous assessment, analysis and feedback in the implementation Of each part of the higher education policy that may be adopted.

— A mechanism to coordinate the collection of a multitier integrated information system has to be evolved at block, district and state levels in collaboration with the Economics and Statistics Departments as well as the District Resource Centres and SCERTs at the district and state levels. Computers should be used with great benefit for storage, retrieval and analysis of the MIS.

REDUCING DISPARITIES

Equalisation of Educational Opportunities

1. Reducing Regional Imbalances

   Schools in rural and slum areas do not have the minimum facilities for a descent educational environment. It is desirable that attractive environment should be provided for these children so that they are enthused to attend the schools.

2. Resources, for minimisation of regional disparities should be worked out at district level because state as a unit of planning does not provide a logical sequence.

3. Specific programmes to cater to the needs of weaker sections, including physically handicapped be offered in existing of special institutions to enhance their productivity.

National Seminar on Elementary Education held at Shillong Oct. 31 - Nov. 2, 1985 on Planning, Management and Finance

The Working Group deliberated upon three main aspects of

elementary education i.e. planning, management and finance. While discussing these aspects, the group also considered various issues listed in the background note as well as those that emerged out of deliberations held in plennary session. The Group recommends the following suggestions for consideration for the proposed new national policy on elementary education.

Structure of Elementary Education

The structure and duration of elementary education is riot uniform in the country. In sixteen States and Union Territories, the elementary stage consists of seven classes (4+3) in others, it is eight classes i.e. 5+3. To achieve a common national goal of elementary education, it is suggested that a common pattern of elementary education be adopted:

— Elementary Education: I-VIII Classes/6-14 years

— Primary Education: I-V Classes/6-11 years

— Middle Education: VI-VIII Classes/11-14 years.

Keeping in view the national objective of providing free and compulsory education upto the age of 14 years, the group suggests that the age of admission to class - I should not be less than 6+.

Time Frame for Universalisation of Elementary Education

The group felt that a realistic time framework to achieve the goal of UEE should also have accessibility, retention and achievement UEE, we should also have accessibility, retention and retention targets for targets which would help to measure the internal efficiency of the system. The group Suggests that enrolment and retention targets for UEE, may be achieved in two phases:

Primary stage (6-11) = 1990

Middle stage (11-14) = 1995

Those targets should be further disaggregated in a realistic manner for various levels of planning below the state level.

Legislation for UEE

i) Some of the States have enacted compulsory primary education act but it has been experienced that it is difficult to enforce them. Therefore, on practical grounds the act for compulsory elementary education at national level would not service the required purposes. however, intensive efforts be made to create awareness about the need for universal elementary education through mass media films, posters etc. and it should be a massive drive.

ii) To help children attend school the act concerning child labour should be strictly enforced. If unenforceable on economic grounds then it should be made obligatory on the part of the employees to compulsory provide educational facilities to working children.

Schooling Facilities

i) All habitations with minimum population of 300 should be provided schooling facilities within distance of one Kilometer. The plan to expansion and rationalisation of educational facilities should be prepared for all areas on the bases of prescribed norms for minimum thresh-hold facilities through school mapping.

ii) For small habitation, scattered houses, mobile population or unreached habitations etc. it is suggested that special efforts should be made to provide educational facilities, such as mobile schools, seasonal schools, use of existing facilities for mobile population and other non- formal facilities etc.

iii) For optimal utilisation of existing educational facilities, noneducational inputs be provided as providing transport facilities and construction of small bridges culverts over streams roads etc.

iv) Residential schooling facilities particularly at the middle stage of education may be provided wherever it is cost-effective.

Special Facilities for Working Children

To provide educational facilities to working children, such as those working at houses, in agriculture form in organised and unorganised industrial sector etc. variety of approaches may be adopted e.g. providing non-formal education centres, changing, school timings, setting up three hour schools etc.

Pre-Primary Education Facilities

While the group revised the importance of pre-primary education as a preparatory stage for elementary education, the group felt that due to resource constraints it may not be possible for the govt. to undertake this responsibility. The group, therefore, suggests that the non-government agencies should be involved in this pros Also like ICDS programme with pre-primary education through Anganwadi Institutions.

Non-formal Education and others Diverse type of Educational Facilities

To achieve the UEE, multiple approaches should be resorted to Like NFE, short duration schools, while you learn scheme, basic education etc. however, it should, be ensured that the quality education is maintained in all these approaches.

Neighbourhood Schools

As Every child has the right to set quality education, idea of neighbourhood schools as advocated in the Education Commission Report should not be faithfully implemented.

10. Incentives to Children

THE GROUP SUGGESTED THAT THE FOLLOWING INCENTIVES BE GIVEN TO CHILDREN :

a) Free text books and uniform be made available to all needy children.

b) Attendance scholarship should be awarded to special target group like SC/ST and girls to reduce incidence of drop outs.

c) Mid-day meal scheme is laudable but its management and finance aspects should not be the responsibility of the Educations Department.

Education of Girls

a) The group suggests that at primary level all schools should be mixed school.

b) At middle stage, policy of education may be followed subject to the condition that whenever girls students are there, lady teachers should be provided. It should be ensured that separate toilet facilities for girls are provided in the schools.

c) If need be, separate schools may also be provided for girls at middle stage.

Supervision Systems

Supervision at primary level is a neglected area. To ensure quality education and to assist primary school. teacher supervision may be done through school-complex system. The lead school of the complex may be provided some additional staff to assist in performing these functions.

Decentralised Administration

a) District should be regarded as basic unit of planning, monitoring and management of elementary education.

b) Whenever local bodies are responsible for managing elementary education, the district and block level education committee, should be set-up strengthened/stream lined.

c) In states where local bodies are not involved in elementary education, district elementary education committee be Bet-up for planning, managing and monitoring of elementary education in the District.

d) For professional support, District Institutions education should be established in each district.

e) As education is instrument of development, education districts/blocks should be co-terminus with development district/blocks.

Education of Backward Areas

a) Instead of lobelling the whole state, as educationally backward state educationally backward districts should be identified.

b) The indicators for educationally backward district should be enrolment, retention and literacy rates.

c) The Central Government should provide special grants for educational development to those districts.

Financing Elementary Education

a) At least 50% of the Central and/or State educational development budget should be earmarked for elementary education. No diversion to the other sectors within or outside sectors be permitted.

b) Setting up of a national foundation for financing of elementary education should be explored. Foundation should raise funds through local contributions and by putting educational, cess on items such as agriculture income, petroleum products transport, exports made development oriented and multi-level in character.

Role of NFE

a) For student who can or will not like to take advantage of formal education NEF be made available.

b) Quality of learning skills in terms of competencies should not be get diluted in NFE.

c) Funding to NFE should be just mantigual, substantial funds, calculated on per capita expenditure as in formal education.

d) Non-conventional approaches be injected into formal system like using para professional in primary/middle schools.

e) There should be linkage horizontally and vertically between non-formal and formal education.

EXTRACT FROM RECOMMENDATIONS OF THE STATE LEVEL WORKSHOP ON NATIONAL EDUCATION POLICY, ORGANISED BY DIRECTORATE OF SCHOOL EDUCATION HARYANA, CHANDIGARH (NOV. 9-11, 1985)

Restructuring and strengthening the Administration and Supervision

a) The District level education offices should be drastically strengthened, upgraded and diversified. The post of DEO should be designated as Chief District Education Officer. tie should be in the scale of a Joint Director.

b) A sub-division from the education point of view may normally be co-terminus with the C.D. Block. But with the expansion of education there may be two or more sub-divisions within a C.L. Block.

Organisation of a sub-division should be based upon a 100 point scale while giving weightage of:

— One point to a primary school;

— Two points to a middle school; and

Three point to a high school.

As soon as the points cross the 133 mark in the point scale another sub-division will be formed. In this situation the block level become rebundant.

c) In view of the substantial quantitative expansion of education, the Director School Education should be assisted by four Additional Directors one each for:

   i) Elementary Education;

   ii) Secondary Education;

   iii) Adult and Non-formal Education; and

   iv) Coordination & Planning

   Besides, the above mentioned 4 additional Directors, there should be one, Education Adviser in the rank of an Additional Director, who would look after purely academic activities in the state. All the Additional Directors should have adequate supporting staff comprising Deputy/Assistant Directors. All the above mentioned posts be manned by personnel from Education cadre.

Norms of Inspection and Supervision

Every school should be inspected atleast thrice a year each subsequent inspection should be a follow-up of the previous one. Primary, middle and high schools should be inspected by the SDED and senior secondary schools by the CDED.

Decentralisation

All the financial and administrative powers should be decentralised with a view to:

i) improving working of the schools;

ii) economizing time and energy;

iii) avoiding frustration among the employees; and

iv) avoiding administrative bottlenecks and delays.

All the drawing and disbursing officers should have the powers to deal with financial sanctions like House Rent allowance GPF Advances, Loans, medical reimbursement, TA bills, journey beyond jurisdiction etc. All DDCs should become empowered to make purchases out of the grants and pupils, funds, made available to them. They should also be invested.

Management of the Plus 2 Stage

it is strongly felt that the proper place for the plus two stage is in the senior secondary school only and nowhere else. This point has already been emphasized by several Education Commissions and Committees. The present policy of split arrangements is obviously conducive to failure. The college education may start only with the plus 3 stage.

Senior secondary schools should be headed by Class-I Principals. Till the plus 2 stage is exclusively put on the schools side, the plus 2 stage. both in schools and colleges should be supervised and regularly inspected by Chief Distt. Education Officer who may, of course, associate some selected teachers from both sides (senior secondary schools and colleges).

Educational Institutions to identify themselves with the Community as a whole, rather than any political party or Sector.

Active participation of the institutions in west and woe of the community, community service involvement of community in the celebration of school functions and festivals and lively functioning of Parent-Teachers Associations will bring community and school closer to each other. These are, it is hoped, will enable the educational institutions to respond effectively to the environment and the aspirations and expectations of the community and chances of their leaning towards any political party of sector and vice versa are minimised.

Feasibility of Independence of Educational Organisation on the Analogy of Judiciary

It will be an ideal situation if independence of educational organisation is granted on the analogy of judiciary. But the group has strong reservations on its legal and constitutional implications. Even if the independence of the analogy of judiciary can't be given, there is still a strong case for according independence to educational organisation in matters of educational planning, administration and formulation of policies by depoliticisation of education on the lines suggested above and by creating Indian Education service.

9

CURRICULUM AT ELEMENTARY LEVEL

The main thrust areas of Indian school education, as mentioned in the National Curriculum for Elementary and Secondary Education : A Framework, 1988, demand a fresh look. Some of these merit reformulation in the light of the country's experience in the field of school education and the others have to be re-affirmed. Some new thrust areas may also need to be added in the light of the changes all around. School education in the present scenario has to have the main thrust on the following :

— Inculcation and sustenance of personal, social, national and spiritual values like cleanliness and punctuality, good conduct, tolerance and justice; a sense of national identity and respect for law and order and truthfulness.

— Elimination of poverty, ignorance, ill-health, casteism, dowry, untouchability, and violence, and ensuring equity, health, peace and prosperity.

— Thinking, experiences and innovations which are rooted in the Indian tradition and ethos and relating these with global thinking.

— Establishing uniformity of structures of school education, ie., 10+2+3 throughout the country.

— Broad based general education to all learners up to the end of the secondary stage to help them become life long learners and acquire basic life skills and high standards of Intelligence Quotient (IQ), Emotional Qoutient (EQ), and Spiritual Quotient (SQ)

— A common scheme of studies for the elementary and secondary stages with emphasis on the skill of "learning how to learn" with flexibility of content and mode of learning to suit all learners including those with special needs.

— Inclusion of Fundamental Duties and the core curricular areas at all the stages of school education.

— Human Rights including the rights of the child, especially those of the girl child.

— Ensuring the minimum essential level of the acquisition of knowledge, understanding and skill at all stages, commensurate with the learners' abilities and the societal context.

— Freedom, flexibility, relevance and transparency in the selection of content, transaction and procedures at different stages of school education.

— Nurturance and sustenance of multiple talents and creativity among all learners in various domains of knowledge.

— Shift of emphasis from information-based and teacher centred education to process centred and learner friendly education.

— Development of a responsive and supportive system of evaluation.

VALUE EDUCATION

Since India is the most ennobling experiment in spiritual co-existence, education about social, moral and spiritual values and religions cannot be left entirely to home and the community. School education in the country seems to have developed some kind of neutrality toward the basic values and the community in general has little time or inclination to know about religions in the right spirit. This makes it imperative for the Indian school curriculum to include inculcation of the basic values and an awareness of all the major religions of the country as one of the central components.

Value education and education about religions would not form a separate subject of study or examination at any stage. These would be so judiciously integrated with all the subjects of study in the scholastic areas and all the activities and programmes in the co-scholastic areas that the objectives thereof would be directly and indirectly achieved in the classrooms, at the school assembly places, play-grounds, cultural centres and such other places.

A comprehensive programme of value inculcation must start at the very earliest stage of school education as a regular part of school's daily routine. The entire educational process has to be such that the boys and girls of this country are able to know 'good', love 'good' and do 'good' and grow into mutually tolerant citizens. The comparative study of the 'philosophies' of religions can be taken up at the secondary and higher secondary stages.

Common Core Components

The need for strengthening national identity is being felt now much more than ever before. As such there is a strong plea for promoting national integration, and social cohesion by cultivating values as enshrined in the Constitution of India through school curriculum. With this in view, the ten core components identified in the National Policy on Education, 1986 need to be reaffirmed. They are as follows: The history of India's freedom movement; The Constitutional obligations; the content essential to nurture national identity; India's common cultural heritage; egalitarianism, democracy and secularism; equality of sexes; protection of the environment; removal of social barriers; observance of the small family norm; and inculcation of scientific temper.

The Fundamental Duties as laid down in Article 51A of Part IVA of the Indian Constitution, also have to be included in the core components. These are to:

(a) abide by the Constitution and respect its ideals and institutions, the National Flag and the National Anthem;

(b) cherish and follow the noble ideals which inspired our national struggle for freedom;

(c) uphold and protect the sovereignty, unity and integrity of India;

(d) defend the country and render national service when called upon to do so;

(e) promote harmony and the spirit of common brotherhood among all the people of India transcending religious, linguistic and regional or sectional diversities; to renounce practices derogatory to the dignity of woman;

(f) value and preserve the rich heritage of our composite culture;

(g) protect and improve the natural environment including forests, lakes, rivers, wild life and to have compassion for the living creatures;

(h) develop the scientific temper, humanism and the spirit of enquiry and reform;

(i) safeguard public property and abjure violence, and

(j) strive towards excellence in all spheres of individual and collective activity so that the nation constantly rises to higher levels of endeavour and achievement.

These core components need to be integrated in school curriculum in a suitable manner. It is envisaged that they would help in instilling a nationally shared perception and values and creating an ethos and value system in which a common Indian identity could be strengthened.

Toward an indigenous Curriculum

In order to make education a meaningful experience, it has to be related to the Indian context. Now, more than ever before, there is a realisation of the fact that by intellectual standards, India cannot flourish merely by importing or borrowing what is happening abroad, or by showing proficiency in solving problems that have been faced abroad.

In concrete terms, this shift in thinking calls for evolving an approach to curriculum preparation based on thinking, experiences and innovations rooted in its indigenous tradition. While doing so adequate attention shall have to be paid to the country's cultural plurality and the enormous amount of wisdom and experience that can be drawn from the various regions and sections of the Indian society. It may also mean making judicious use of and drawing from traditional knowledge systems and solutions to issues of health, water management, population explosion etc.

At a time when there is worldwide recognition and patenting of items like neem and turmeric, this kind of information must become an integral component of learners' knowledge. It is also desirable that learners are introduced to the advances made by the country in the past in various areas of knowledge. Besides, the knowledge and appreciation of folk cultures, songs, traditional dance forms, costumes, and musical instruments must become part of the school curriculum.

The Minimum Levels of Learning

In order to ensure access to the education of a comparable standard to all learners irrespective of caste, creed, location or sex, the concept of the Minimum Levels of Learning (MLLs) has emerged as one of the basic concerns. An effort to combine quality with equity, keeping in view the developmental needs of learners from all the sections of society including the disadvantaged and deprived ones, the dropouts and the working children and girls, has generated a need for identifying certain essential levels of learning for each stage of school education. These have been called the Minimum Levels of Learning. The MLLs are expected to be achieved by one and all.

Since the MLLs provide a sense of direction and a certain amount of accountability, these are considered to be an effective tool for programme formulation for school improvement. The quality of a school or educational system, in real sense, has to be defined in terms of the performance capabilities of its students. The Minimum Levels of Learning can be stated in a variety of ways to specify the learning outcomes. One of the important ways of doing so is to state MLLs in terms of competencies. Whichever approach is followed, the specification of the MLLs should meet the purpose of enhancing the learning attainments and serve as performance goals for the teacher and output indicators for the system.

Accordingly, the MLLs must have, apart from relevance and functionality, the attributes of achievability, understandability and evaluability. Learning has to be seen as a 'continuum' in which units are sequenced in a functional manner. The approach must help the learners progress systematically through this continuum by mastering the specified sets of competencies in each unit before moving on to the next one. Learning each subsequent unit will then be enjoyable and meaningful.

The concept of the MLLs is holistic rather than fragmentary in nature. MLLs should be envisaged as learning outcomes to be achieved at the end of a particular stage. Specifying further details and their gradewise sequencing need not be considered as a rigid prescription. The concept provides enough room for flexibility. The marshalling or sequencing of skills representing learning outcomes is to be done in such a way that it involves in a balanced manner the analytico- synthetic processes.

Moreover, 'learning' is to be understood in the broader sense of 'skill', 'quality', 'attitude', and 'value' too. That way, the term would embrace all the cognitive, psychomotor and affective area learning outcomes of education.

The emphasis on defining the MLLs highlights the importance of the integrative nature of learning and evaluation to ensure effective diagnostic interventions and assessment procedures. Thus, the MLLs do not merely serve as the indicators of a learner's progress or guide evaluation alone, these also help in identifying the appropriate sequencing of learning, suitable transactional processes and desirable assessment techniques which would enable a teacher to provide remedial teaching on the one hand and enrichment programmes on the other as per the needs of individual learners. Teachers can get very specific clues for organising peer learning, goal directed learning and encouraging self-learning in a conscious and concerted manner.

The MLLs approach is based on the elements of mastery level learning, child-centred and activity-based teaching, continuous and comprehensive evaluation, diagnostic and remedial teaching, differential treatment to optimise achievement levels of all and action research. All these elements need to be practised to achieve the goal of quality elementary education for all.

Emphasis has been laid on the introduction of the MLLs and the adoption of a common scheme of studies at the different stages. Simultaneously, flexibility is envisaged in the selection of strategy for curriculum transaction. This will make learning relevant to the needs and environmental contexts of the learners and allow scope for initiative and experimentation on the part of the teacher, the school and the local educational authorities. However, the scope for flexibility in the methodology and approach to curriculum transaction is not expected to be used for introducing differential courses or similar measures which would create disparities in the standards of education in different parts of the country.

General Objectives of Education

Education liberates human beings from the shackles of ignorance, privation and misery. It must also lead to a non-violent and non-exploitative social system. School curriculum, therefore, has to aim at enabling learners to acquire knowledge, develop understanding and inculcate skills, positive attitudes, values and habits conducive to the all-round development of their personality. Young girls and boys, are to be empowered through education to increase their capability. Paradigm shifts are therefore necessary to support a curriculum that values the interaction of the process and the content. Besides, the development of intrinsic values and the emotional intelligence of learners is also crucial.

School curriculum has therefore, to help to generate and promote among the learners:

— language abilities of listening, speaking, reading, writing and thinking and communication skills – verbal and visual- needed for social living and effective participation in the day to day activities;

— mathematical abilities to develop a logical mind that would help learners perform mathematical operations and apply them in every day life;

— scientific temper characterised by the spirit of enquiry, problem- solving, courage to question and objectivity leading to elimination of obscurantism, superstition and fatalism, while at the same time, sustaining and emphasising the indigenous knowledge ingrained in the Indian tradition;

— understanding of the environment in its totality both natural and social, and their interactive processes, the environmental problems and the ways and means to preserve the environment;

— appreciation of the sacrifices and contributions made by the freedom fighters and social workers from rural, tribal and weaker sections from all the regions of the Indian society, particularly from the North-East and the Andaman and Nicobar Islands, in India's freedom struggle and social regeneration, and readiness to follow their ideals;

— appreciation for the need of a balanced synthesis between the change oriented technologies and the continuity of the country's traditions and heritage;

— knowledge of and respect for the national symbols and the desire and determination to uphold the ideals of national identity and unity;

— deep sense of patriotism and nationalism tempered with the spirit of Vasudhaiva Kutumbakam;

— understanding of the positive and the negative impact of the processes of globalisation, liberalisation and localisation in the context of the country;

— qualities clustered around the personal, social, moral, national and spiritual values that make a person humane and socially effective, giving meaning and direction to life;

— knowledge, attitude and habits necessary for keeping physically and mentally fit and strong in perfect harmony with the earth, water, air, fire and the sky;

— qualities and characteristics necessary for self-learning, self-directed learning and life-long learning leading to the creation of a learning society;

— capacity not only to process information but also to understand, reflect and internalise and develop insight;

— willingness to work hard, enterpreneurship and dignity of manual work necessary for increasing productivity, obtaining job-satisfaction and creating wealth generating systems;

— acquisition of pre-vocational/vocational skills;

— appreciation of the various consequences of large families and over population and need for checking population growth; and

— cultivating proper understanding of and attitude toward healthy sex related issues and respectful attitude toward members of the opposite sex.

The emphasis on the 'learner-centred approach' necessitates careful determination of the objectives of education to be achieved at a particular stage/class in keeping with the norms of physical, mental, social, and emotional development of the learners of the relevant age-group. However, the level of achievement with regard to a particular objective will be rising from one class to another in a spiral fashion.

The Learners' Profile

Learners are not passive objects. They are active and inquisitive persons. It is not that only the environment shapes them, rather they too shape the environment to a great extent. The learners do not come to school with a blank mind but with pre-conceived ideas. Their classroom experiences are interpreted in the context of these pre-conceived notions. Thus, the prior experiences, beliefs and emotions affect the individual's perception and interpretation of events. This knowledge acquisition is a constructive or generative process and each student's knowledge is personal and unique.

For long, the child or the learner was viewed as a natural or given category. This undermined the importance of the fact that the development of the learner is intimately linked to changes in the socio-cultural and historical conditions in a given society. Thus, differences across groups and changes within a group may affect the nature of the learning. As such, a monolithic view of the learner and learning is untenable. On the other hand, an integrated approach for understanding the characteristics of learners seems appropriate and helpful.

During the pre-primary stage, enormous changes take place in the children's physical growth and mental development. From a state of dependence and helplessness the children gradually attain independence and become curious learners. As their bodies grow and respond to the social and cultural cues, their nervous systems mature and their cognitive experiences are enhanced. They quickly adapt to the world and slowly begin to imagine and discover methods for storing away the memories of the past and present events. Play fosters the overall development of the learners who may engage in functional play, i.e., simple and repetitive movements with or without an object, and constructive activity— physically manipulating objects in order to construct or create something. This period is marked by the development of language, the use of symbols and egocentric thinking, i.e., failure to distinguish between one's own point of view and that of another individual. Children at this stage also engage in fantasy play.

When children enter the primary stage their physical development seems to slow down and becomes less eventful. They become slimmer, more muscular and master new skills which enable them to compete effectively against their peers. Depending upon the children's eco-cultural system and developmental niche, which emphasises different motor skills, children now become better coordinated. Their thinking is governed by the fundamental rules of logic. Here, the concept of the zone of proximal development (ZPD) acquires significance.

The ZPD refers to the distance between a child's actual development level and the higher-level potential. It is the difference between what children can achieve independently and what their potential level of development might be if given help or guidance. The cognitive capacities of the learners are enhanced when instruction is focused on individual potential rather than on the level of their actual development. This concept strengthened the view that social influences contribute significantly to the development of children's cognitive abilities and mentoring or guidance facilitates their development. From egocentric speech (which serves to control one's own behaviour, and is usually verbalised), the children move on to inner speech which consists of self-talk.

During this phase children rehearse what they are going to say before actually saying it. Their social development is regulated by the peer group. In the company of their peers, children learn to cope with everyday conflicts, anxiety and fears through fantasy play. Interaction with peers also gives them social values of cooperation and sharing.

At the upper primary stage, several physical changes take place in children as it is a period of biological transition from childhood to adolescence. At the cognitive level, the children are gradually able to think logically in terms of all the hypothetical situations related to a particular problem. They also endeavour to establish an identity of their own. The process of identity formation requires taking into account one's own view as well as the views of others and of the society. Thus, the importance of the peer group increases considerably. The children now experience frequent mood swings and conflicting thoughts.

At the secondary level, the characteristic developments that have taken place during the upper primary stage get strengthened. Thinking with abstract concepts, establishing social identity, and giving importance to the peer groups increase all this considerably. Therefore, at this crucial stage it is also necessary to promote social interactions among children. For effective learning and for intellectual development, learners have to cooperate with their friends, share their experiences, discuss their discoveries and argue out their differences of opinion.

Characteristics other than the intellectual ones also provide important guidelines for designing curriculum which could be geared to the all-round development of the learners as individuals, and their development also in the context of the national goals and the socio-cultural priorities. Learners' physical, social and emotional characteristics, attitudes and interests that emerge in them during childhood, early adolescence and mid-adolescence, should be carefully taken into consideration while determining the objectives, content and strategies of curriculum and its transaction at the pre-primary, primary, upper primary and secondary stages.

For the development of beliefs, habits and attitudes associated with physical well-being, emotional maturity and proper social orientation, the years of pre-primary and primary education are the most impressionable and formative period of the child's life. This fact has to be realised in all seriousness by the curriculum designers and practitioners so as to provide appropriate and adequate learning experiences to the learners.

By the time children enter school, they have in the normal course, already developed a readiness for participation in group life with their peers. However, a discerning outlook toward social conventions and social events, and appreciation for lofty social ideals are yet to emerge in them. Similarly, though they begin at this stage to distinguish between the right and the wrong, they have not as yet developed the higher moral ideals involved in the process. The children demonstrate in their behaviour a desire not to depend on others, but the crystallisation of this desire takes place gradually through the years of secondary education.

In the normal course, learners, during the secondary stage of education, are expected to develop a philosophy of life that would provide them appropriate motives and directives of behaviour as future adults. Toward the end of the upper primary stage, the learners start critically evaluating the contradictions they observe in the words and deeds of individuals and the society. The awareness that one needs to stand on one's own and choose an appropriate career is normally reflected in the learner's behaviour.

These developmental features indicate the need for gradual introduction of learning experiences related to ideas, attitudes and skills associated with moral values, national ideals and priorities, socio-cultural cohesion and global fraternity. Systematic provision of information and guidance that would help the youth in making right choices of career and vocation for themselves must be ensured toward the end of the upper primary stage and particularly during the secondary stage of education. For a large number of students, some kind of orientation to work education may be required as a part of their curriculum during the secondary stage.

During the period of secondary education, emergence of desire and inclinations of sexual nature is a normal feature of students' psycho-physical development. This dimension deserves careful attention of the curriculum organisers. The idea that the Indian society does not approve of promiscuity and that self-control or 'Samyam' is one of the highly valued qualities ought to be underlined. This will generate among the youth healthy attitudes toward sex and respect for members of the opposite sex.

Curriculum designers could hardly afford to overlook the emotional dimensions of the child's life during the school period and the importance of emotional maturity in the life of a person. It is only gradually, through growth, that the child achieves emotional stability and emotional independence. There are occasions, particularly toward the end of upper primary and during the secondary education, when the learner has to face intense stress and strain which may result in emotional crisis. Curriculum should provide for appropriate activities and experiences, of scholastic and co-scholastic nature, and counselling and guidance in this regard.

Scheme of Studies

The general objectives of education will be realised through the content and learning experiences related to different subject areas. However, the emphasis would shift from factual knowledge to the process of understanding, thinking and internalising. Toward all-round development of personality, value education, health and physical education, art education and work education, have to be given appropriate importance in the school curriculum. The inter-connections among various subject areas have to be clearly established. A common scheme of studies, therefore, is advocated for classes I to X.

The core component areas and values shall form an integral part of the curriculum at all the stages and may suitably be integrated in different subject areas. Flexibility in the selection of content and organising learning experiences must be inbuilt in the system.

Early Childhood Education (ECE)—Preparation for Primary Education (2 years)

This stage of education helps in preparing children for school and constitutes an important element of Early Childhood Care and Education (ECCE). It is available as a pre-school education component under Integrated Child Development Scheme (ICDS) through a net working of 'Anganwadis'. It is also available in various other forms such as preparatory schools, nursery and kindergarten classes etc. both in private and government sectors in varying degrees. It is to be realised that the experiences to be provided at the very beginning of education play a very crucial role in the development of child's personality and have strong bearing upon later education of children.

Learning at this stage may be characterised by group activities, play–way techniques, language games, number games and the activities directed to promote socialisation and environmental awareness among children. Accordingly, pleasure, perception and participation need to be duly emphasised. It will ensure readiness to learn among children and reduce unhealthy and harmful load on children whose neuro-muscular capacities are not yet adequately developed. Formal teaching of subjects and reading and writing must be clearly prohibited. ECE needs to be made uniformly available to all children of the country to ensure equity.

During this period there should be more and more opportunities to use the language orally and listen to it in the natural interactive mode. Children should be provided with ample opportunities for developing essential skills of identification, comparison, matching, naming, seriation, drawing and counting without subjecting them to formal ways of learning numbers etc. With a view to instilling social awareness among children, child to child interaction and child nature interaction be promoted besides organising activities helpful in developing positive attitudes, and habits for healthy social participation. They should be encouraged to play with pets, knowing common birds, animals, plants and means of transport and some celestial bodies such as sun, moon and stars.

Elementary Education (8 Years)

Primary Stage (5 years): Primary stage of education has been visualised in two segments with inherent internal continuity. The first segment comprises classes I and II, where children are just introduced to formal teaching and are at a stage of development which requires a smooth transition from informal and non-formal environment to a formal one. The second segment consists of classes III-V wherein the children get prepared to understand the environment and learn in a systematic way. The scheme of studies for these two segments is given below:

A. Classes I and II

(a) One Language — the mother tongue/the regional language

(b) Mathematics

(c) Art of Healthy and Productive Living

Experiences to be provided in areas (a) and (b) will constitute an integrated whole taking into its fold, the natural and the man-made environment. Teaching and learning of language and mathematics would be woven around the environment of the learners and integrate environmental concerns as well.

Experiences to be provided for art of healthy and productive living will further contribute toward all-round development of the personality of the child. These will be organised keeping child in central focus involving students in activities commensurate with their developmental stage. Activities related to health will get a prominent place so that children acquire necessary skills, attitudes and habits to keep themselves healthy and participate in games and sports suitable for their age. Children will be initiated into preliminary yogic exercises and will be exposed to various soothing experiences in the field of music, drama, drawing and painting and clay modelling.

In organising these activities local factors may be given due importance. They will be encouraged to participate in creative activities such as free hand drawing and painting. Besides this, children will be involved in the activities related to work education so as to enable them to be free from inhibitions and like to work. For value inculcation stories and anecdotes would play an effective role. These will also generate and strengthen the element of curiosity, imagination and a sense of wonder. All the experiences will need to be presented in an integrated manner for which themes will be identified and teachers will make use of locally available resources and harness community support wherever necessary.

B. Classes III to V

(a) One language — the mother tongue/the regional language

(b) Mathematics

(c) Environmental Studies

(d) Art of Healthy and Productive Living

Children will be provided with experiences to help their socio-emotional and cultural development with a realistic awareness and perception of the phenomena occurring in the environment. This may be accomplished by emphasising, observation, classification, comparison and drawing of inferences through activities conducted within and outside the classroom. The integrated approach would be most suitable to achieve the desired objectives.

The experiences gained earlier will be further strengthened by ensuring participation of all children in the activities related to music, dance, drama, drawing and painting, puppetry, health and physical education, games and sports, yoga and productive work. Integrated approach will be used. Autonomy and flexibility incorporating the locally developed curriculum and materials will be encouraged. Concerted efforts will be made to ensure proper value orientation among children.

Upper Primary Stage (3 years)

(a) Three Languages — the mother tongue/the regional language, modern Indian language and English

(b) Mathematics

(c) Science and Technology

(d) Social Sciences

(e) Work Education

(f) Art Education (fine arts: Visual and Performing)

(g) Health and Physical Education (including games and sports, yoga, NCC and scouting and guiding)

Secondary Stage (2 years)

(a) Three Languages — the mother tongue/the regional language, modern Indian language and English

(b) Mathematics

(c) Science and Technology

(d) Social Sciences

(e) Work Education

(f) Art Education (fine arts: Visual and Performing)

(g) Health and Physical Education (including games and sports, yoga, NCC and scouting and guiding)

10

Meaning and Significance of Minimum Level of Learning

THE Yashpal Committee went around the country a few years ago to elicit peoples' perceptions of the problem of curriculum burden, following the great Indian tradition of *janapada mataanveshana*. As a research assistant to the committee, I too talked to teachers and educators in several parts of the country to try and understand how they perceived the problem. One common opinion I heard was that, yes, there is a load, but that it is also necessary: 'We have to catch up with the world and be prepared for the twenty-first century.'

Let us for now bypass the debate of whether the millennium begins this year or the next, or that we would have been spared this confusion if only the West had been introduced earlier to counting from the great Indian Zero. The 21st century is now officially here, and our national educators have taken on a new challenge: moving from a 'burdened curriculum' towards a 'curriculum of the unknown'. They are like their counterparts in the great Indian tradition, the ajnatanvestas or seekers of the unknown, as they stand now on the shores of the vast brahmandam of the third millennium, and boldly, yet humbly, seek to make sense of and prepare for it.

The recently released discussion document – the National Curriculum Framework for School Education – gives an idea of the entire scope of the issues that our educators grappled with when it was drafted. The philosophical underpinnings of education had to be definitively moved back more than 3000 years, from the 1960s development discourse to 'the Great Indian Tradition'. And to demonstrate that the 'Indian way of thinking' is up-to-date in matters such as secularism and social welfare for the under-privileged, Mahatm[illegible] included in good measure.

As regards the curriculum itself, [illegible] ensure the pre-servation of the behaviouristic core with which our national curriculum planners and textbook writers are most comfortable; at the same time one had to demonstrate familiarity with modern concepts like the 'zone of proximal development', 'multiple intelligence', 'indigenous knowledge' and 'culture specific pedagogies', many of which are fundamentally anti behaviouristic. Perhaps it is because of the lack of time and the 'compelling circumstances' which have necessitated immediate renewal of syllabi and textbooks (Preface), that the resulting document was forced to sacrifice the great Indian tradition of brevity – the *sutra* or aphoristic form.

Written in the style of traditional Indian popular wisdom, the text consists of self-affirming, empty tautologies, viz. the need to 'adequately provide appropriate learning experiences to learners.' It is of course an indisputable truth that learning experiences need to be adequate and appropriate. But one is no wiser at the end as to what adequacy or appropriateness entail. Other recommendations include well-known mantras such as 'simple to complex', 'immediate to remote'. Still others reflect little more than the syndrome of keeping-up-with-the-international-Joneses. The plethora of fashionable concerns includes the 'alarming deficiency: emotional illiteracy', 'girl child' and 'children with special needs'. Perhaps the only one missing from the document is the nationwide District Primary Education Programme's favourite: 'community participation'.

At the end, one put down the document with mixed emotions – amused, irritated, surprised, but most of all, deeply disturbed. In matters of how knowledge, the learner and the process of learning is to be conceptualized, or the direction that Indian education must take, there were profound contradictions and a veritable lack of clarity. The only agenda expressed with any consistency was the assertion of the great Indian tradition.

From the 1950s, curriculum development in India approached both knowledge and learning from an essentially behaviourist paradigm. Although no official document presented *any* explicit model of the child as learner, implicitly curriculum developers and textbook writers drew on the behaviourist-connectionist framework wherein knowledge is treated as a given and broken down into a hierarchical taxonomy of 'specific learning objectives'. This approach is marked by a minimalist model of the child – essentially in terms of 'previous knowledge' and the ability to respond and show 'observable behaviour' when motivated, which the teachers can then select and shape.

Children can be easily evaluated against these learning objectives; failure is handled with remedial teaching. The process is teacher-centred. There is no need for a theory of cognition and learning; only one of altering and reinforcing responses with appropriate feedback – rewards such as praise and punishment like teacher disapproval. These concepts and vocabulary can be traced back to the influence of Benjamin Bloom and other American curriculum experts of the 1950s on the newly created NCERT.

The debate that gathered force 1970s onwards – whether to model the child's learning in behaviourist or constructivist terms – passed Indian curriculum developers by. According to constructivism, the child like any other human being is regarded as engaged in making sense of the world, acting upon it, and producing knowledge. A curriculum based on this model is interactional; the child's present and potential development determine the kind of learning experiences the teacher must provide.

By the early 1990s, it was difficult to ignore the fact that a paradigm shift had occurred everywhere else in the world. The cult of 'specific learning objectives', however, survived by reinventing itself, in the form of 'minimum levels of learning' (MLL).These levels, it was claimed, would not only establish standards of achievement, they would also help to free the teacher from textbook and evaluation-centred teaching and practice child-friendly pedagogy.

But by their very nature, the MLL is no different from the highly specific, fragmentary learning objectives in terms of observable behaviour. It comprises of long, detailed subject-wise lists for classes I to V. For example, the list in Mathematics for class I begins with 'Count 1-20 using objects and pictures'. Other items in the same list include: 'Identify zero as the number representing nothing or the absence of objects in a collection', 'Arrange numbers 1-100 in ascending and descending order', and so on.

Not surprisingly, the MLL has not brought about any Copernican revolution in which the child replaces the teacher as the centre of the curriculum. Post-MLL curriculum related activities continue to be narrowly teacher-defined and led, and are geared to evaluation. The problem is not one of creating standards or defining objectives. Education needs both. Rather it is one of defining these standards and objectives based on a model of the child as essentially receiving knowledge as also a model of learning as exhibiting 'observable behaviour' according to a narrowly defined timetable.

Compare the two objectives given above to 'national standards' defined by the NCTM for the same area, numeracy, from kindergarten to grade 4: 'Construct number meanings through real-world experiences and the use of physical materials'... 'Interpret the multiple uses of numbers encountered in the real world'). This is followed by a discussion of what abilities and understanding can be developed, with what kind of learning experiences. Such a statement of standards reflects a perspective in which mathematical knowledge, even of numbers, is not fragmented into logical bits, but seen as growing out of the child's efforts at 'mathematizing' her experiences; using what she knows, interpreting and learning. Learning is not seen as the outcome of specific pedagogic acts, but as emerging over a period of time.

Given the formidable presence of the MLL in all new curricular initiatives of the state, it was a pleasant surprise to see on page 17 of the new National Curriculum Framework, a section titled 'Child as a Constructor of his Knowledge'. Finally it appeared that the foundations of school curriculum would be shifted away from archaic misconceptions of the child as a learner. Just how can we aspire to be 'a knowledge-centred India' or 'learn to learn' unless children are made active participants in their learning? Espousing the constructivist paradigm should have led to its logical conclusion of reorienting the approach to the curriculum – in matters of selection, organization, transaction and evaluation.

After 50 years of post-Independence educational effort and understanding we need less patronizing ways of responding to the need for universalizing elementary education. The document noted the 'worldwide recognition of the indigenous knowledge system'. It also recognized the need for consciously incorporating 'the fundamental rights of minorities and people coming from disadvantaged groups like scheduled castes, scheduled tribes and other backward communities', and 'using culture-specific pedagogies'. And yet it failed completely in combining them and making a conceptual breakthrough in the matter of educating children in their cultural contexts.

'Contextualization' is not simply a matter of detail that can be taken care of in textbooks or through pedagogic exercises such as story telling, dramatics and puppetry. Instruments such as MLL which measure students against narrow, decontextualized standards, will continue to show tribal and lower caste people as 'disadvantaged' and 'deprived' in educational settings. And no amount of remedial teaching, and/ or condensing the core curriculum for migratory children, will mitigate its disastrous consequences for identity, personal and collective. Never mind that children across the country are burdened by the total lack of meaning of what they learn in school, mostly through the great Indian tradition of memorization. There was barely a mention of this central problem of the Indian school curriculum.

Periodically there were articulations akin to the dangerous political discourse that feeds off Indian chauvinism. The Indian tradition can be depended upon to find ancient equivalents for all modern conditions: *Vasudaiva kutumbam'* for the global village, and *sehriddya sarvabhutam* for social cohesion and learning to live together. Perhaps it is only to bring out the continuity between cultural tradition and information sciences that 'computer simulation and drill' is specially highlighted as an important learning tool for social science study.

More ominous was a sentence buried deep in the section on science as a subject of the core curriculum. At the end of the 'hefty' 125 pages, one wonders what holds together the variety of ideas and intentions expressed in this document. The answer lies within the document itself; another great Indian tradition, which is gaining popularity – a more politically expedient technique derived from *purna ganita* or holistic mathematics. Here, in order to synthesize a whole from some parts, you simply put all the parts together and give it an appropriate name. In the past this great Indian method for adding dissimilar things had been used to create the subject 'Environmental Studies': 1 subject (Environmental studies) = 1 subject (science) + 1 subject (social studies); 1= 1+1.

In the accounting ledger for curriculum load, this looks very neat. Of course in reality, this 'subject' is represented by two separate books – one for science and the other for social studies. Similarly, 1 subject (social studies) = 1 subject (history) + 1 subject (geography) + 1 subject (civics?) + 1 subject (economics).

We find this technique being repeatedly invoked in the document to add new areas to the curriculum without attracting the attention of the load-watchdogs: 'The three areas of work education, arts (fine and performing), and health activities may be put together *and a suitable name be given to them*'.

This then seems to have been the technique to produce the discussion document. First list everything that must be included, then write them up, sort them into chapters, and finally bind everything into a document. Universalisation of Elementary Education (UEE) has been accepted as a national goal in India since Independence. The founding fathers of our Constitution recognised UEE as a crucial input for nation building. The Directive Principles of State Policy envisage that the state shall endeavor to provide free and compulsory education for children up to 14 years of age within a period of 10 years. The National Education Policies so far have reiterated the constitutional directive. The National Policy on Education 1986 resolves to provide free and compulsory education of satisfactory quality to all children up to 14 years of age before the commencement of the twenty first century.

The colonial regime prior to our Independence in 1947 established a system of education that had limited access and denied mass education. It gave greater emphasis on conformism to socio-political and economic systems obtaining in the country in those times. Macaulay explicitly stated that the objective of the education system was to create a new breed of Indians as similar to Europeans as possible. It was on account of this that the Indian National Movement developed a strong critique of the British System that only imparted 'learning skills' and not 'life skills' and that did not respect Indian traditions. The national movement also expressed the global sentiment of education for all and Gopal Krishna Gokhale's Compulsory Education Bill reflected the spirit of India's freedom movement.

The imperatives of the colonial education policy promoted alternatives, notable being Mahatma Gandhi's "education for life" and Rabindra Nath Tagore's approach of education for self-development, reflected through Shantiniketan. Dr. Zakir Hussain's thrust on 'Nayee Taleem' was also based on Gandhiji's philosophy of education for life. Gandhiji's emphasis on "Swawalamban" sprang from his belief that the State was not the best agency to promote education. He believed that education is a process of empowerment. It integrates physical, mental and emotional development. He stressed that education must promote respect for manual labour rather than abhorrence for it.

FRESH APPROACH

The fervour for freedom and patriotism to achieve "swawalamban", made our leaders search for an alternative approach to elementary education. Article 41 and 45 of the Constitution enunciating the Directive Principles of State Policy on education provided the basis for the new approach. 14 States and 4 Union Territories enacted Legislation for free and compulsory primary education. All States have exempted children from tuition fee up to upper primary classes. However, compulsion has not been enforced due to socio-economic and political considerations.

Expansion and Growth

The thrust of the Central and State Governments in universalising elementary education so far has been on three aspects namely, universal access, universal retention and universal achievement. Concerted efforts made in these areas have resulted in significant expansion of elementary education in the country. The number of primary schools has increased from 2.10 lakh in 1950-51 to 5.90 lakh and number of upper primary schools from 13,000 to 1.71 lakh respectively in 1995-96. During this period, Gross Enrolment Ratio (GER) at primary levels has increased from 43% in 1950-51 to 104.% in 1995-96. 95% of the rural population in the country have a primary school within 1 kilometre and 85% an upper primary school within a distance of 3 kilometres. With 15 Crore children enrolled and 3o lakh teachers, we have one of the largest elementary education systems in the world. The proportion of girls in classes I-VIII as also women teachers has increased steadily.

Quality Improvement

The quality of elementary education has been one of the major concerns right from 1950s. The National Policy on Education, 1986 brought to the forefront the need for quality improvement in terms of learning achievement of children. As a result, greater efforts have been made to impart competency based learning, particularly from 1990 when the Minimum Levels of Learning (MLLs) were introduced. A clear shift from teacher dominated teaching to a child centred approach has been observed in most states. Integrated Textbooks which include workbooks are replacing traditional books. A large number of teaching, learning and reading materials have been developed, with active participation of teachers and NGOs. Efforts are continuing to promote competency based learning both at primary and upper primary levels by re-orienting and training teachers. Results so far have been encouraging.

Policy and Planning

The period after Independence saw a linear expansion of the elementary education system through allocation of additional resources. It was in 1964 that the Central Government recognised the need to take a holistic view of education and appointed the Education Commission. The Commission was entrusted with the task of evolving a national system of education. It recommended a radical transformation in the prevailing education system and highlighted the need for the "common school approach" to promote equity and social justice.

The first National Policy on Education, 1968 recommended free and compulsory elementary education and equalisation of educational opportunities especially for girls and children belonging to SCs and STs. The National Policy on Education 1986 and its Programme of Action,was enunciated on the basis of a detailed review of the country's educational performance. The policy resolves to achieve UEE by 2000 AD.

The plan allocations for elementary education have increased steadily, though still not adequate to fulfil the constitutional commitments. Fifty years of freedom have seen higher levels of spending by the Central and State Governments to provide quality of education for all. Better school infrastructure, more and better-paid school teachers, timely availability of subsidised or free text books in regional languages, provision of scholarships, uniforms and mid day meals have all received attention of state governments who are the main providers of elementary education. The Central Government increased its allocations for elementary education after 1976 when education became a concurrent subject. These allocations were aimed at providing additional funds to resource poor states on the basis of the principle of equalisation and for quality improvement.

The period following the adoption of National Policy on Education (NPE), 1986 saw the introduction of a number of centrally sponsored schemes to cater to the specific needs of the elementary education sector. These included Operation Blackboard to improve school environment, enhance retention and learning achievement of children by providing minimum essential facilities in all primary schools; restructuring and strengthening of Teacher Education to upgrade pedagogical skills of teachers through establishment of dedicated teacher training institutes at District level (DIETS); Non-formal Education Programme to provide alternative education facilities for girls, working children and children in far flung areas; Minimum Levels of Learning to improve learning achievements of children; and the National Programme -of Nutritional Support to Primary

Education, commonly known as Mid-day Meal Scheme, to provide nutritional support to children in primary classes.

Plan expenditure on elementary education has increased to nearly 50% of Central expenditure on Education. States continue to discharge the main responsibility for management, expansion and maintenance of schools. Since there is considerable variation in their fiscal capacity to do so, there is need for targeted interventions to improve primary education in such states.

External Assistance

Following the World Conference for Education for All (EFA) in Jomtien (Thailand) in March 1990 there is a greater commitment and willingness on the part of multilateral and bilateral aid agencies to invest in primary education in developing countries. A major internationally assisted programme namely District Primary Education Programme (DPEP) was launched in 1992 with assistance from World Bank and European Union. The programme adopts a holistic approach to promote primary education through decentralized planning and integrated programming at district level. The programme has been extended to 149 districts in 14 States in 1997.

The Lok Jumbish and Shiksha Karmi Projects are two other successful internationally assisted projects. Lok Jumbish, meaning a people's movement for UEE, has a holistic understanding about the problem of UEE and is implemented by establishing an interface between the local community, the teaching profession, the educational administration and the learners. The Shiksha Karmi Project envisages a paradigm shift in delivery of primary education. Inspired by the concept of barefoot teachers, the project has effectively responded to the problem of teacher absenteeism in the remote and inaccessible areas of Rajasthan.

Internationally assisted projects for basic education have focussed attention on decentralisation, people's participation, construction of school buildings, development of innovative teaching learning materials, participative teacher training, enhancement of institutional capacities and improvement in learning levels. The overall strategy and approach of these projects gives priority to low literacy areas, girls and disadvantaged sections of society.

Decentralisation and Community Mobilisation

The process of decentralisation has been an encouraging feature of our efforts to universalise elementary education. NPE, 1986 visualises direct community involvement in the form of Village Education Committees (VECs) for management of elementary education. The POA, 1992 emphasised micro-planning as a process of designing a family-wise and child-wise plan of education by which every child regularly attends a school or a NFE centre, continues his or her education at a place suitable to him/her and completes at least eight years of schooling or its equivalent at the NFE centre.

The Seventy-third and Seventy-fourth Constitutional Amendments have hastened the process of community management of elementary schools. These amendments have created a congenial ambience for the Panchayat Raj Institutions (PRIs) to play a more dynamic role. These institutions now provide a greater voice to women, scheduled castes and scheduled tribes. Increasingly PRIs and VECs are becoming involved in social mobilisation, planning and supervision for UEE. The introduction of micro-planning and school mapping have brought the school closer to the community while sensitising people to issues and problems in their local schools.

Recent trends in community participation indicate a greater thrust on empowerment of communities. Mobilising the communities to take responsibility to ensure quality education for every child is the core strategy of several innovative initiatives in elementary education including DPEP, LJP, SKP and BEP. Genuine community involvement is the key factor for the success of LJP and SKP in Rajasthan. LJP has had a positive effect on the empowerment of locally elected people, especially women at village level who are often active members of the LJ core teams and Mahila Samoohs.

The VECs, carefully formed and trained through environmental building activities in the LJ, are actively involved in school matters. SKP has constituted VECs in 2000 villages to promote community involvement in primary education and encourage village level planning. DPEP is making useful investments in orientation and training of VEC members. An important role of the VEC is to mobilise resources for maintenance, repair and construction of school buildings. The VECs also help in determining the school calendar and school timings in consultation with the local community.

Partnership with NGOs

NGOs are emerging as important partners in efforts of the Central and State Governments towards UEE. They have been instrumental in mobilising social support for UEE, development of socially relevant curriculum, contextual teaching learning materials, innovative teacher training, pedagogic renewal, review and evaluation of educational experiments, action research for UEE, and designing of alternative education programmes. The participation of NGOs together with community support has helped to improve the physical conditions and environment of elementary schools as well as promotion of education for girls and children belonging to SCs and STs and working children. As of now, nearly 750 NGOs are supplementing the Governmental efforts towards UEE by rendering cooperation and resource support to Non-formal Education with assistance from the Government.

Future Challenges

The country has undoubtedly been successful in evolving a

national structure for elementary education in the last fifty years. Primary education is now provided in the mother tongue or regional language in all the States and UTs. There has been substantial increase in access to elementary education, with reduced class, caste and sectional disparities. First generation learners, girls and the under privileged sections of society have been provided with unique opportunities for vertical mobility. Literacy standards have substantially improved across all the States and UTs. National Literacy rate has increased from 15.% in 1951 to 52.% in 1991. An impressive academic support system has been built up at national and state level through NCERT, NIEPA, NCTE, SCERTs, CIEMATs, DIETs, BRCs, and CRCs to provide technical support and guidance to the elementary education system.

Despite substantial achievements, the task of UEE is far from complete. Schools and enrolments have certainly increased but so have the number of out of school children. The country today has one of the largest illiterate populations in the world. Caste, gender, class and regional disparities in UEE though reduced, are still glaring and persistent. While the demand for quality education is showing perceptible increase because of improved awareness and social mobilisation through organised efforts such as TLCs and PLCs, supply is generally inadequate.

The educational administration in most states and UTs is yet to effectively tackle endemic problems concerning shortage of teachers, teacher absenteeism, inadequate and improperly designed school buildings, lack of teaching learning equipment, need based teacher training, and a curriculum related to real life requirements. Teachers' esteem in a society that worshipped Gurus is low. They are called upon to do variety of non-teaching jobs, leaving little time for teacher-pupil interaction. Teacher education, considered crucial to improve quality of education, has not made the vital difference in the classroom.

A traditional style of administration and the tendency for centralisation is impeding genuine people's participation and effective partnership with NGOs. Lack of transparency and rigid procedures have not facilitated confidence building measures necessary for empowerment of women and the poor. Imperative in these shortfalls is the need to consolidate the gains, design specifically targeted programmes to reach the unreached, improve quality of education making it contextually relevant and related to real life, and make UEE a social movement. We need to redouble our efforts in promoting education for girls, SCs and STs and minorities. Research in educational planning, management and training should be given greater attention in our endeavour to improve learning achievement of children in schools.

The recent measures initiated by the Government, namely DPEP, Mid–day Meal Programme and the proposal for NEEM, the National Programme Media advocacy and Publicity for UEE and the Joint GOI-UN System Education Programme are expected to address some of these challenges more effectively. The proposed National Elementary Education Mission should evolve strategies for reaching the unreached and achieving the goal of UEE within a given time-frame in a systematic, sustained and integrated manner by involving all segments of civil society in this national endeavour.

The resolve of the Government to make elementary education a fundamental right of all children of 6-14 years is expected to spur the government and non-government sectors to take necessary measures to achieve UEE. It is a demonstration of political will and administrative resolve to achieve UEE and eradicate illiteracy. Efforts of the Government to mobilise resources for education to the extent of 6% of GDP will also help in hastening the process of universalising elementary education.

Undeniably, we face a gigantic challenge to achieve UEE. Nevertheless, in the last fifty years we have expanded our base and built many assets to complete the unfinished task in the foreseeable future. We have a strong policy framework, significant political and administrative commitment and a national desire for UEE. It is hoped that with a clear vision, firm will, higher investments, greater dedication, rapid decentralisation and increased people's participation, we would be able to fulfil our goal of providing satisfactory quality of education to all children in the country within the next decade.

11

CHILD-CENTRED TEACHING-LEARNING PROCESS

Educational policy and progress have been reviewed in the light of the goals of national development and priorities set from time to time. In its Resolution on the National Policy on Education in 1968, an emphasis on quality improvement and a planned, more equitable expansion of educational facilities and the need to focus on the education of girls was stressed. It was also stated that of all the factors which determine the quality of education and its contribution to national development, the teacher was undoubtedly the most important. It was on the qualities and character, educational qualifications and professional competence of the teacher that success of all educational endeavours must, ultimately, depend.

About a decade and a half later, the National Policy on Education (INPE-1986) was formulated which was further updated in 1992. The NPE-1986 provides for a comprehensive policy framework for the development of education up to the end of the century and a Plan of Action (POA) 1992, assigning specific responsibilities for organising, implementing and financing its proposals. Among the distinguishing features and recommendations of this policy are:

— emphasis on pre-primary education,

- formulation of strategies based on micro planning at the grassroots level to ensure children's retention in school.
- recommendation to lay down Minimum Levels of Learning (MLLs) for each stage of education.
- integration of adult literacy and Non Formal Education (INFE) programmes with vital national concerns such as the small family norm. health care. environment and nutrition,
- provision of essential facilities in schools,
- adoption of a child-centred, activity-based approach, and
- establishment of District Institutes of Education and Training (DIETs) for the pre-service and in-service education of teachers for elementary schools and for personnel working in non-formal and adult education programmes.

In the NPE 1986, improvement in the status and professional competence of teachers is envisaged as the cornerstone of educational reconstruction. It emphasises that teacher education is a continuous process which new programmes of teacher education must reflect

To ensure greater participation in education by all sections of society and also to improve quality, decentralised management structures are being introduced in states. This is in pursuance of the 73rd and 74th Constitutional Amendments of 1992 regarding *Panchayati Raj* and *Nagar Palika* institutions.

EDUCATION FOR ALL: INTERNATIONAL POLICY AND PROGRAMME INITIATIVES

The World Conference on Education For All (EFA) held at Jomtien, Thailand in 1990 affirmed the will of participating nations- including India-to meet the basic learning needs of all children, youth and adults. To achieve this objective a two-pronged strategy was designed, i.e., Universalisation of Elementary Education IUEE) and universal adult literacy, which has since been the priority policy and action areas for the participating nine highly populated countries.

Three years later in December 1993, India's commitment to EFA (Education for All) was reaffirmed in its adoption of the Delhi Declaration and Framework of Action at the EFA Summit. The Declaration calls for ensuring a place for every child in a school or an appropriate education programme according to his or her capabilities, consolidating efforts towards basic education for children, youth and adults from public and private sources, improving and extending literacy and Adult Education (AE) programmes within the context of an integrated strategy of basic education for all people, eliminating disparities of access to basic education, improving the quality and relevance of basic education, and in all actions and according to the highest priority at national and other levels, ensuring that a growing shore of national and community resources is dedicated to basic education, improving the management of existing resources for education, and collaborating with other notions in the development of distance education.

At a Special Conference convened in February, 1994 following the summit, the Chief Ministers of all the States and Union Territories (UTs) decided that coordinated and concerted action would be needed on the part of the local community, state governments and the central government in the mobilisation of resources for education so that there was a substantial increase in budget allocation and so as to accord higher priority to primary and AE

The process of affirmation of the goals of EFA was reinforced at the Mid Decode Review of EFA which took place in Amman, Jordan in June 1 996, at which various initiatives were discussed in a country-specific context to review achievements of EFA.

Elementary education

Ensuring accessibility of educational opportunities has been the principal policy plank of governmental strategy. While special efforts were aimed at educationally disadvantaged groups, particularly, Scheduled Costes (SCs) (comprising roughly 17 per cent of the population and Scheduled Tribes (STs) (constituting about 8 per cent of the population, various measures including monetary and other incentives, and recruitment of more teachers from disadvantaged communities, and flexible school timings provided the fillip to the expanding coverage of enrolment. As on incentive to enrolment, attendance and retention, besides improving the nutrition of children, a nation-wide mid-day meal programme has been launched during 1995-96. More than 33.5 million children benefited from the scheme. By 1997-98 all government run/aided schools in the country would be covered.

The Indian education system is also unique in that it seeks to give due recognition and importance to the social organisation, traditions, customs and value systems of the various communities-particularly SCs and STs. This is supported by the development of materials and curricula in tribal languages, residential schools for tribal children and the encouragement of the young, educated members of the community to participate in the educational process.

Various initiatives have been token to reduce the academic burden on students while improving the quality of education. Not only is curriculum development being decentralised but an increasing involvement of teachers in the development of textbooks, child-centred and activity-based methods of teaching in schools and examination strategies ore being formulated to assess the ability to understand rather than the ability to memorise. The system of examination, too, is continuously under review through introduction of continuous and comprehensive evaluation.

The Government in 1 996. has renewed its commitment and resolve to UEE and to spend at least 50 per cent of the allocation on education which is to grow to 6 per cent of Gross Domestic Product (GDP) by the turn of the century as against the current level of about 3.23 per cent of GDP. Opening of residential schools for the poor children in each district and Teacher Housing Scheme are the thrust areas of the new policy.

New initiative: District Primary Education Programme

The District Primary Education Programme (DPEP) is the major initiative undertaken to effect improvement in the quality and UEE. The programme is distinguished by its holistic approach and the principle of contextuality in planning. This, in effect, implies that education is planned and organised in the specific context of the area concerned-a shift from macro to micro planning with the district as the unit of planning. The programme lays great emphasis on people's participation and management, has a marked gender focus and seeks to enhance school effectiveness by increasing infrastructural facilities, developing instructional materials and training of teachers.

Non Formal Education

The NPE 1986, while taking the enormous challenge of achieving UEE in its entirety [access, retention as well as achievement!, recognised the fact that schools would not reach all children, particularly, millions of girls and working children whose participation in the school system is thwarted by socio-economic conditions. The Policy, therefore, called for a large and systematic programme of NFE as an integral component to achieve UEE with enough flexibility for learners to learn at their own pace and at the same time having quality comparable with formal education.

Secondary education

In keeping with the role of secondary education in preparing students for further academic or professional studies, the policy has been focused on improvement of quality through specific inputs such as the schemes for improvement of Science

Education, Environment Education, Population Education and Computer Literacy. Government run schools, Kendriya Vidyalayas (Central Schools) have added to promotion of national identity throughout the country. The Government has accelerated the process of creating infrastructure and teacher training facilities so that these chains of schools act as pace setters for other schools in the country. Residential coeducational secondary schools [Navodaya Vidyalayas] have been established in each district to nourish talent in the rural areas. These schools have a positive bias in favour of girls and currently, about 1,20,000 students are enrolled on the basis of merit, in these schools

Open school

A major initiative to expand access of education was to promote distance education. To this end, the Open School system also provides alternative schooling to neo literates who have acquired functional literacy and also to drop-outs from the school and the NFE systems so that their schooling continues at their own pace and at a time convenient to them. The National Open School (NOS) and the State Open Schools provide alternative means to acquire secondary level education in a flexible manner.

Vocational education

Vocational education is the policy framework that seeks to provide diversification of educational options, increase potential employability and reduce the mismatch between demand and supply of skilled manpower. At present, about 10 per cent students take up vocational courses in the last two years of the schooling phase. The endeavour is that 25 per cent students be diverted to the vocational stream by the end of the present century. A Central Institute of Vocational Education (CIVE) under The National Council of Educational Research and Training (NCERT) has been set up to support courses and develop instructional material. The Institute has accomplished this in about 150 vocations. It is also proposed to set up State Institutes of Vocational Education and strengthen existing ones. Pre-vocational education is being introduced at the lower secondary stage (classes IX and X). The scheme aims at covering 1,000 schools during the Eighth Plan 11992-971

Non-formal vocational education and training programmes are also being introduced through Non Governmental Organisations (NGOs), specially, in rural areas. These are intended for girls in the 14-18 age group and are designed to emphasise entrepreneurship and introduce new and emerging technologies to, women

Higher education

Higher education policy in India has been characterised by upgradation strategies that provide for quality improvement, and consolidation of facilities for existing Universities and Colleges. The higher education sector, considered vital for the national economy, has witnessed a steady growth since Independence in 1947. The enrolment of students too shows an increased share of women and SCs and STs in all stages of higher education. The utilisation of distance education as a cost-effective and easily accessible medium for upgradation of education and skills, particularly in remote areas, forms part of the thrust area in the higher education policy.

Technical education

Technical education is one of the most significant component of the human resource development spectrum with great potential for adding value to products and services, for contributing to the national economy, and for improving the quality of life of the people. In recognition of the importance of this sector, the successive five year plans laid great emphasis on the development of technical education. Technical education includes courses in engineering, technology management, pharmacy, applied arts and crafts, etc. Policy guidelines in technical education have sought to streamline courses and syllabi in relation to the manpower needs of the country as well as changing technological scenario across the globe.

Initiatives in technical education

Policy initiatives to revamp the technical education system include promoting institution-industry interaction, providing continuing education to update the skill and knowledge of technical personnel working in the industry and service sectors, the transfer of technology to the rural sector and setting up Technology Development Missions to meet the emerging challenges in science and technology.

In order to update and upgrade technical education in the Indian Institutes of Technology (IITS), Regional Engineering Colleges (RECs) and other institutions/polytechnics, obsolete machinery and equipment is weeded out, modern machinery and new equipment relevant to curricular needs introduced and opportunities for hands-on experience for student created]

A new policy measure has also been initiated to mobilise funds, particularly, for higher and technical education from non-governmental sources. in tune with the economic liberalisation of the economy, institutions are being encouraged to generate resources, raise fees which often have not been revised in the last three or four decades and embark on judicious financial management with the overall objective of reducing government subsidies.

A National Technical Manpower Information System has been developed by the Government to monitor the absorption of trained engineering and technical manpower and, thereby, create a data base in order to streamline and plan the development of technical education.

During the past few years, the number of institutions in the private sector has increased considerably. A number of industrial houses have also established technical and management institutions. The government, however, has taken suitable measures to regulate education in the private sector to check its commercialisation and maintain standards through setting up All India Council of Technical Education (AICTE).

Adult education

AE, an essential component of EFA is seen as an imperative for the growth of the individual and the nation. The National Literacy Mission NLM), set up in 1988 with the goal of helping 80 million persons achieve literacy by 1995, has adopted the Total literacy Campaign (TLC) as the dominant strategy for achieving its literacy goals. This has resulted m a rich and varied experience that has become an international resource. The Mission has now been extended to cover 100 million non-literates by 1997, that is, by the end of the 8th Plan period.

Value-based education

The NPE 1986 recognises that importance should be given to value-based curriculum incorporating the notion of an equitable society, secularism, democracy, and a scientific temper. These are reflected in the core elements of the school curriculum and also include observance of the small family norm, protection of the environment and gender equality. Human rights have also been now included. Both at the national and state levels, textbooks have been reviewed to eliminate passages that were inimical to human rights or that distorted them. Steps have, simultaneously, been initiated to include alternative material which shows sensitivity to human rights issues. Universities are also in the process of introducing courses on human rights. The NCERT has published a Source Book on Human Rights as a guide for teachers

Early childhood education

The importance of Early Childhood Care and Education (ECCE)

has been recognised as a crucial preparatory aspect of a child's development. In India, this programme has evolved to provide a holistic service. Besides, educational facilities for learning through structured and unstructured play activities, health care and nutrition are also catered for. Day Care Centres are provided as a support service to enable girls taking care of siblings to attend school. These Day Care Centres also assist working women belonging to the poorer sections.

Supplementing education at this level, the National TV Network has transmitted a serial which introduces pre-school children to reading, numbers, geometric shapes, health care concepts, sanitation and food using songs, animation and puppets. The number of pre-primary schools has increased from 303 in 1951 to nearly 14 million in 1991-92 while the enrolment in these has gone up from 28,000 to 3.9 million for the corresponding years.

The elementary education system in India is the second largest in the world with 149.4 million children of 6 -14 years enrolled. This is about 82 per cent of the children in this age-group. The emphasis, however, is not on enrolment alone, equal attention is paid to retention and achievement. An estimated 95 per cent of the rural population now has access to primary schooling facilities within a walking distance of 1 km; 84 per cent of the population is served by middle or upper primary schools within a distance of 3 kms. The Gross Enrolment Ratio {GER) for classes I-V is 104.0 and for classes VI-VIII if is 67.2 for the year 1994-95. There has been a substantial increase in girls' enrolment: from 40.4 million in 199~91 to 46.8 million in 1994-95 in primary schools and 52.9 million in 1990-91 to 62.6 million in 1994-95 in upper primary schools.

Facilities for expanding enrolment

The expanding enrolment has necessitated a growing number of teachers as well as schools in the country: from 5.6 million primary schools in 1990-91 to 5.8 million in 1994-95 and from

16.6 million in 199~91 to 17.14 million teachers at the primary level in 1994-95. There are four types of schools in the country: government managed, government aided, government recognised but unaided, and unrecognised.

A common structure of education is being followed in most states: i.e., the 10, + 2, + 3 system. Thus a child who joins class 1 at the age of six goes through five years of primary school, and three years of upper primary/middle school to complete eight years of elementary education. Two years of secondary education and two years of higher secondary education bring schooling to an end. Three years of further studies enable the student to obtain his/her first degree.

Curriculum development for elementary schools The states are free to develop their own curricula and instructional materials within the framework developed at the national level by the NCERT. To cope with this, a strategy has been evolved to impart MLLs, i.e., the development of competency based teaching and learning to suit local situations This approach integrates various components of curriculum, classroom transaction, evaluation and teacher orientation. It is expected to achieve greater relevance and functionality in primary education

Non Formal Education

Despite enormous strides in school education, 28 million out of 153 million in the age-group *5-14* are still out of school. Of these, 14 million are working children who cannot attend school full time Hence, NFE is seen as a vital aspect of India's current strategy on education as it can reach out to working children, school drop outs, girls and those who cannot attend full-time schools due to several socio-economic factors. Under the NFE programme there are three types of centres:

— Co-educational centres where the contribution of the union government and state government is *50:50;*

— Girls' centres with the contribution of union and state governments being 90: 10; and

— NFE centres run by NGOs In these the assistance from the union government is 100 per cent

The life of a centre is, generally, two years. These centres are organised for two hours a day at a time convenient to the learners. Each centre is run by an instructor who takes care of the various groups of learners learning at various grade levels. Children learn each unit at their own pace. This is also true of NFE centres at the upper primary level

The NFE course is condensed into four semesters of six months each for which specially developed teaching-learning materials and stationery are provided to children free of cost. Compatibility with the formal school system is ensured through a focus on MLLs. There is a provision for testing and certification of children of NFE centres to facilitate their entry into formal schools. Implemented through state governments and voluntary organisations, the NFE programme draws on a high level of community participation and is characterised by flexibility, relevance and a decentralised administrative structure.

Secondary education

There has been a steady expansion of secondary education in India. Between 1986 and 1993, the enrolment growth for secondary and higher secondary was 32.45 and 37.72 per cent, respectively. Girls' enrolment, too, increased greatly, registering an increase of 50.99 at the secondary level and 53.97 at the higher secondary level. In addition to expansion, secondary education is being strengthened through various schemes such as, those for improving education in science, vocational areas and work experience, population education, culture, values, computer literacy, education technology, yoga, physical education and sports. A number of programmes have also been formulated for promoting enrolment of girls, SCs/STs and disabled children.

12

Multi-grade and Multi-level Teaching-learning Process

Organizing learning is one of the many challenges faced by primary teachers. The occurrence of interest in whole-class teaching deviates many primary teachers from child-centered approach of teaching-learning to teacher-centered approach in the existing set-up, which leads to poor learning among children. In spite of various learning levels of learners, primary classrooms are commonly treated as a grade specific/age specific structure in our country both in rural and urban set-ups. Even in the cut and thrust of single grade/age classrooms, there are many parameters that teachers have to manage and many vital and practical decisions that they have to take right from the planning stage to the transactional stage in the classroom.

When the above mentioned teaching-learning variables/ parameters i.e., curriculum, pedagogy, instructional time, teaching-learning materials, etc. in single-grade classrooms are so complex and challenging, why have pedogogists, practitioners and even modern educationists propagated multiage classrooms, instead of grade-specific-classroom teaching in many developed and developing countries? The multiage classrooms are usually opted for over single-grade classrooms by most developed and developing countries like Australia, Indonesia, Vietnam, New zealand due to sound pedagogical reasons. Educational practitioners claim that this situation definitely provides opportunities for employing multilevel teaching at the primary stage. Various researches conducted in this area by Ketz, Evangelou Hartman, 1993; Veenman, 1997; Smith Warburfon, 1997 have also suggested that this approach facilitates

- creation of more learning culture than teaching culture;
- creation of mixed-ability group, which encourages peer-learning;
- opening of scope for self-learning, cooperative learning for children;
- learning to learn.

This school of thought believes that multiage grouping is superior to single-grade or horizontal grouping as it helps to develop the group into a more social and family-like structure, in which students who are at least a year apart in age are placed in the same classroom for several years.

In India, the concept of gradeless/multiage classroom is not new. Many Indian schools in ancient times were indigenous, non-graded schools and had functioned as a single-teacher school in the country. The Indian Education Commission also recommended the introduction of the 'ungraded unit' as one of the measures to improve quality and reduce the incidence of wastage and stagnation at the primary stage. Many state governments took up the suggestion and introduced ungraded classrooms at the primary stage, particularly combining Classes I and II and Classes III and IV as a unit under the guidance of the State Institution of Education in collaboration with NCERT in 1977. The results were reported to be satisfying and encouraging in improving the quality of education along with reducing the incidence of wastage and stagnation particularly at the lower stage (Classes I and II). But such practices and innovative efforts were not continued/sustained by the state governments due to certain administrative reasons.

WHY MULTIAGE/GRADELESS CLASSROOMS?

Before initiating a discussion on this issue it would be necessary to know the conceptual meaning of multiage classrooms. The terms 'combination class,' 'gradeless', 'multiage', are commonly used synonymously in education. 'Gradeless' or 'multiage' refers to a situation in which children are not grouped on the basis of their chronological age. In such classrooms learners of different age and ability are grouped together and further subgrouped on the basis of their levels instead of chronological or physical age. It is referred to variously in the literature as 'multilevel,' 'multiage', 'vertical group' or even 'family class.' It is distinguished from monograde graded classroom in which students within the same grade are assumed to be more similar in terms of age and ability. The multilevel type of classrooms are deliberately created in developing countries. The reason being the age of entry to school, particularly in rural and tribal areas, varies and grade repetition is common.

In our country also grade repetition and admission throughout the year are common phenomena in rural and tribal areas. Now the question emerges: Why have some schools opted for this approach? As we know, government and private schools have their own limitations like fixed time table, examination-based evaluation, rigid curriculum and common methodology for all children, which are unsuitable for children's learning in different situations—rural, urban, tribal, and slum. For example, the problems like admission throughout the year, grade repetition, chronic absenteeism, etc. are more common in rural and tribal areas in comparison to urban areas. If we follow the urban practices in such situations, the efforts would be futile.

To overcome the problem of rigidity, this approach believes: 'No two individuals are alike and therefore individual attention to each child is desirable'. Thus, the learning level should be the basis of grouping rather than age (which is the criterion of the grade-specific classroom). The approach also believes that the number of children in such classrooms should not be more than 20-25. It claims that this approach is very useful in multigrade classrooms where students who are apart in grades, are placed in the same classroom. The advantages of this grouping as experienced by the organizations were as follows.

— Mixed Crouping (2-3 levels): This provides the younger learners the opportunity to observe, emulate and imitate a wide range of behaviour, while the older students have the opportunity to take responsibility for the younger learners.

— Multi-level Grouping: It widens the scope of the curriculum and makes assessment more flexible and practicable.

— Social Maturity: It leads to a greater sense of belonging, support and confidence among the learners.

— Ample scope for low-level learners to attend high-level material, while high-level students can profit from the opportunities to review their lower-stage materials.

— Encourages cooperation and learning to live together among the learners.

The most important reason for adopting ungraded or mixed-ability classroom by these experimental schools was that children did not learn at the same pace even if they were in the same age group. Thus, homogeneous classes are possible only if one does not recognize freedom of pace of learning. Their schools recognized the principles of freedom of pace of learning of the child and therefore had discarded the convenient practice of organizing schools in homogeneous classes.

More so in grade-specific classrooms (homogeneous classes), the pace is controlled by the teacher. She/he teaches the same chapter of the book to all the children at the same time. In such a situation, if the child is absent for a long period for whatever reason (illness, visiting relatives, marriage in the family and so on), she/he feels lost when she/he comes back to school. By allowing freedom of pace, this situation would be avoided. Similarly, the scope of the bright child who finishes the course before one year, is not feasible in the grade system. This approach provides the opportunity to bright children and has provision for differential treatment at different levels.

HOW TO MANAGE THE MULTIAGE CLASSROOM

Multiage classes or gradeless classes challenge teachers' ability to plan, organize, manage and monitor children's work. Thus the task for teachers is not only very challenging but demanding also. The field experiences suggested that the knowledge required to work effectively within such classrooms could not be gathered via textbooks, teaching methods, curriculum, teacher's guide, etc. The knowledge required for effective multiage classroom teaching is rendered irrelevant by those with a responsibility for training and supporting teachers in their work.

Classrooms at the primary stage have a low pupil-teacher ratio as the low pupil-teacher ratio was considered as one of the crucial factors for effective teaching-learning. This school of thought believed that smaller groups were not only handled administratively better, but also allowed the teacher to understand the behaviour of each child individually. A smaller group also facilitated the use of child-centered approach in the classroom, which could help to address children at different levels of learning. This approach also propagated the single-teacher method (teacher moves with grade), which made the teachers more secure in improving the student-teacher relationship. Also, the child does not perceive the environment in segments or compartments but views the environment as a whole; the subject-teaching approach, according to them, tends to unnecessarily fragment the child's knowledge and cause confusion in his/her learning.

The curriculum is one of the significant elements, which links the child with the world of knowledge. The organizations believe that "the central concern of the primary-stage curriculum is to develop an understanding of basic life skills among the learners so that they can develop a holistic view about the environment and are able to function effectively in the environment in which they live". They also believed that "the conceptual structures always evolved through the process of development.

Following the Piagetian thought, as the child gathers more information and experiences which help him/her to improve the existing conceptual structures through a process of assimilation and accommodation, transfer of knowledge is a misnomer and knowledge can only be reformed and constructed". Thus the nature of the text materials, the child's environment, the quality of teacher education were found to be very significant in the child's conceptual learning.

A significant characteristic of their curriculum, therefore, was not only enriching the experiences of the learner but also improving the process of acquiring experience. It was found that their curriculum was flexible. They believe that the curriculum shouldn't be based only on knowledge and skills but should include a large number of activities derived from the child's daily-life situations.

In classrooms, children were found to learn at their own pace, hence, a multilevel approach of teaching was followed in the classrooms. Their teaching-learning approach was found to be based on the principle of 'learning to learn' rather than what to learn.

The fundamental principles of their classroom teaching-learning process were

— shift of focus from teaching to learning in approach;

— freedom of pace to learn for each child;

— the child's mother tongue, the medium of initial learning, followed by Hindi or the standard language;

— group activities followed by individual activities; cooperative learning encouraged in all respects;
— encouraging concrete experiences as primary school children are at the concrete operational stage (7-11 years);
— the teacher not to remain as the only source of wisdom, but was to be more of an intervener or a facilitator rather than an instructor or evaluator;
— discouraging grade promotion or annual evaluation which had no meaning for a child in teaching-learning;
— a friendly and informal teacher-pupil relationship;
— encouraging learning through errors and without fear in all respects.

Major Implications

The above experiment of the organizations has provided an innovative model at the primary stage which was experimented in the rural and slum areas on a limited sample. The above experiment could be upscaled or used for the wider system and would possibly be very suitable for multigrade situations wherein, while the number of children may not be too large, the number of levels will inevitably be more. Some of the major implications are:

— employing mixed-age grouping as demonstrated by sets of schools of the organizations has advantages as discussed and has relevance for multigrade situations. The approach definitely widens the scope of such classrooms where absenteeism, grade repetition, multiage situation (due to regular admission throughout the year and age variation at the entry level) are prevalent, especially in the multigrade classrooms.
— A variety of graded self-learning materials, which could involve the learners meaningfully, are needed for such classrooms. Textbooks alone cannot serve this purpose. The

materials, which could be syllabus-based, should be graded and should promote active learning of the required competencies. The older children would require more of self-learning activities. These would be best developed by the teachers themselves to a large extent during training so that they feel a sense of ownership and also have the motivation and competence to use them and evaluate them as part of a feedback and feed-forward cycle.

— To be able to successfully implement the child-centered approach, the teacher would need sufficient time to plan and prepare activities to suit different levels. This is a very crucial area and needs to be considered for all schools. While the 'chalk and talk' method requires no prior preparation, activity-based teaching, particularly through the multilevel, dynamic grouping approach, needs not only careful and thorough preparation but also the time to do it in.

— a very significant lesson that can be derived from these case studies is that the training of teachers must lay emphasis on 'do-how' rather than on 'know-how' with a major component of 'hands-on' practice in model situations for acquired skill development. Also important is the provision for recurrent training and 'sharing' workshops, which serve to further enrich teachers' skills and knowledge and sustain their motivation.

The number of schools adopting this approach in India is limited. The challenge would be to be able to replicate and sustain many of these innovations in the phenomenally large number of multigrade schools across the country for which the major resource support would be the Cluster Resource Centres. Building up the professional base of the Cluster Resource Centre coordinators, therefore, becomes a crucial link.

The organizations' experiments are basically on limited and selected samples (mainly rural and slum). The lessons which have been derived/learned from the above study, could be tried out in multigrade, particularly in traditional multigrade, schools through Action Research–Intervention Studies. The field-tried strategies along with teacher training package should be disseminated to different schools for real functioning in the field.

Rishi Valley is situated in the rural interior of South India, in a chronic drought area in the state of Andhra Pradesh. The population consists largely of marginal farmers, shepherds who have tended their flocks since Neolithic times and daily wage earners on seasonal employment. For more than twenty-five years, Rishi Valley Education Centre has engaged in a variety of educational programmes that reach out to its neighbours in this impoverished countryside. These educational innovations have found wide application and are presently being adapted in several parts of India in programmes for universalising elementary education.

SATELLITE SCHOOLS

The Rishi Valley Institute for Educational Resources (RIVER) maintains a network of "Satellite Schools" in sixteen villages in the vicinity of Rishi Valley. These schools have their source in an outreach programme that began more than fifteen years ago. It was founded on a conviction that community participation and landscape regeneration could bring about more effective and robust elementary education. These factors seem to be very important in a country like India, where the majority of the population lives at subsistence levels in village communities.

Within a village, education can be a means of securing both livelihood and social capital. Based on these convictions, the Rishi Valley Satellite Schools have developed a community-based curriculum that is taught by village youth who have been trained in classroom management and multigrade methodology based on educational materials that have been specifically designed for multigrade classrooms.

Motivation

The point of departure for RIVER in 1987 was a close study and analysis of elementary school curriculum. This study helped to identify several initial problems:

— The student population in a typical school was heavily concentrated in the earliest stages of learning. Half of the entire student body was at Class I stage, and enrolment tapered off strongly at higher stages, with many children remaining at the same stage from one year to the next. This indicated not only a high dropout rate but also a very low rate of learning among those who stayed in school.

— Most of the schools had only one or two teachers to handle all the five Grades. Within each grade, children were at very different levels across the learning continuum. In effect, this was a multigrade, multilevel situation. And yet children were being taught with monograde methodology. This turned out to be a very common and widespread mismatch.

— Children were not enjoying the learning process, as it was fully teacher-directed, with no provision for individual differences in learning pace and no scope for co-operative learning.

— Teachers were demoralised and often frustrated because they didn't have systematic support materials and methodologies to help them handle multigrade, multilevel situations in a meaningful and interesting way.

— Having studied the status quo, RIVER aimed to work within the given constraints of financial and human resources imposed by the situation it faced. RIVER wanted to design a programme specifically tailored for one-teacher, one-room schools, to serve children in mixed-ability groups, using materials and methodologies that would be interesting, enjoyable, and locally conceptualised. At the same time, RIVER kept in mind the need for a programme that would be widely replicable.

Community - based Language Curriculum

In order to sustain community interest and enthusiasm for education, opportunities have been created for various forms of interaction between the local population and the school. These interactions have helped to energise the schools as well as enrich the language curriculum.

In view of the rich folk tradition in which our villages are steeped, folk art, folk songs, local stories and legends have been incorporated into the curriculum. Drawing upon the rich knowledge of folk and oral traditions of mothers (and the fathers too!), several stories have been written down and "published" in the form of handmade booklets illustrated by children. Each booklet carries the name and photograph of the author. Children have shown a great interest in reading these stories "written" by people whom they know and can relate to. This kind of input facilitates learning, reduces alienation, and plays a part in motivating the first generation learners in confidently facing the reading materials.

The Language curriculum is based on the recognition of the easy facility that young children have in absorbing and using their own 'mother tongue' for both oral and written communication. Hence, the programme allows ample scope for the child to respond to stimuli built into the cards/activities by expressing herself in her own specific dialect/local language. At the grade 1 level more time is spent on "readiness activities", and listening and speaking are the prime areas that need to be addressed. Reading and writing is introduced only in the later months of the grade 1 level and then developed steadily through a series of activities and exercises.

Thus, Folk songs and stories form a storehouse of natural language learning materials and these are liberally incorporated into the curriculum, along with their enactment through puppet theatre. The movement from the local dialect towards the standard regional language is made gradually as the reading and writing skills are expanded, to enable communication with a wider circle.

Built into the very curriculum of mathematics is an activity of "Metric Melas", which are daylong community festivals. The aim of the festival is to convey to children and uneducated adults the concepts of mass, length and time and their units. Within a festive atmosphere, children record measurements and produce statistical and other findings that they later use in their classes. Similarly, the Environmental Studies curriculum includes extensive village surveys - of local flora and fauna, types of housing, festivals and farming patterns. Later, the data collected in this manner is categorised, systematically analysed, and attractively displayed so that this provides content for the Language Arts programme. In these and other ways, local culture is drawn into the language classroom. This interface of the school and the community at the curriculum level yields rich, authentic data about the whole community and its natural surroundings, which can be interestingly, used later, as language learning materials.

Teaching Learning Materials

The Rishi Valley elementary school programme has been developed over the past fifteen years to address the educational needs of first generation learners. Here the academic curriculum is graded for individual levels of learning, grounded in up-to-date information, and framed in the local idiom.

The learning resource materials designed by Rishi Valley are the material basis for a systematic and comprehensive education programme encompassing a variety of enrichment activities and community participation. It provides more than one thousand systematically designed study cards and activities, together with a default task planner or what we call the `Achievement Ladder'. This is a wall chart that pictorially displays all the cards/activities in a clear sequential organisation that permits every child to progress at his or her own pace, with a clear understanding of their movement through the curriculum.

Categories of Language Activities

The Rishi Valley programme scales down the learning process into a meaningful sequence of concrete and manageable steps or tasks. These multiple steps of the learning process are gathered into units called "milestones". Each milestone is reached through a sequence of five types of activities - "Introductory activities," "Re-inforcement activities," "Evaluation activities," "Remedial activities," and "Enrichment activities". These five types of activities leading to a milestone make up a unit of learning. Milestones are organised into an ascending order, beginning with the first rung of the Learning Ladder and ending with the topmost rung, which denotes the end of a class. This whole learning continuum - an ascending series of milestones, with steps leading up to each milestone - is visually represented in a "Ladder of Learning".

Classification of Language Cards

Each of the learning cards/activities carries an identifying picture or logo. There are Bull logo cards, Elephant logo cards, Monkey logo Cards, and so on. Each logo symbolizes an activity. Rabbit logo cards are flash cards for introducing words. Tortoise logo stands for dictation. Monkey logo represents matching pictures with words. Bull logo represents story cards to introduce the sounds associated with letters. Elephant logo cards reinforce reading and writing skills. Dog logo cards contain evaluation materials. In addition to logos, each card has a number to represent the ascending levels of learning. Thus, a yellow card marked 'Elephant 3' represents the third level of reading and writing activities.

Core & Local-Specific Materials

Sixty percent of the materials are fixed in advance to provide a "core" for the curriculum. The remaining forty- percent is left in a schematic form, leaving details to be supplied locally by teachers with the help of students. A set of 'Preparation formats' is provided to facilitate creativity among young trainee teachers and to help them design some of their own materials with the help of resource persons during the training programmes. Trainee teachers are made keenly aware of the key principles on which the system is based. Materials designed on these principles are further refined and modified on the basis of field tests carried out by teachers in their respective schools.

Value-Based Model

The programme covers four main subject-areas: Language, Mathematics, Environmental Studies and Integrated Arts&Crafts with an achievement ladder in each area. Children at different levels share the same materials across the grades (grades 1 to 4) within a single classroom. This methodology promotes self-learning, co-operative learning, and self-evaluation. It makes it possible for one teacher to guide learning for each child at his or her own pace within a mixed-ability group.

Respect and tolerance for other cultures, and concern for the natural environment are values woven into the material. This model of education uses the school and its curriculum to communicate good personal habits of cleanliness and hygiene, and social values of caring for the natural environment, preserving local knowledge and medicinal traditions, and sustaining cultural heritage. The material and the methodology has been especially designed and tested for first generation learners, and has sufficient flexibility of approach and richness of content to make it suitable for use in all primary schools.

Integrated Approach

A key feature of the approach is that subjects are not strictly compartmentalised. Wherever possible concepts and skills from various subjects are co-ordinated and woven together. With this in mind, many materials have been designed for multi-purpose use, so that a given set of materials may find use across subjects and across different grade levels. This design helps to build confidence in children who meet familiar materials in differing situations; each one building different skill based on familiar stories, pictures, and other content. A final but important advantage of this Multiple-usage not only facilitates learning but also streamlines the materials and makes it more economical.

Classroom Processes

Students learn in groups, at there own pace. Each child knows his or her current place on the Ladder and with the help of the Wall Chart can identify the appropriate card for the next learning activity. Students actively participate in the learning process, with older students helping younger ones. They work either in groups or alone. The teacher intervenes when new concepts are introduced, when work is to be evaluated, or when a student needs special attention. Thus, the classroom management is an essential part of the RIVER approach and is considered to have both administrative and pedagogic significance. The children are divided according to the level of the teacher's role and the child's autonomy in a particular cognitive task. Normally, there are five groups in each classroom. They are as follows:

— *Partially teacher-supported*: The teacher initiates the children into these activities and then lets them work on their own, making a picture, introducing words, completing sentences, sorting letters etc.

— *Completely teacher supported*: Identifying words in a song, Tracing the rubber letters, writing, situational stories etc

— *Partially peer- supported*: Children initiate/support each other, largely working on their own, like sight and sound games, threading cards, matching words and pictures etc.

— Completely peer- supported: Children teach and learn from each other, include picture words, abstract words etc.

— *Self-Learning*: Children practise reading and writing and test their own abilities, using the cards containing evaluation materials.

In addition, there are whole class and small group interactions for several of the activities connected with language expression through oral and written exercises. The composition of the groups is dynamic, with the children moving in and out of groups, depending on their activity. This system is based on the strong belief that real and meaningful learning takes place through the dynamic interaction between teacher and children and among children themselves.

In this approach, rote-learning and dry reading-writing exercises are replaced by activity-based learning. Work cards supported by learning aids are designed to require serious involvement from the child. Children are to be actively engaged in the learning process. Learning becomes a joyful experience, raising motivation levels and using classroom time more effectively. Apart from the obvious effect of raising academic standards, RIVER classroom processes have contributed to a dramatic reduction in dropout rates. The present dropout rate in the Rishi Valley Satellite Schools is negligible - less than two percent in the worst case.

Evaluation and Assessment

The RIVER programme uses a variety of evaluation procedures. Materials and methodologies are provided to help teachers identify learning difficulties, and to direct students to address specific problems. Child level monitoring formats and ongoing/terminal evaluation materials allow parents, teachers and children to monitor learning achievements in a simple way. Subject wise milestones designed by the practicing teachers themselves, along with an approximate time-range indicate within which a child is expected to learn certain concepts. When the child compares the time she has taken with the average time indicated she could gauge for herself the pace of her learning.

Teachers too could have a clear idea of the pace of learning of each child; of selected groups of children, or of an entire class. At the administrative level, these procedures enable monitoring authorities to track the progress of all students and to compile statistics comparing different schools so as to evaluate the achievements of their students, the effectiveness of their teachers/trainers and the quality of their curriculums.

Role of Teacher

The mechanics and contents of the RIVER multilevel programme have to be actualised into learning interactions between teacher, students and the learning materials. This involves a specific kind of dynamic, which is unique to the multigrade multilevel situation. Here the teacher's role shifts from being a purveyor of knowledge to a facilitator of learning for a group of children who are each at a different level in their learning and thus often involved in diverse tasks and activities at any given time.

On a wider scale, he must also see himself as rooted in the community, willing and able to draw upon local resources, and create local-specific materials of his own to supplement the common educational materials. The teacher has to organise the classroom, seeing to the appropriate storage of materials and display of teaching aids and data from field trips. He also needs to make a timetable and a weekly plan and orient students initially in how to use the learning materials and how to take care of the classroom and its surroundings.

On a day-to-day basis, the teacher would find himself involved in a variety of actions: initiating children into their learning tasks, creating groups for peer supported and participatory learning, evaluating students who have completed a certain stage in their learning and helping the slower ones in understanding and completing their tasks. He would need to keep an eye open to see that every child is profitably engaged, even as he involves himself with the learning of specific children.

More time needs to be spent with children at grade 1 and 2 level, while older students who can read should be able to follow instructions on cards and move ahead more easily on their own. The teacher should also plan and make time for whole-group activities such as singing songs, doing craft-work, presenting puppet shows, conducting the mime and mimicry activities, and undertaking the village survey and the metric mela. In a well-managed multilevel classroom, disciplined learning for all should arise from the very sense of joyful engagement that children experience in their learning.

For a new teacher, yet inexperienced in the dynamics of the RIVER multilevel programme, this multi-faceted role may indeed look daunting and almost impossible to fulfil. That is the reason why observation of actual classroom dynamics is given so much stress in the RIVER teacher training programmes. "Seeing is believing", and it is through introducing the trainee as an observer into the classroom that his initiation into the RIVER methodology is envisaged. A frank discussion forum is then organised for any questions arising from this experience, related to classroom discipline, groupings and much else besides. Through dialogue and discussion, the trainee is empowered to feel more confident about his role in the multilevel classroom. Thus the training programme is not envisaged so much as one for imparting "knowledge" as one where the trainee discovers within himself the confidence and the wherewithal to meet the challenges of his new role.

Teacher Training

RIVER has developed teacher education programmes rooted in hands-on practice; exposure to Satellite Schools, teaching in actual schoolroom situations, all transacted with the help of the self-learning materials. The trainee teacher learns the discipline through an idiom that is familiar. The Programme demonstrates how complex concepts can be communicated in concrete terms, in a step-by-step process, from the simple to the complex. Initially, potential teachers are required to reproduce teaching/learning materials by hand and use them in practice sessions. They are encouraged to examine the materials critically and to suggest improvements. Colour coding and Logos on different materials enable trainee teachers to work with children of different age groups and mixed abilities in one class. Here they learn to handle vertically grouped classes, where children are at many different levels.

Diagnostic materials in the Programme help them to identify the ability level of individual students, and place them correctly on the Ladder of Learning. Schematic Formats in the programme encourage trainees to develop local specific materials by creatively interacting with the community where they will teach. The Programme also includes Art Education resource pack that aids trainee teachers in learning the basics of school Arts and Crafts programme. Training programmes stress the primacy of "how to learn" over "what to learn" in each subject. Trainees develop skill in "how to learn" and a general understanding of how learning can be facilitated through the Ladder of Learning with its associated materials and activities.

SCALE OF OPERATIONS AND CURRENT STATUS

RIVER has been working for the past 15 years in the area of multi-grade/multi-level education. In collaboration with various state government agencies, it has helped establish multi-grade programmes in Karnataka, Kerala, Andhra Pradesh, Uttar Pradesh and Tamil Nadu. In addition, the Institute has provided resource support to Government and Non-Government Organizations from Maharashtra, Assam, Gujarat, Rajasthan, Pondicherry, Orrisa, Haryana and more recently, from Ladakh and Jharkhand. The interactions with educational agencies across the country have greatly enriched RIVER's experience in the field and helped evolve programmes that are flexible and sensitive to the great variety of cultures India has.

International Initiatives

RIVER has been approached by agencies in Ethiopia, Spain,

Nepal, Bangladesh, Columbia and Maldives, to study its materials and methodology for its potential applications in their countries. Collaborative Education Projects modelled on the RIVER approach are being explored to initiate similar programmes for primary school children in Southern Ethiopia and in the 22-school project of Maldives to provide child entered quality education. A core group consisting of two educationists from Ethiopia and two administrators from their sponsoring group in New York and the core group from the Maldives Education Ministry visited Rishi Valley, to draw up plans for adapting the self-learning Multi-level approach, training teachers, and supervising their projects through the initial stages.

Each of the above programmes has thrown up a variety of innovations to the basic methodology as each programme has adapted the basic elements of the methodology to suit their local/particular needs. The leaders of these innovative processes have been very often the teachers themselves, along teacher trainers and academic resource persons. The work initiated in these programmes has helped RIVER enrich its own programmes and to evolve constantly finding solutions for difficult situations as well as to introduce and cross-fertilize ideas among various programmes.

ADAPTATIONS FOR OTHER LANGUAGES

Designer Workshop Concept

There was no way to automatically transfer this materials and methodology, which existed mainly in Telugu, to Malayalam, Tamil, Kannada, or Hindi. A meaningful transfer of this methodology involves a radically new way of looking at the pedagogical situation¾right from the physical organization of the classroom, to the roles of the teacher, the student, the interaction between them, as well as at the content of the subject matter itself. All these factors would have to be understood and internalised by new teachers. In sum, there is a whole spectrum of attitudes that had to be unlearned and another set learned.

A process of "transcreation" through capacity building had to therefore to be initiated with the help of a team of resource persons, educators, storytellers, writers, and illustrators. The entire focus of the capacity building process is to make respective groups understand the cardinal principle of the whole exercise, namely, that the content should reflect local contexts, which really endow the programme with vibrancy. An exact replication of the programme in a new socio-cultural and linguistic milieu would in fact detract from the very warmth and vibrancy of the programme. That is why one needs to strengthen the network of teachers who come from a different geographic, linguistic and cultural zone and start a process of exchange in which the basic concepts and principles underlying this methodology were explicated.

For the teachers who are new to the principles and practice of multi-grade learning, it is necessary to communicate and develop a wide range of new concepts, skills and attitudes. As these often go against the grain of traditional teaching practices in mono-grade classrooms, inculcation of this new methodology is by necessity a process that involved experiential learning in a context where this approach is already in use. They would be invited to observe the multi-grade classrooms of the satellite schools and encouraged to adapt what was the most suitable for their own context. Eventually, depending on the interaction time available to respective teams a range of activities would be planned to promote an active, integrated learning on the part of the participants, while also focusing on individual elements of the multi-grade approach. It would also be necessary to leave ample room for raising doubts and seeking clarifications.

The core of the capacity building programme would broadly consist of field observations, intensive discussions, as well as simulation and actual creation of materials and activities, covering the whole ambit of the multi-grade, multi-level learning programme of Rishi Valley.

13

Programme of Mass Orientation of School Teachers (PMOST)

Four and a half decades ago, we in India had taken a pledge through our Constitution that within a period of ten years from 1950, free and compulsory elementary education would be provided to all children up to 14 years of age. Since 1950, determined efforts were made towards the achievement of this goal. Over the years, there have been very impressive increases in the number and spread of institutions as well as enrolment. Today, India has about 574,000 primary schools (classes I-V) and 156,000 upper primary schools (classes VI-VIII), the number of teachers in them being 1.705 million and 1.082 million respectively. The enrolment at the primary and upper primary stages is 109 million and 40 million respectively.

The Indian elementary education system is thus one of the biggest such systems in the world, providing accessibility within 1 km to over 825,000 habitations covering 94 per cent of the country's population. During the past one decade the enrolment rate has grown close to 100 per cent at the primary stage.

However, universalisation of elementary education (UEE) in its totality is still an elusive goal and much ground is yet to be covered. Drop-out rates continue to be high (36.3 per cent in classes I-V and 53 per cent in classes VI-VIII), retention of children in schools is poor, achievement levels are low, and wastage is considerable. Despite increased participation of girls, disparity still exists, more particularly among scheduled castes (SCs) and scheduled tribes (STs).

In the National Policy on Education (NPE) 1986, with revised modifications in 1992, we resolved to achieve the goal of UEE by the turn of the century, emphasising three aspects: universal access and enrolment, universal retention up to 14 years of age, and a substantial improvement in the quality of education. The resolve is spelt out unequivocally and emphatically in the programme of action (POA) 1992, which gave unqualified priority to UEE. One is therefore pinning great hopes on the new innovations and alternative strategies which are being applied to ensure that the shortcomings and inadequacies, which did not allow us to realise this goal so far, are overcome, and the new resolve will not have to be extended further.

The Education for All (EFA) Summit of the nine high-population countries held in New Delhi in December 1993, which was an offshoot of the World Conference on Education for All held in Jomtien, Thailand, in March 1990, culminated in a policy declaration and framework of strategies for its implementation. The policy declaration called for providing basic education facilities for every child and consolidating efforts towards basic education for children, youth and adults. In the context of an integrated approach of basic education for all people, literacy and adult education programmes are to be improved and extended, eliminating disparities of access and improving the quality and relevance of basic education. It can be said that the Indian NPE 1986 and its POA 1992, while resolving to ensure free and compulsory education of satisfactory quality to all children up to 14 years of age by the year 2000, adumbrated the policy statement made at the EFA Summit.

New Innovations and Alternative Strategies

Some of the major initiatives and strategies are:

— Disaggregated target setting and decentralised microplanning, which will provide the framework of universal access and community participation.

— Strengthening alternative channels of schooling such as the non-formal education (NFE) system for those who cannot avail of conventional full-time schooling.

— Introduction of minimum levels of learning (MLLs) at primary and upper primary stages to improve learner's achievement.

— Improvement of school facilities by revamping the scheme of Operation Blackboard (OB) and connecting it to the MLL strategy.

— Establishing linkages between programmes of early childhood care and education (ECCE), primary education, literacy and UEE.

— Addressing the more difficult aspects of access, particularly to girls, disadvantaged groups and out-of-school children.

— Restructuring of teacher training in view of the changed strategies and programmes.

— Availing of external financial support for basic education.

— Launching the National Elementary Education Mission (NEEM).

Disaggregated Target Getting and Decentralised Microplanning

Our experience with UEE encompasses the entire Third World experience. On the one hand, we have States like Kerala, which have achieved universal literacy as well as UEE in terms of school participation with social indicators as good as those of the best among the Third World countries. On the other, we have States like Bihar and Madhya Pradesh, with indicators as bad as those of the Sub-Saharan countries. One of the new strategies to achieve UEE is adoption of disaggregated target setting and decentralised planning. Our long experience with the pursuit of UEE has established that UEE is contextual. The contextuality varies widely across the country. Even in a State like Kerala, where participation is near universal, much requires to be done in respect of quality and achievement.

In such states, the pursuit of UEE would be mainly in the areas of quality, facilities and achievement, while in other states participation and demand aspects would need more attention. Therefore, the attempt would be to prepare district-specific and population-specific plans for UEE within the broad strategy frame of microplanning through people's participation. Microplanning has been defined as a family-wise and child-wise design of action to ensure that every child regularly attends a school or an NFE centre and completes 8 years of schooling at a pace suitable to him or her and attains an essential level of learning.

Guidelines for operationalising microplanning have been prepared and distributed to the state governments. The concepts of microplanning and local level capacity building have been given currency and efforts launched to decentralise educational planning and management. Microplanning exercises have already been undertaken in several states to ensure that all children receive primary education of satisfactory quality either through formal schools or through part-time NFE centres.

To operationalise the strategy for UEE through disaggregated target setting and decentralised planning, a new scheme titled District Primary Education Programme (DPEP) has been evolved. The concept of DPEP is a beachhead for effecting improvements and full-scale development of the entire elementary education sector. The overall goal of the programme is the reconstruction of primary education as a whole in the districts instead of piecemeal implementation of the various schemes. The fundamental principle of DPEP is capacity building at all levels to evolve further strategies which are replicable and sustainable. The specific objectives of the programme are:

- to reduce differences in enrolment, drop-out and learning achievement among gender and social groups to less than 5 per cent
- to reduce the overall primary drop-out rate to less than 10 per cent
- to raise average achievement levels by at least 25 per cent over measured baseline levels and ensure achievements of basic literacy and numeracy competencies and a minimum of 40 per cent achievement levels in other competencies by all primary school children,
- to provide, according to national norms, access for all children to primary education classes (I-V), i.e., primary schooling wherever possible or its equivalent non-formal education.

The programme would strengthen the capacity of national, state and district institutions and organisations for the planning, management and evaluation of primary education. NEEM has recently been set up to oversee, among other things, the implementation of this programme throughout the country.

Alternative Channels of Education such as the Non-Formal Education (NFE) System

Non-formal education has become an accepted alternative channel of education for children who cannot attend full-time schools due to various socio-economic constraints. To reach this large segment of marginalised children, we in India have been running, since 1979-80, a programme of NFE for children in the 6-14 age group, who have remained outside the formal system. These include drop-outs from formal schools, children from habitations without schools, working children, children who have to remain at home to do domestic chores, and girls who are unable to attend formal schools for a variety of reasons.

The enlarged and modified version of the NFE programme now in operation visualises NFE as a child-centred, environment-oriented and flexible system to meet the diverse educational needs of the geographically and socio-economically deprived sections of society. Non-formal education is designed to overcome the shortcomings of the formal school and make education a joyful activity. Decentralised community participation through village education committees (VECs) in planning, running and overseeing the programme has been considered crucial for its success. Although the focus of the programme is on the educationally backward states, it also covers urban slums and hilly tribal and desert areas in other states as well.

Today, the programme is being implemented in 20 states and union territories through the state governments and voluntary organisations. While there are more than 226,000 NFE centres in the state sector, there are about 29,000 run by voluntary agencies. About 44 per cent of all the NFE centres are exclusively for girls, who are the main victims of socio-cultural and socio-economic factors. The estimated enrolment capacity is about 6.3 million children. Under the NFE programme, efforts are now being made to further improve quality, allow greater flexibility to implementing agencies and relocate NFE centres on the basis of microplanning/area survey. The NFE programme is being linked to ground realities, allowing for continuous experimentation. Development and scaling-up of effective NFE models that can help the learners to learn at their own pace is a major thrust area.

Minimum Levels of Learning (MLL)

The need to lay down minimum levels of learning (MLL) emerged from the basic concern that irrespective of caste, creed, location or sex, all children must be given access to education of a comparable standard. The MLL strategy is an attempt to combine quality with equity. It lays down learning outcomes in the form of competencies or levels of learning for each stage of elementary education. The strategy also prescribes adoption of measures that will ensure achievement of these levels by children both in formal schools and in NFE centres.

The focus of the MLL strategy is development of competency-based teaching and learning. Preliminary assessment of the existing levels of learning achievements has revealed that they are quite low across several districts. Minimum levels of learning in respect of three subjects, namely language, mathematics and environmental studies, have already been laid down for the primary stage. It has been stressed that the emphasis should be on concept formation rather than on content. The burdens of non-comprehension and overload of content are forcing children to resort to rote memorisation. The issues of content versus concept, understanding versus rote memorisation, unachievable content load versus achievable set of competencies, have been integrated into the new MLL approach.

Minimum levels of learning have been specified in terms of competencies expected to be mastered by every child by the end of a particular class. The programme has been initiated throughout the country with the help of voluntary agencies, research institutions and others concerned. Minimum levels of learning for the upper primary stage are now being finalised.

Revamping the Scheme of Operation Blackboard (OB)

Recognising the unattractive school environment, unsatisfactory condition of school buildings, inadequate physical facilities, and insufficiency of instructional materials in primary schools, which function as demotivating factors for enrolment and retention, a scheme symbolically called Operation Blackboard was introduced in 1987-88 to bring all existing primary schools in the country to a minimum standard of physical facilities. Under this scheme, each school is provided with: (i) at least two reasonably large all-weather rooms along with separate toilet facilities for boys and girls; (ii) at least two teachers (one male and one female); and (iii) essential teaching and learning materials including blackboards, maps, charts, a small library, toys and games, and some equipment for work experience.

External evaluation of the scheme indicated the lack of training of teachers in using the teaching materials, specification of a large number of uniform facilities to be provided without modification according to local needs, and lack of provision for breakage of equipment. Effective steps have since been taken to remove these drawbacks. The scheme of Operation Blackboard has also been modified and expanded to provide a third room and a third teacher to primary schools where enrolment exceeds 100, and it has been extended to upper primary schools. The scheme is concentrating on rural areas and SC/ST areas, and girls' schools are being given the first priority.

Establishing Linkages between Programmes of early Childhood Care and Education (ECCE), Primary Education, Literacy and UEE

Early childhood care and education (ECCE) is viewed as a crucial input in the strategy of human resource development, as a feeder and support programme for primary education, and as a support service for working women of the disadvantaged sections of society. Since the age-span covered by ECCE is from conception to 6 years, emphasis has been given to a child-centred approach and play-way and activity-based learning in place of formal methods of teaching including introduction of the 3 Rs. Keeping in mind the role of ECCE as a support service in UEE, it is deliberately directed to the most underprivileged groups, those who are still outside the mainstream of formal education.

The aim of ECCE is that every child should be assured access to the fulfilment of all basic needs. It involves the total development of the child in every aspect including the physical, psychomotor, cognitive, language, emotional, social and moral. The present ECCE programmes include:

- — the integrated child development service (ICDS)
- — the scheme of assistance to voluntary organisations for running early child education (ECE) centres
- — *balwadis* and day-care centres run by voluntary agencies with government assistance
- — pre-primary schools run by state governments, municipal corporations and other agencies
- — maternal and child health services through primary health centres, sub-centres and other agencies

The ICDS is today the biggest programme of early childhood development, serving about 15 million children and 3 million mothers. Appropriate linkages are being established between ECCE programmes, primary schools, NFE centres and other related schemes of UEE.

Promotion of Access to Girls and Disadvantaged Groups

As with all educational indicators, gender disparities are conspicuous in regard to enrolment and retention. Over the past 25 years, enrolment of girls at the primary stage has grown from 5 million to 47 million and at the upper primary stage, from 0.5 million to 16 million. But disparities persist. Today girls account for only 46 per cent of the enrolment at the primary stage and 38 per cent at the upper primary stage. The drop-out rates of girls at the primary and upper primary stages are higher than those of boys. Regional disparities are also conspicuous. The very low female literacy (20 to 29 per cent) in some of the major north Indian states causes grave concern. The rural girls are doubly disadvantaged by non-availability of educational facilities and by their domestic chores.

Concerted efforts are now on to reach out to the girl child in rural and remote areas and urban slums by designing special NFE programmes with a view to getting them back into the formal stream. The NFE programmes are being dovetailed into the total literacy campaigns (TLC) to reach out to the girls in the 10-20 age group. Programmes for continuing education are being designed to ensure that neo-literates and school-going girls have access to reading materials.

An important constraining factor for female education is the lack of women teachers in rural areas. Therefore, special efforts are being made to recruit women teachers and to augment teacher training facilities for women so that adequate numbers of qualified women teachers are available. Co-ordinated efforts are also on to provide the necessary support services to enhance their participation and performance.

We in India are unambiguous about removal of disparities and attainment of equality of education opportunities for SCs, STs and other backward sections including girls. A number of strategies aimed at accelerating their rate of enrolment and retention have been detailed and are being implemented. Because of the affirmative policies of the government, the enrolment of these categories has increased considerably at the primary stage. The participation of SCs and STs at the primary level is more or less in proportion to their share in the population. Drop-outs, though declining, continue to be significantly large [primary stage (classes I-V), SC 49 per cent, ST 64 per cent; upper primary stage (classes VI-VIII), SC 68 per cent, ST 79 per cent]. Gender disparities are conspicuous among SCs and STs.

To ensure universal access and enrolment of SC children in rural areas, priority is given to the needs of SC habitations and hamlets in opening primary and upper primary schools. For SC children access and enrolment are assured primarily in the formal schools. Where they are not able to attend these, provision is made for non-formal and distance education centres. Every ST habitation is being provided with a primary school or other suitable institution. In tribal areas, the educational plan is being implemented in an integrated manner. Pre-school education, non-formal education, elementary education and adult education are being organically linked and integrated to ensure achievement of total literacy of the entire population.

Adequate incentives are given to the children of SC, ST and other backward sections in the form of scholarships, uniforms, textbooks, stationery and midday meals. All schools, NFE centres, and pre-school centres in SC/ST habitations are being equipped with necessary infrastructural facilities in accordance with the norms laid down for Operation Blackboard and for achieving MLL. Operation Blackboard has already covered almost all schools in tribal areas. Indigent SC/ST families are given incentives to send their children, particularly girls, to school.

Restructuring of Teacher Training

Teacher performance is the most crucial input in the field of education. In the ultimate analysis, the national policies on education have to be interpreted and implemented by teachers as much through their personal example as through teaching-learning processes. With a view to improving the quality and competence of teachers, a centrally sponsored scheme of Restructuring and Reorganisation of Teacher Education (RRTE) was launched in 1987.

During the period 1987-90, nearly 1.8 million teachers were trained under the programme of mass orientation of school teachers (PMOST). Most of them were primary and upper primary teachers. The main objective of the programme was to orient teachers in the main priorities and directions envisaged in the NPE 1986 and to improve their professional competence.

Among the other main components of the RRTE, as far as elementary education is concerned, are:

setting up of District Institutes of Education and Training (DIETs) in all districts to provide good quality pre-service and in-service training to elementary school teachers and adult education/non-formal education personnel and to provide resource support to these systems organising Special Orientation Programmes for Primary Teachers (SOPT) with a view to providing training to teachers in the use of OB materials and orienting them towards MLL strategy with a focus on teaching of language, mathematics and environmental studies

More than 300 DIETs have already become operational and have started conducting training programmes. The SOPT launched in 1993-94 is now going on in almost all states and more than 115,000 teachers have already been trained. A National Council for Teacher Education (NCTE) was set up in 1993 with statutory status for the effective implementation of all teacher education and training programmes and to achieve planned and co-ordinated development of the entire teacher education system throughout the country. The regulation and proper maintenance of norms and standards in the teacher education system is the responsibility of the NCTE.

Availing of External Financial Support for Basic Education

As a matter of policy and principle, India had not been seeking financial support from external agencies to implement its programmes of basic education. This situation changed in 1991-92, when a conscious and strategic decision was taken to avail of external assistance to achieve the goal of Education for All (EFA).

Today a number of agencies including the World Bank, Unesco, Unicef, Swedish International Development Agency (SIDA), International Development Association (IDA), and the British Overseas Development Agency (ODA) are sharing our concerns in this area. A new phase has, therefore, emerged — a phase of partnership between the inherent potential of the country and financial and other support from external agencies.

Launching the National Elementary Education Mission (NEEM)

With the objective of mobilising all the resources — human,

financial and institutional — necessary for achieving the goal of UEE by the year 2000, a National Elementary Education Mission (NEEM) was set up in August 1995 with the District Primary Education Programme (DPEP) as its core. This Mission will monitor and implement all the meticulously formulated strategies based on microplanning, and will ensure that free and compulsory education of satisfactory quality is provided to all children up to 14 years of age by the turn of the century.

14

OPERATION BLACKBOARD (OB)

The scheme of Operation Blackboard, started in 1987-88 to bring about substantial improvement in facilities in Primary schools with the aim of improving retention, has three inter-dependent components, namely

(i) Provision of a building comprising at least two reasonably large all-weather rooms with a varandah and separate toilets for boys and girls

(ii) at least two teachers in every primary school, as far as possible one of them a women; and

(iii) provision of essential teaching learning equipment including, blackboards, maps, charts, toys and equipment for work experience.

Funds for construction of school buildings are provided by the State Govts. However 48% funds for construction are also provided by Ministry of Rural Development as central matching share under Jawahar Rozgar Yojana if States raise 12% JRY s are and 40% Non JRY share. Funds for other two component are provided by this Department. The scheme envisaged coverage of primary schools in all the blocks/municipal areas in the country in a phased manner.

In the period 1987-88 to 1992-93, the scheme was implemented in 91.5% of the blocks in the country comprising

91 per cent of the primary schools. An assistance of Rs. 853.95 crores was released by this Department. Of this Rs. 154.91 crores was released in 1992-93. There is a provision of Rs. 179 crores for Operation Blackboard during 1993-94. It is proposed to cover the remaining primary schools during 1993-94 itself.

In order to operationalise the revised policy and Programme and Programme of Action 1992 regarding school facilities, the following three sub-schemes are proposed under Operation Blackboard during the eighth plan :-

i) Continuation of the on-going Operation Blackboard to cover the remaining schools identifi d in seventh plan.

ii) Expansion of the scheme of Operation Blackboard to provide three teachers and three class rooms to the primary schools where enrolment exceeds 100.

iii) Extension of the scope of Operation Blackboard to Upper Primary schools.

MINIMUM LEVELS OF LEARNING (MLLS)

The strategy to improve learning acquisition in schools focuses attention on what is happening in the classroom, and seeks to bring the principles of equity nd quality to bear up on it. The strategy aims at laying down learning outcomes expected from basic education at a realistic, relevant and functional level, and prescribing the adoption of measures that will ensure that all children who complete a stage o schooling achieve these outcomes. These outcomes define the MLL common to both school and equivalent NFE programme.

The following are the different steps for introduction of MLL in sch ols :

(i) an assessment of the existing level of learning achievement;

(ii) a definition of the MLL for the area and the time-frame within which it will be achieved;

(iii) reorientation of teaching practices to competency based teaching;

(iv) an introduction of contiguous, comprehensive evaluation of students learning;

(v) review of textbooks and revision, if required;

(vi) provision of inputs as necessary including provision of physical facilities, teacher training, supervision and evaluation, etc., to improve learning acquisition of MLL.

The aim of the MLL strategy is also to provide to the system a measure for performance and efficiency analysis. The endeavour will be to monitor learning achievement to direct greater resources where levels of learning are lower and to consciously accelerate the pace of development in the needy areas, thereby reducing the disparities and equalising standards. Ultimately this will lead to improvement of the quality and the performance of the system.

Immediately after the publication of the Report of the Committee defining MLL statement, the Ministry organised three Seminars at Delhi, Ahmedabad and Ajmer to explain the whole concept and chalk out strategies for implementation of MLLs programme. 15 agencies were identified and sanctioned projects with 100% central assistance. These projects cover 2000 primary schools, 10,000 teachers and about 3.86 lakh students. A sum of Rs. 121 lakhs has been sanctioned so far to these projects during the period 1991-94. A small team of resource persons has also been constituted to provide necessary guidance to projects and to the Ministry in implementation of this programme.

In addition, it has been decided to involve District Institutes of Education and Training in the programme. Faculty members of SCERTs and DIETs of Andhra Pradesh, Delhi, Gujarat, Haryana, Jammu, Kerala, Punjab, Rajasthan and Tamilnadu have been provided necessary orientation. The MLL competencies have been translated in many regional languages in the States and distributed to teachers. Handbooks for teachers, pupils' workbooks and evaluation material in the subjects of Language, Mathematics and Environmental Studies have also been prepared to enrich the class-room teaching environment.

Scheme of Operationalising Microplanning

The National Policy on Education (NPE) 1986 and revised Policy Formulation (1992) envisaged an array of activities by teachers and other field level educational workers to undertake a Microplanning exercise to ensure that every child receives primary education of satisfactory quality through the school system as far as possible or through part-time non-formal education programmes wherever necessary. The Programme of Action drawn up in pursuance of NPE explained Micro-Planning as "a family-wise and child wise design of action to ensure that every child regularly attends school or NFE Centre and completes 8 years of schooling at a pace suitable to him/ her and attains essential levels of learning".

Universalisation of Elementary Education has been one of the goals of India's educational development. Provision of free and compulsory education-to all children until they attain the age of 14 years is a Directive Principle of the Constitution. The National Policy on Education 1986, also envisages a large and systematic programme of non-formal education. The programme of Non-Formal Education is an organised programme of education for the school drop-outs and unschooled children outside the formal system at a place and time convenient to divergent learner clientele who cannot attend full-time day school. The assumption is that this kind of arrangement may result in provision of education comparable in quality with formal schooling. NFE has been envisaged as an alternative strategy to formal education and provide complementary role in achieving the goals of Universalisation of Elementary Education.

The objective of the programme is to make provision for education comparable with formal schooling for children of 6-14 age group who remain outside the formal system due to various socioeconomic constraints.

The programme caters to the children in the age-group 6-14 years particularly the school dropouts, working children, children in habitations without schools and girls who cannot/ do not attend formal schools on account of domestic chores.

The programme is being implemented through the State Governments and Voluntary Agencies. Instructions under this programme are imported at a time and place convenient to learners in small groups. Part-time Instructors are locally recruited and trained for this purpose. NFE courses are condensed courses of 2 years duration. The curriculum used is relevant to local environment and learner's interest. Moreover, it is comparable to formal system. There is a system of testing and certification for enabling entry of NFE learners into formal stream. The most important features of the programme are community participation, flexibility and decentralisation.

A Centrally Sponsored Scheme of Non-Formal Education was started by this Department in 1979-80 to make provision for education of the target group children.

The programme was, initially, started, on experimental basis, in 9 educationally backward States Andhra Pradesh, Assam, Bihar, J & K, Madhya Pradesh, Orissa, Rajasthan, Uttar Pradesh and West Bengal. In 1987, the 10th educationally backward State viz. Arunachal Pradesh, has been covered under the purview of the scheme. Moreover, the scheme also covers NFE programmes in urban slums, hilly, desert and tribal areas and projects for education of working children in other than the above mentioned educationally backward States. The programme is, at present, in operation in the States of Andhra Pradesh, Assam, Bihar, Gujarat, Haryana, H. P., J & K, Karnataka, M.P., Manipur, Mizoram, Maharashtra, Orissa, Rajasthan, Tamil Nadu, U.P. and UT of Chandigarh. During

1992-93, the Govt. of India provided central assistance of Rs. 45.17 crore to 13 States/UTs for running about 2.15 lakhs NFE Centres under State Sector and Rs. 10.19 crore to Voluntary Agency for running about 23,000 NFE centres under Voluntary Sector.

The programme also provides for financial assistance to voluntary agencies for Experimental & Innovative projects to promote experimentation and innovations for achievement of goals spelt out in National Policy on Education, 1986 for Universalisation of Elementary Education. During 1992-93, Central assistance was provided to 31 voluntary agencies for 1,34,15,957 such projects. In 1993-94, Central assistance of 35,12,563. to 14 voluntary agencies for 16 projects has been sanctioned upto 31.12.93. During the remaining period of the current year, further Central assistance amounting to Rs. 1.65 crore is likely to be sanctioned to 50 voluntary agencies for projects.

The programme is being monitored through quarterly Progress Reports, Joint Evaluation Teams and field visits of central Govt./State Govt./NCERT officials. Moreover, seven external agencies have been engaged for evaluation of the scheme in eight States viz. Andhra Pradesh, Bihar, Gujarat, Madhya Pradesh, Orissa, Rajasthan, Uttar Pradesh and West Bengal. Final Reports have, so far, been rece- ived in respect of Andhra Pradesh, Madhya Pradesh, Orissa, Rajasthan, Uttar Pradesh and West Bengal. The reports are being examined. On the basis of the feed back received, necessary action has been initiated to remove the deficiencies and ensure more effective implementation of the Programme.

The proposal for revision of the Scheme and its continuation in the 8th Plan has been approved in June, 1993, with an outlay of Rs. 704.00 crore. The budget for 1993-94 is Rs. 110.16 Crore. Essential features of the NFE scheme, as determined during the revision in 1987, have been retained. Certain aspects of the scheme have been further improved and strengthened. The revised scheme envisages intensified project approach and provides for greater financial and administrative decentralisation of management. Moreover the revised scheme also envisages more intensive training, development of quality teaching- learning material, semesterization of NFE courses etc. The cost parameters have also been revised and a new scheme of cash incentive to Instructors is proposed to be introduced with view to provide better infrastructural facilities and enhance motivation of Instructors. As per revised cost parameters the total cost of one NFE project comprising of 90 primary and 10 upper primary centres has gone up from Rs. 5.50 lakhs to Rs. 12.10 lakhs in the first year and from Rs. 4.80 lakhs to Rs. 11.85 lakhs in subsequent years. As a special incentive for education of girls, the ratio of number of NFE girls centres to co-educational centres has been enhanced from 25:75 to 40:60.

The Central assistance for co-educational centres and administrative resource support to States/UTs has also been increased from 50% to 60% to off-set the enhanced administrative cost.

The revised scheme of NFE lays more emphasis on consolidation of existing programme rather than its expansion during the 8th Plan. However, marginal expansion of the programme will be inevitable. The revised scheme has been implemented from 1.10.1993. However, the component of cash incentive to instructors will be effective from 1994-95.

It is proposed to increase the no. of NFE Centres to 3.5 lakhs during the VIII Plan (1992-97) subject to availability of adequate funds.

The NFE programmes are thus expected to cover all children who fall outside the pale of formal education either because of non- enrolment or dropping out for one reason or the other. Taking into account the special socioeconomic factors of the families of the target group children, the NFE programmes in India give emphasis on linking the programme with other micro-planning exercise for development, giving considerable flexibility in implementation of the NFE projects and the active participation of voluntary agencies and the village level opinion leaders.

The Centrally Sponsored Scheme of Restructuring and Reorg- anisation of Teacher Education being implemented since 1987-88 was revised during 1993-94 for implementation during the VIII Plan. Its main objectives are to provide academic and resource support at the grass root level for the success of various strategies and programmes being undertaken in the areas of elementary, secondary and adult education and to institutionalise in-service teacher training. The revised scheme has following components :-

— Setting up of about 450 Districts Institutes of Education and Training (DIETs) by the end of VIII Plan either by upgrading suitable existing Elementary Teacher Education Institutions or establishing new one so as to provide good quality pre-service and in service training to elementary school teachers and AE/NFE personnel besides providing resource support to elementary education and adult education systems.

— Upgradation of about 250 Secondary Teacher Education Institutions (STEIs) into Colleges of Teacher Education (CTEs) and converting about 50 of them into Institute of Advanced Study in Education (IASE) in order to provide training and resource support to secondary school system and to complement the work of SCERT.

— Strengthening of State Councils of Educational Research and Training (SCERTs).

— Special Orientation Programme for School Teachers (SOPT) covering 4.5 lakh Teachers per year during 1993- 97 with a view to provide training to teachers in the use of OB materials and orienting the teachers towards Minimum Levels of Learning strategy with focus on Teaching of Language, Mathematics and Environmental studies.

15

Special Orientation Programme of School Teachers (SOPT)

Electronic media has a time-tested, large and definite role to play in the field of Distance Education. In fact, the latest innovations in the arena of teachers' training through distance education are based on electronic media. Educational Television is more than 35 years old in India. Educational Radio is still older. In terms of response of the students, it is in favour of educational television which broadcasts both image and voice. Teachers and students have graduated from pure audio to the image and voice learning media. Next logical step is two way interaction - and expectation will be interaction with image and voice - preferably two way video - otherwise at least one way video and two way audio.

Indira Gandhi National Open University (IGNOU), with a national jurisdiction, state of the art media production facilities, fairly well-established student support services and expertise in teacher education has been making attempts to provide teacher education/training packages for teachers in the institutions of higher education and primary education through distance education. With the aim to cater to the training needs of the primary sector, the School of Education, IGNOU went into a collaboration with National Council of Educational Research and Training (NCERT) in 1993. It is offering a Certificate

Programme in Guidance for primary school teachers and parents and is in the process of developing a comprehensive programme titled "Diploma in Primary Education (DPE)", following a modular approach, for training the untrained primary school teachers in the North-Eastern States of India. There is also a plan to extend this programme in other State in subsequent years. The University makes use of self-instructional print materials, audio and video programmes, theoretical and activity oriented assignments, tutorials and academic counselling, contact session and internship, Radio and TV broadcast and teleconferencing for its professional programmes.

At the Centre level, Government of India has funded a successful experimentation in introduction of distance education mode in delivering training packages to the primary teachers under the existing "Special Orientation Programme for Primary School Teachers"- a training programme with cascade model. This distance education mode has made use of the interactive video technology. Two pilot projects have been taken up by the implementing agency - the National Council of Educational Research and Training (NCERT). The first pilot project was taken up during January, 1996 in the state of Karnataka. 850 primary school teachers who had been assembled in 20 centres, were trained. The learning centres were almost at a distance of 2500 kms from the Teaching Centre.

The seven day programme had 14 sessions, each of which was on various topics such as Minimum Levels of Learning, Teaching Aids, Multi-Grade Teaching and strategies for teaching Mathematics, Environmental studies and Languages. Each of the sessions was of about 210 minutes (120 minutes of live interaction and 90 minutes of individual and group activities). Each session comprised of self-study, presentation and demonstration (live and pre-recorded) by experts, panel discussions, teachers interaction with panelists through telephone and fax and also group activities. NCERT's Central Institute of Technology (CIET) had also conducted a Classroom 2000+ experiment in May 1993 which demonstrated the potential of

Interactive Video Technology in direct teaching of Physics and Mathematics concepts to group of students spread at various distant locations in the country. It made use of Television set, a telephone and computer key pads for trainees making responses. The similar mode had now been tried for teacher training.

Keeping these developments in mind, India's National Action Plan (NAP) for Inservice Education of Primary Teachers through Distance Education - a perspective plan to integrate all the ongoing programmes in this direction, has been prepared. In this plan it has been felt that only by pressing into service the distance education mode, equipped with modern training technology, it will be possible to provide inservice training to all primary teachers every year and their trainers and supervisors every second year. Thus the technology aspect has to play a big role in implementing this plan. Therefore, it has been also felt necessary to test-run yet another pilot project to train teachers through distance mode using interactive technology. With the collaboration from UNESCO and the International Telecommunication Union (ITU), Government of India has taken up a pilot programme on Inservice Primary Teacher Training (IPTT) through application of interactive television (ITV) in distance education.

The project will aim at designing and pilot testing a continuing inservice education of primary teachers and teacher educators (DIET Staff). It will simultaneously validate and standardise technology specifications for interactive television system for application in distance education in the developing countries. The major objectives of the project are:

— to design and implement an interactive distance education programme for primary teachers and DIET staff throughout a wide geographical area in the selected States,

— develop print, audio and video software according to the requirements of the proposed distance education programme,

— to use interactive television (ITV) to improve quality of interactivity in distance education programme and standardise technology specifications for ITV for application in distance education,

— to gain insight into the organisational managerial and technical constraints and problems to interactive distance education for inservice training of primary teachers, and consider the trade off between large number of learners and the level/quality of interaction.

Some of the major outputs of this project will be standardisation of ITV technology for application in distance education; training of at least 8000 teachers and teacher trainers; gain of experience and insight during the implementation, learning centres would get equipped with reception facilities in addition to the existing educational technology aids and equipment. Strategically, this project will be built upon available programmes, experience and infrastructure. It does not propose training set up de-novo. Another component of the strategy is to involve the State Governments and State level institutions in administrative and academic decision making in the project. This is important, because, the training of primary teachers has to be dealt by the State governments and State agencies.

During the implementation phase, five one-week programmes each in two different Indian Languages (Gujarati and Hindi) will be held for teacher educators and teachers. These programmes will be carefully staggered so that each programme or a group of programmes are followed by intensive review and programme modifications. The five programmes in each language will be spread over 24 weeks of implementation allowing on an average four weeks of interim period for review and modifications - both from the angle of pedagogy as well as technological application. The ultimate beneficiaries of the project are the primary school students and hence, the country as a whole. Direct beneficiaries are the professional staff in the DIETs and the primary teachers. Interactivity will be the main feature of the programme delivery. Several levels of interactivity have been proposed. They are:

a. Face to face interaction;

b. Satellite based interactive learning;

c. Inter-centre information exchange; and

e. Computer assisted interactive learning.

Special feature of the project will be experimentation with alternative interactive modes at different locations. The learning Centres will comprise urban, semi-urban and rural sectors. Although the self-study and face to face interactions will remain the same in different learning centres, the return path of the ITV component will vary. Five centres each will have satellite based talk back facility, voice-mail, STD/FAX and data network. Subject to availability, a few Centres will use ISDN facility/video telephone. This will provide 3x4 i.e. 12 different modalities within the project for experimentation of effectiveness and cost-efficiency of different approaches.

Pre-school teacher education prepares teachers for teaching pre-school classes, i.e. nursery and kindergarten. The minimum qualification for admission into the pre-school teachers' education programme is a secondary or a senior secondary examination i.e. ten or twelve years of schooling. The duration of the course varies from one to two years. Pre-school teacher training institutions are mostly unaided private institutions. In the case of course for nursery and primary teachers, State Education Departments prescribe a minimum percentage of marks in the qualifying examination as a requirement for admission.

Elementary teacher education in for training teachers to teach primary classes (grades One to Five). The minimum qualification for admission to the elementary teachers' education programme is either ten or twelve years of schooling. Recently, most States have prescribed twelve years of schooling as the minimum requirement, though some of them still have a pass in the secondary school examination as the entry qualification . The duration of the programme is generally two years. Normally, the first year of training is devoted to the teaching of subject-matter or 'Content' and the second year to the 'methodology of teaching'. These programmes are given certificates such as the J.B.T. (Junior Basic Teachers' Training) or B.Ed (Diploma in Education) or T.D. (Teaching Diploma etc.).

Elementary teacher training institutions are of three types: government, private aided and private unaided. Recently, District Institutes of Education and Training (DIET) have been set up in all the states. An important features of the DIETs is that, besides providing pre-service teacher education, they conduct programmes of in-service education of teachers. As of date, the number of DIETs is 433 and these institutes are fully financed by the Central Government. The total number of elementary teachers' training institutions in India is 1,179.

Secondary teacher education institutes prepare teachers for teaching at the upper primary and secondary levels (grades Six to Twelve). The minimum qualification required for admission into the secondary teachers' education programme is graduation in science, social sciences, humanities, commerce, agriculture etc. A large number of postgraduates also seek admission to these training institutions. Secondary teacher education is offered by secondary colleges of education, which are affiliated to different universities. Some university departments also offer a secondary teachers' education programme. The minimum qualification for admission to this programme is a graduation. These institutes are of three types-government, private aided and private unaided. There are around 600 secondary colleges of education.

Four Regional Institutes of Education (RIEs), constituent units of the NCERT, offer a four-year integrated course for secondary teachers. The minimum qualification for admission to this programme is a pass in senior secondary examination i.e. after twelve years of schooling. Recently, the University of Delhi, Delhi has started a four-year programme in elementary education in five colleges leading to the Bachelor's degree in Elementary Education (B.Ed.). The duration of the Delhi University programme is also four years. The products of the programme are qualified to teach classes I to VIII.

In- service training of teachers is offered at the central, state, regional, district and sub-district levels. At the national level, in-service training programme are offered by institutions such as NCERT, the NIEPA, the Central Institute of Indian Languages (CIIL), Mysore, among many others. At the regional level the Regional Institutes of Education of the NCERT conduct inservice programmes for teachers of their region .

At the state level, programmes are mainly offered by the State Council of Educational Research and Training (SCERT), State Institute of Education (SIE), State Institute of Science Education (SISE), Institute of Advanced Study in Education (IASE), Colleges of Teacher Education (CTE) and State Institutes of Educational Technology (SIET). At the district level, District Institutes of Education and Training (DIET) conduct inservice training.

As follow up to the 1986 National Policy on Education (NPE), the Government of India financed a national scheme for in-service training of teachers (primary and secondary school teachers). The objectives of this scheme, known as the Programme of Mass Orientation of School Teachers (PMOST), were to sensitize teachers in the emerging concerns in education, the use of a learner-centered approach, as well as action research and enrichment of knowledge in curricular areas and the core components as given in the NPE. The duration of the PMOST training was ten days. The programme was implemented during 1986 to 1990. About 1.8 million teachers were given inservice education under the PMOST scheme. Video films relating to various modules of the PMOST training were telecast on the national network when training camps were held. The programme was implemented by the NCERT in collaboration with the SCERTs in different states.

After the PMOST, another programme known as the "Special Orientation Programme for Primary School Teachers" (SOPT) was launched in 1993-94 to improve the quality of the elementary education. The emphasis given in this programme is on training of teachers in pedagogy for developing the minimum levels of learning (MLLs) for the primary stage, training in the use of materials provided to primary school teachers under the scheme of Operation Blackboard and in child-centered approach to teaching-learning. Under this scheme 0.45 million teachers are to be provided inservice training each year. As in the case of PMOST, this programme too has been provided with media support.

The certification of prospective teachers is done by the different examining bodies on successful completion by award of a professional degree/diploma.

The certification at the elementary teacher preparation level (Junior Basic Teacher's Training/ Diploma in Teaching/ Elementary Teacher Training/Diploma in Nursery Teacher Training) is done by the Directorates of Primary Education of the States.

The certification in the form of an award of degrees, such as the Bachelor of Education (B.Ed.) is done by the universities. The teachers, who attend the inservice programmes are given the certificate of attendance.

States follow different recruitment procedures. In some States, the recruitment is made on the basis of candidates' performance in a competitive examination, whereas, in some other States, recruitment is made on the basis of the academic and professional background of candidates. The merit of each candidate is determined on the basis of his/ her score in the examinations he/ she has passed in addition to previous teaching experience, if any. In some other states, a combination of the two procedures, i.e. performance in a competitive examination and academic achievement is suitably integrated. The performance of candidates in oral examinations through interview is also practiced.

The pay scales of teachers are determined by States. Most states follow the national guidelines for salary scales of teachers working in state schools and private aided schools. In addition to the salary, a price-index linked "dearness allowance" is given to teachers. Various other allowances such as the city compensatory allowance, house rent allowance, hill allowance, winter allowance; backward, remote and tribal area allowance, island allowance etc. as applicable in different working conditions are added to the salary. These allowances differ from State to State and, within a State, from stages of education. Entry-level salaries for trained primary teachers are only slightly higher than those for untrained teachers. The maximum salary for a trained teacher is three to four times his/ her entry-salary, and it is usually reached after 16 to 20 years of service in most stages.

In addition, most States provide a fixed medical allowance or a reimbursement for medical expenses, advances for house building and for purchase of conveyance, free education for children of teachers, as well as retirement benefits, gratuity and group insurance. States also offer incentives to some special categories of teachers. For instance, in Assam, Bihar, Gujarat, Maharashtra and Tamil Nadu, female teachers working in rural and remote areas are given residential accommodation.

At the entry level, the annual income of teachers in India at different school levels such as Primary, Secondary and Senior Secondary are Rs.80,000/, Rs.1,00,000/ and Rs.1,20,000/, respectively. The average per capita gross domestic product (on current prices) was Rs.11,975/ in the year 1995-96*. The status of primary teachers is generally low

16

DISTRICT PRIMARY EDUCATION PROGRAMME (DPEP) CONCEPT

District Primary Education Programme (DPEP), launched in India in 1994, is one of the largest education projects of its kind in the world. The Programme aims to achieve the long cherished goal of Universalisation of Elementary Education (UEE) in the country through district-specific planning with emphasis on decentralised management, participatory processes, empowerment and capacity building at all levels.

Ever since Independence in 1947, India has strived to achieve the goal of UEE in accordance with the Constitutional commitment to provide education for all children of 6 to 14 years. Primary education has been one of the focus areas in successive five year plans. True, India has made enormous progress in terms of increase in the number of schools and enrolment at the primary stage since independence. The Gross Enrolment Ratio (GER) at the primary stage in India has exceeded 100 per cent. Despite all these achievements, a large number of children were still out of school and the goal of UEE continued to be elusive.

High drop out rate ranging upto 60%, large number of out-of-school children (about one-third), lack of access in 17% (1.8 lakh) of habitations with in one km radius and high wastage (33%) taking 7.2 years for 5 years of primary schooling were some areas of concern. Then there were problems relating to low levels of learning achievement and low participation of girls, Scheduled Caste (SC), Scheduled Tribe (ST) and other disadvantaged groups. Coupled with it were various systemic issues relating to effectiveness and efficiency of primary education like poorly functioning schools, inadequate school infrastructure and facilities, high teacher absenteeism, large number of teacher vacancies, poor quality of education and inadequate funds.

The Government had taken several initiatives to tackle these problems. The National Policy on Education (NPE), a landmark in the history of Indian education, framed in 1986, recognised the need to make concerted effort to expand and improve basic education. As an outcome, various schemes were initiated. Operation Blackboard was launched in 1986 with focus on providing additional class rooms, teachers and a package of teaching materials and aids. District Institutes of Education and Training (DIETs) were established in districts under a centrally sponsored scheme in 1988, to look after teacher training. The Total Literacy Campaign (TLC) was also launched in 1988 to eradicate illiteracy. Minimum Levels of Learning (MLL) programme was started in 1991 to identify basic competencies in language, mathematics and other subjects and to develop new text books.

Meanwhile, various states also initiated basic education projects around this time. The Andhra Pradesh Primary Education Programme (APPEP) with DFID assistance was the first of its kind. The Lok Jumbish Project with SIDA Assistance was initiated in Rajasthan while Bihar and Uttar Pradesh also started similar basic education projects. Although these projects vary in their design, they share the objectives and strategies of 1986 policy.

The Programme of Action (POA) 1992 provided fresh insights and directions for achieving Universalisation of Elementary Education. It called for an integrated and decentralised approach to the development of primary education with focus on building capacities, particularly at district and sub - district levels. Imbibing the spirit of this policy initiative, emerged DPEP in 1994.

The objectives of District Primary Education Programme are to:-

— Provide all children with access to primary education (class I to V)

— Reduce primary dropout rates for all students to less than 10 percent.

— Reduce differences in enrolment, dropout rates, and learning achievement among gender and social groups to less than 5 percent.

— Raise the average achievement levels of students by at least 25 per cent in language and mathematics and at least 40 percent achievement levels in other subjects.

— DPEP also seeks to strengthen the capacity of national, state and district institutions and organisations for planning, management and evaluation of primary education.

The criteria for selection of districts under DPEP are:

— Educationally backward districts with female literacy below the national average (39.29 percent) and

— Districts where Total Literacy Campaign (TLC) have generated demand for elementary education. (Out of 536 districts in the Country TLC covers 450 districts as on March 31,1999).

The Programme was initially launched in 1994 in 42 districts spread over 7 States - Assam, Haryana, Karnataka, Kerala, Madhya Pradesh, Maharashtra and Tamil Nadu. Later, it was extended to Uttar Pradesh, Bihar, West Bengal, Andhra Pradesh, Orissa, Gujarat and Himachal pradesh. At present, the programme covers 60 per cent of the child population in the country, spread over 176 districts in 15 states. Further expansion to 60-65 districts is in the pipeline and with this the coverage will go upto 230-235 districts. In addition, similar basic education project covers 17 districts in Uttar Pradesh under the Uttar Pradesh Basic Education Project (UPBEP).

Majority of the DPEP districts - with high share of tribals and socially disadvantaged population - are among the most educationally backward districts in the country with low female literacy. States and districts covered under DPEP are:-

Salient Features

DPEP is different from other schemes in several ways.

a. *Holistic View* : DPEP adopts holistic approach, from the schematic to the integrated, with emphasis on convergence of existing programmes and resources.

b. *District Specific* : It adopts area - specific approach with district as the unit of planning and implementation. The key strategies of this district-specific planing have been to retain the contextuality and sensitivity to local conditions. This means plans are tailored to the specific needs of the districts.

c. *Decentralized Planning*: Corollary to the area – specific approach is the local area planning or decentralized planning with disaggregated target setting.

d. Participatory Process: Consistent with the philosophy of decentralisation, plans are prepared at districts through participatory process involving district and sub-district functionaries, teachers, parents and community members.

e. *Sustainability* : DPEP has a marked focus on sustainability, sustaining the benefits beyond the project period.

f. *Equity*: Equity is a major concern in DPEP. All plans strategies and intervention are tailored to address the specific needs of the disadvantaged groups such as Scheduled Caste (SC), Scheduled Tribe (ST), minorities, girls and the disabled.

g. *Community Ownership*:The Programme stresses on community participation and community ownership.

h. *Home grown Idea*: DPEP, which has adopted innovative practices and approaches, is a home grown idea.

i. *Additionality:* DPEP is an additionality to the existing resources for education. A basic requirement of DPEP is that at least 1991-92 levels of expenditure on elementary education should be maintained in real term.

j. *Convergence:* The programme encourages convergence of services in education, health, NFE, ECCE etc. rather than replicating them.

Learning scores of class students in all project districts improved substantially both in language and mathematics over the baseline of 1994. In many cases, the target of achieving 25 per cent improvement was crossed. Similar improvement was witnessed among children of Class III and IV as well. The hike in achievement in language and mathematics in class I varies from 1% to 44% and in class III/IV, the increase varies from 1% to 25%. The average performance of students in class – I in majority of the districts has crossed 60% mark.

PROGRAMME MANAGEMENT STRUCTURE

DPEP has evolved a management structure from the Centre right upto the village level with substantial autonomy, high degree of flexibility, and above all, space to experiment with different methods and models. The Programme is working towards institutionalization of an appropriate management culture across the primary education system in the country. The management structure of the Programme has several levels-national, state, district, block, cluster and village. Details of these structures are given below.

National Level: The role of National Level Structure (NLS) of DPEP is in facilitation, capacity building, appraisal, co-ordination and overall direction of the programme. Till adequate capacity is built in states, it would also assist in planning and implementation. The NLS includes:- The role of National Level Structure (NLS) of DPEP is in facilitation, capacity building, appraisal, co-ordination and overall direction of the programme. Till adequate capacity is built in states, it would also assist in planning and implementation. The NLS includes:-

Mission General Council (GC) headed by the Union Minister of Human Resource Development, is the apex body which provides policy direction to DPEP and reviews the progress. It also facilitates centre – state co-ordination and promotes debate o n issues with policy implications for primary education development. GC meets annually and is adequately represented by NGOs, educationists, public men and representatives of state and central government.

Project Board (PB) headed by, the Union Education Secretary, is the empowered executive body with full financial and administrative powers to implement the Programme. It recommends to the Government policies on DPEP, considers Annual Work Plan, promotes convergence, approves norms and reviews DPEP quarterly. PB meets at least once every quarters. Joint Secretary of DPEP will be the Member Secretary of both GC and PB.

DPEP Bureau in the Ministry is a dedicated cell to implement the programme. Much of the background work relating to policy, servicing of PB, release of finances to states, overall review of the programme is done by this Bureau. It also provides for appraisal, supervision, monitoring, research and evaluation, reimbursement, procurement and technical support. The Bureau is accountable to the General Council and the Project Board for implementation of the Programme.

The Technical Support Group (TSG) of the Educational Consultants India Limited (Ed.CIL) provides professional and technical support. The National Resource Centres - National Council of Educational Research and Training (NCERT), National Institute of Educational Planning and Administration

(NIEPA) and Lal Bahadur Shastri National Academy of Administration (LBSNAA), also provide support, apart from Indira Gandhi National Open University (IGNOU) and Indian Institutes of Management (IIMs).

State Level: At the state level, the Programme is implemented in a mission mode through a registered autonomous society, which has two organs. At the state level, the Programme is implemented in a mission mode through a registered autonomous society, which has two organs.

General Council (GC) with Chief Minister as ex-officio president and Executive Committee (EC) headed by the Chief Secretary/Education Secretary of the State. The Project is implemented by the State Project Office (SPO) and the executive responsibility rests with the State Project Director (SPD) being the Member Secretary of the GC and EC. Government of India is represented in the GC and EC. As the plans are formulated and implemented with the association of the community, NGOs, teachers, universities, national apex institutions and educationists, they are given adequate representation and voice in management of the project at all levels – state, district, block and village.

Management Structure of DPEP have many common features across the states. These include small staff size, linkages with the State Department of Education and other related departments and consultancies for accessing expertise in key functional areas. The state project management structure is supported by State Council of Educational Research and Training (SCERT), State Institute of Educational Management and Training (SIEMAT), State Resource Groups (SRGs), Textbook Corporations and other Institutes.

District Level: District and sub-district level programme planning and management are carried out by the District Project Committee headed by the District Collector or the Chief Executive Officer of the Zilla Parishad. The Committee reviews the progress of DPEP in the district and works towards widening the network of supportive agencies. The committee has representation of NGOs, panchayats, educational institutions, Village Education Committees and functional specialists apart from government departments. Besides, there is a District Implementation Committee which functions as the executive body at the district level.

District and sub-district level programme planning and management are carried out by the District Project Committee headed by the District Collector or the Chief Executive Officer of the Zilla Parishad. The Committee reviews the progress of DPEP in the district and works towards widening the network of supportive agencies. The committee has representation of NGOs, panchayats, educational institutions, Village Education Committees and functional specialists apart from government departments. Besides, there is a District Implementation Committee which functions as the executive body at the district level.

District Project Office (DPO), headed usually by the District Primary Education Officer, have been established as a separate structure in all the districts. Day-to-day implementation is managed by a full-time District Project Co-ordinator (DPC) assisted by Assistant Project Co-ordinators. Staff of the Department of Education posted in the district including supervisory officials and functional specialists work closely with the district DPEP units. District level structure is also supported by District Institute of Education and Training (DIET), District Resource Groups (DRGs), NGOs and other institutes.

Sub-District Level :Some of the Project districts also have Block Project Implementation Committees. Block Resource Centre lends academic support, so also Cluster Resource Centre at cluster level (group of villages). Some of the Project districts also have Block Project Implementation Committees. Block Resource Centre lends academic support, so also Cluster Resource Centre at cluster level (group of villages).

Village Level: At village level, there are Village Education Committee (VEC), Mother – Teacher Association (MTA) and

Parent - Teacher Association (PTA) to oversee implementation of the Project.

Programme Components and Interventions

The Programme is structured to provide additional inputs over and above the provisions made by the State Governments for expenditure on elementary education. DPEP fills in the existing gaps in the development of primary education and seeks to revitalise the existing system.

The Programme components include community mobilisation, creation of community based structure, construction of classrooms and new schools, opening of non-formal and Alternative Schooling centres, appointment of new teachers, setting up of Cluster Resource Centres (CRCs), and Block Resource Centres (BRCs), teacher training, development of Teaching Learning Material, distance education and special intervention for education of girls, the disabled children and Scheduled Caste and Scheduled Tribe Children.

Community Mobilisation

Community participation is an inbuilt intervention in DPEP. The Programme elicits the involvement of the community including minorities, women and the socially deprived groups, making them stakeholders in the primary education system. This is the first large scale attempt to involve community participation for achieving universal primary education. Given the social, economic and cultural diversity in India, community participation is an enormous challenge.

A wide range of communication and media options are adopted for community mobilisation in the programme. DPEP has drawn upon the experiences of Kala Jathas (cultural troupes) mode of the Total Literacy Mission (TLM) for community mobilisation. Kala Jathas have been extensively organised using folk forms, puppet shows, traditional media, street plays, films and songs to create awareness. Rallies, workshops, meetings, house to house campaigns and camps are also held to motivate parents to send their children to school. Opportunities such as weekly market, Melas (fairs), and religious gatherings have also been used, apart from the media channels of radio, television and print media.

Special melas take Mahila (women), Ma-beti (mother-daughter), Bap-beti (father-daughter) and Sishu (child) are organised to sensitise the community on needs of primary education. Posters, banners, hoardings, pamphlets, folders and brochures also create an environment of a campaign. The states implementing the programme, today, have rich repository of print and audio-visual material.

Studies have shown that these campaigns have generated interest and enthusiasm resulting in increased enrolment. Before DPEP, the community perceived the existence of the school as its only area of concern. Recent developments show that the community is increasingly participating in issues related to the school environment, pedagogical renewal, learning achievement levels of children etc. The increasing involvement of parent and wider community is also having a salutary effect on the teaching-learning process. DPEP's experience has shown that when interventions are designed by the community and are tailored to a village's distinctive characteristics, then the best results follow. In fact from Gujarat to Assam and from Himachal Pradesh to Kerala, instances of community members volunteering there time, energy and resources can be related.

Village Education Committees (VECs)

DPEP has set up community structure commonly known as Village Education Committee (VEC) in all villages to function as an interface between the community and the primary education system. This generates community's interest and involvement leading to community ownership of the programme. Studies have shown that VECs have played an important role in mobilising the community, motivating parents to send their children to school and even managing Early Childhood Care and Education (ECCE) and Alternative Schooling (AS) centres. In some places VECs are supervising construction of schools and classrooms. These committees have assisted in enrolment, retention and reduction of drop-out rate, besides strengthening and maintaining the physical infrastructure of the school. In some places, they raise contributions for schools, prepare village educational plans, appoint para teachers and conduct house-to-house surveys and micro planning.

The tenure of VECs range from 3 to 5 years. VECs meet once in a month, and review functioning of the school. They also discuss about enrolment and drop-out position, progress of civil works and effectiveness of mobilisation campaigns. These committees are adequately represented by women, disadvantaged groups, parents, social workers and prominent persons. In some states, women comprise half of the total members. The head-teacher of the village school and member of the Village Panchayat (local body) are ex-offico members of the committee. DPEP provides school grant of Rs. 2000 per annum to each VEC for improving school facilities, furniture, health check up etc.

The Programme has undertaken to orient and train VEC members to enable supervision, school improvement and also for bringing about attitudinal changes among parents and the community. Studies have revealed that active participation of women resulted in better functioning of VEC as also school. Wherever women headed VECs, widespread information sharing and consultation with larger community has been witnessed. Village Education Committee has been set up in all villages of the project area.

Besides VECs, there are other community based structures like Mother Teacher Association (MTA), Parent Teacher Association (PTA), and Mahila Samakhya Sanghs (Womens clubs formed under the scheme for women's empowerment) which also assist the Programme.

The interface between Panchayat Raj (local self government) Institutions and VECs needs to be strengthened and harmonised for wider participation of the community in education.

Physical infrastructure

Provision of necessary physical infrastructure is a basic requirement for ensuring universal access and enrolment of children. DPEP undertakes construction of new schools buildings, classrooms, repair work, provision of drinking water and toilet facilities and also developing infrastructure for Block Resource Centre (BRC), Cluster Resource Centre (CRC), District Institute of Education and Training (DIET), State Institute of Educational Management and Training (SIEMAT) and State Council of Educational Research and Training (SCERT). DPEP also supports construction of ECCE centres, residential schools, multigrade centres, partition walls, boundary walls, etc.

DPEP has evolved over 100 innovative district and state specific designs – a distinct improvement over the traditional box-type schools-with facilities for activity based learning. Improvement of learning environment to suit pedagogical needs is central to the new designs, which are child and handicapped friendly. It uses appropriate technologies using local material and skills. These new designs emphasis on making better physical and visual access, creating space other than class rooms like verandah, pavilion, platform etc, and providing external class rooms and display and storage space. An innovation fund has been made available to aii project states to develop new pedagogically – sensitive school construction designs.

Community participation has been one of the successes of the civil works programme and VECs are playing a lead role in construction activities. The community employs labour, buys materials and oversees the construction. Voluntary contribution in terms of land, labour and material can be seen in various places. Some states have constituted Village

Construction Committees (VCC) a sub committee of VEC to oversee civil works. Three fourths of all works under the Programme have been undertaken through the village community. Procedurally, community participation is a significant departure from the conventional system of construction. DPEP recognises the community as the major stakeholder in the provision of infrastructure and this creates sense of ownership and pride in the village. Interestingly, now the community is acting as a watchdog over the works being done departmentally or through contractors.

To facilitate the process of community involvement, training modules and construction manuals have been developed in local languages. The engineers, interestingly, are now acting mainly as technical resource persons to help and guide the community.

As per DPEP guidelines, cost of civil works should not exceed 24 percent of the project cost. This had led to prioritisation of construction needs and ensured that only additional requirements, over and above the normal state government sponsored or Operation Blackboard funded construction activities, are promoted by DPEP. It has also led to convergence of funds for civil works under other programmes like Jawahar Rozgar Yojana and area development programmes. In some states funds of Panchayat, District Rural Development Agency (DRDA) and Tribal Welfare Departments have also been tapped.

Over 7,000 new school buildings, 5,300 additional classrooms, 8,800 toilets and–drinking water facilities have been constructed. In all 3,800 buildings were repaired, in the project area as on January 1, 1999. DPEP has a massive construction programme with outlay of about Rs. 15,000 million. It plans to construct over 26,300 new schools, 22,400 class rooms and over 10000 other buildings in 163 districts of the Project. It also proposes to provide drinking water and toilet facilities at over 63,000 places and to repair over 32,000 schools.

Alternative Schooling (AS)

Studies have shown that physical conditions such as far off schools from habitation, geographical barriers like river in between the village and school; socio-economic conditions such as children engaged in agricultural work; and school related factors like poor school environment, have sometimes limited the access to formal schools. This broad category of out-of-school children includes dropouts, enrolled but not attending classes and non-enrolled children. Most of the out-of-school children are from the disadvantaged groups and they are from backward and tribal areas. Of them, majority are girls. True, there are formal schools in 95% of the villages in the country with in a distance of one kilometre and also there are many Non Formal Education (NFE) centres. But both the systems have been rigid with fixed duration and schedule.

Alternative schools under DPEP, on the other hand is flexible and provides learning at a free pace. It is set up after studies and house to house surveys. A number of Alternative Schools (AS) have been opened for children in remote and small habitations as also for out-of-school children in other areas. This has ensured school participation of working children, street children, children of migrating communities, slum children and other marginalised groups.

Normally, AS centres are run for 250 to 300 days in a year with a minimum of three hours per day. But there are also many AS centres which function like formal schools with five hours daily. The period of Alternative Schooling strategies vary from 2 to 5 years, based on the free pace of learning and multi-level situation. Minimum qualification of Alternative Schooling teachers in most states is matriculation and normally women teachers from the community are prefered. Apart from the foundation training, these teachers are imparted regular in-service training.

Education in AS centres is not inferior to that of formal schools. Stress is given on equivalence in quality with formal schools in terms of teacher's qualifications/training, academic support, school hours, duration and TLM. Infact, studies have shown that quality of education and learning achievement levels in AS are higher than formal schools. In most of the AS Schools, formal textbooks are being used. Most of the project states have evolved separate academic support systems to assist AS teachers.

Community participation is the hallmark of various AS strategies. Teachers belong to the community, they are selected by the community and honorarium is paid by the community. A number of Alternative Schooling models and strategies are in vogue in project states, depending on specific needs and requirements. For instance, there are 7 Alternative Schooling models in Gujarat. Some models of Alternative Schooling are:-

Employment Guarantee Scheme (EGS) of Madhya Pradesh, where Government opens schools within 90 days if an area without school within 1 ½ kilometre radius of the habitation is identified and if there are atleast 40 out-of-school children. It is managed by the village panchayat. of Madhya Pradesh, where Government opens schools within 90 days if an area without school within 1½ kilometre radius of the habitation is identified and if there are atleast 40 out-of-school children. It is managed by the village panchayat.

Back to School Campaign in Uttar Pradesh and Andhra Pradesh, where through intensive camps, children are withdrawn from work and educated to the level, corresponding to their age. They are then brought back to the mainstream school system. in Uttar Pradesh and Andhra Pradesh, where through intensive camps, children are withdrawn from work and educated to the level, corresponding to their age. They are then brought back to the mainstream school system.

Makhtabs and Madrasas in Assam and Uttar Pradesh where Makhtabs (Muslim religious leaders) or para teachers impart formal primary education - especially to Muslim girls who do not come to formal schools-in Makhtabs and Madrasas after the religious instructions. in Assam and Uttar Pradesh where Makhtabs (Muslim religious leaders) or para teachers impart formal primary education - especially to Muslim girls who do not come to formal schools-in Makhtabs and Madrasas after the religious instructions.

Alternative Schooling in Madhya Pradesh under DPEP is run with the help of "Digantar" an NGO. This is a four-hour school based on free pace learning. There are no grades and the teacher is only a facilitator. in Madhya Pradesh under DPEP is run with the help of "Digantar" an NGO. This is a four-hour school based on free pace learning. There are no grades and the teacher is only a facilitator.

Multigrade schools in Kerala. These are opened in collaboration with Rishi Valley School Group in habitations and villages which do not qualify for opening new schools. It emphasises on group learning and use of self learning material. These are opened in collaboration with Rishi Valley School Group in habitations and villages which do not qualify for opening new schools. It emphasises on group learning and use of self learning material.

As in Tamil Nadu have been opened to bring back out-of-school children to mainstream after an input of one year. have been opened to bring back out-of-school children to mainstream after an input of one year. Residential Schools in Gujarat envisages opening Ashram residential schools, seasonal hostels and vocational courses for children of migratory population during harvesting seasons. envisages opening Ashram residential schools, seasonal hostels and vocational courses for children of migratory population during harvesting seasons.

Sugar schools in Maharashtra is for children of families who migrate to the area of sugar factories during the season. These schools are close to sugar fields or sugar factories. In some cases, children are accommodated in the nearby formal school for about 6 to 7 months. is for children of families who migrate to the area of sugar factories during the season. These schools are close to sugar fields or sugar factories. In some cases, children are accommodated in the nearby formal school for about 6 to 7 months.

Other innovative approaches like summer camps and mobile schools are also being planned. The stress is on developing flexible school strategies, tailored to the needs of particular groups. So far over 38,000 AS centres with enrolment of over one million children have been opened in the project areas and 80,000 more such centres are proposed to be set up. By opening large number of schools under AS, many states have achieved universal physical access and universal enrolment.

Pedagogical Renovation and Quality Improvement

Quality improvement is the cornerstone of DPEP and focus is on ensuring improvements in classroom processes. This is being attempted through renewal of curriculum and Teaching Learning Material (TLM), teacher training and empowerment, provision of decentralised academic support and capacity building of institutions. Improving classroom processes have been found not only more cost-effective but also more beneficial than incentives for achieving targets of universalisation.

Route to Quality Improvement

Curriculum and Teaching –Learning Materials/Processes

a. Textbooks Development

DPEP emphasises on improving the quality of teaching and making learning a joyful experience for students. Classroom processes are child centred, activity based, bias free (tribal, gender social and economic), attractive and interesting. It is also a two-way interaction, promoting self and group learning but avoids information overload. This new philosophy meant a review and in most cases an overhaul of curriculum and teaching learning materials including textbooks, workbooks, teachers handbooks, supplementary reading material etc.

Textbook development commenced right in the first year of the programme and states are at various stages in this process. Most of the states have developed and trialled MLL oriented activity based textbooks through a participatory process involving teachers, co-ordinators of BRC and CRC, DIET and SCERT personnel, subject experts, artists and illustrators. Some states have even replicated DPEP textbooks in non-DPEP districts. Development of text books has entailed a very rigorous process of debate, discussion, drafting and review before the final manuscript is arrived.

The processes have been guided by State Resource Groups (SRGs) specially constituted for facilitating pedagogical renewal. Tie-ups with organisations such as Ekalavya (Madhya Pradesh), Centre for Learning Resources (Pune), Digantar (Rajasthan), Development Network (Bihar) and Lok Jumbish (Rajasthan) have also facilitated pedagogical renewal processes in states, besides experts from NCERT and other premier institutions.

In most of the states trialling of textbooks had been undertaken to identify gaps that could be corrected before large scale introduction took place. Trialling has been done in some schools over a specified period of time involving teachers and resource persons specially trained for the purpose. The trialling outcomes were discussed in workshops and changes incorporated accordingly.

The illustration, design and production aspects of text-books, workbooks and handbooks have been given due attention. As a result, books produced under DPEP are far more attractive and interesting while costs have either reduced or remained the same. Some of the DPEP states have developed textbooks in more than one language, depending on the different languages used as medium of instruction in the schools. Other than this, to overcome learning difficulties of tribal children, Bridge Language Inventories (BLI) have also been prepared and teachers trained in their usage. This is particularly helpful for teachers who are not familiar with the mother-tongue of the children. With improved communication between teacher and taught it is expected that the children will gradually be able to follow the formal language of instruction. What is being attempted under DPEP for quality improvement and pedagogical renovations is little short of renaissance, and a quiet one at that.

b. Supplementary Reading Material

In addition to textbooks, supplementary reading materials were also developed to provide additional inputs to both teachers and students. They are usually in the form of:

— Readers/story books

— Graded language reading booklets

— Fun-booklets on mathematics etc.

The other kinds of teaching learning materials developed and used in DPEP include practice work cards, picture-word cards, school readiness packages, activity guides, rhymes and story collections.

c. Pupil Evaluation

Some states have begun work on recurrent pupil evaluation which is in accordance with pedagogy of activity-based, child-centered teaching learning processes, instead of annual examination system.

Alongwith the change in textbooks and workbooks, all teachers in DPEP districts are trained in joyful learning, competency and new pedagogy. Teachers are central to the Programme as they can bring about changes in classroom processes, through commitment, creativity and innovation. In-service teacher training earlier has rarely been undertaken on a large scale. Training in DPEP, is not conceived as a one-time exercise. Instead, the training programme is being followed up with regular and on-going academic support with the help of

CRCs and BRCs. Arguably, the most significant intervention has been the initiation and consolidation of teacher support through decentralised sub-district level resource centres and resource persons.

DPEP has developed, trialled and transacted teacher training modules in all the Project districts. An evaluation study has found a visible shift towards the new training programme, which is motivational and content and need based. The teacher training programmes have been largely participatory in nature. These programmes are usually residential and of different duration, spread over three to ten days and are usually conducted at BRCs. Some states have also integrated the monthly meetings and other block/cluster level activities to support the structured training programmes. The overall training strategy in DPEP has made a major departure from the earlier pattern in which the courses were centrally designed, which followed the lecture mode and were not regularly updated or conducted.

As the cascade model has been generally followed by the states in training their teachers, the services of Master Trainers (MTs) and Resource Persons (RPs) have been utilised in a big way. To minimise transmission loss in the process, the number of levels of training is kept to the minimum and the selection and training of MTs/RPs has been meticulously done. The SCERT and SRGs (which have now been established in almost all the states) train district or block level RPs who in turn train the teachers directly. In some states the CRC Co-ordinators conduct training programmes at the cluster level. The institutions involved in training are SCERT, SPO, DIET, state and district resource groups, NGOs, BRCs and CRCs.

Teacher training packages are introduced only after it is field tested. The feedback received is used to improve upon the package. In some states feedback is taken regularly during the training programmes and efforts have been made to make mid-course corrections.

All states have completed several rounds of training. Till date more than 7,20,000 teachers have been trained. Training of head teachers has also been taken up in some states. In addition to teachers, DPEP has also trained over two million community leaders, 20,000 master trainers, 5,000 action researchers and 2,000 planners and managers. All teachers are given a grant of Rs. 500 per year to prepare teaching learning material and aids.

Academic Support Institutions

Teacher training programmes cannot be the only input for teachers' empowerment. In line with the understanding of teacher development as a continuing process with the requirement of regular academic support, sub-district structures at block and cluster level Cluster Resource Centre (CRC) for a group of 8 to 10 Villages and Block Resource Centre (BRC) for a group of 8 to 10 clusters-have been established in all states. The block and cluster level resource centres have been set up under DPEP to provide on-site support to teachers in terms of school visits, demonstrations and feedback, teacher training, material preparation, discussion of specific problems at monthly meetings etc. Under DPEP, about 14,000 CRCs and about 3,700 BRCs have been set up.

CRC have been involved in conducting training programmes for teachers. In some states they have supervisory powers. In the monthly meetings all the CRC teachers come together to share and discuss their academic and administrative problems. One of the major activities at these meetings has been lesson demonstration followed by discussions. The CRC Co-ordinator facilitates the discussions and sometimes gives lesson demonstrations also.

BRCs are headed by co-ordinators, who are normally secondary school teachers with experience in primary education. BRCs may also have resource persons, trainers, teacher educators, subject experts and academic co-ordinators.

School visits are undertaken independently by both BRC and CRC functionaries, but the nature of support provided by the BRC and CRC are generally different. The CRC Co-ordinators generally make monthly visits to each school. During the visit the CRC Co-ordinators attempt to provide on-site academic support and guidance to the teachers by listening to their problems, giving lesson demonstrations and by helping them to make lesson plans. The BRC Co-ordinators visits to school are less frequent and they generally play a supervisory role. In some states where CRCs are still in the process of evolving their roles, the BRC faculty provides direct on-site academic support to the teacher.

The academic functioning of these sub-district structures would need to be strengthened further. Also linkages with DIETs and the educational administration would need to be improved. Capacity building of personnel of sub-district structures would be an important area of work for the future.

DIETs

District Institutes of Education and Training (DIETs), which provide academic and resource support to elementary education teachers and non-formal instructors in districts, have been identified as the principal technical and professional resource institutions in DPEP districts.

Strengthening of DIETs has been attempted through provision of equipment, books etc. Equipment provided includes photocopiers, overhead projectors, typewriters, duplicating machines etc. In most of the states library books have been provided to the DIETs by DPEP. The initial effort was to ensure adequate staffing in DIETs.

Most DIETs have taken up the following activities under DPEP:-

— In-service teacher training

— Academic monitoring and supervision

— Action Research, TLM preparation etc.

— Facilitating implementation of activities under other functional areas.

Key DIET faculty members have been identified and involved with the programme in most states. They have contributed significantly to the programme. The SCERT, DIETs and the resource groups have been contributing in the areas of developing training packages and materials for training, curriculum and textbook development, supervision and provision of academic inputs to the BRCs and CRCs. District Resource Groups (DRGs), wherever they are functional, are helping BRCs and CRCs in the regular academic support to teachers.

To supplement the efforts of SCERTs and DIETs, state and district level resource groups have been constituted comprising representatives from the State Departments of Education, SCERT, SIE, DIET, Universities, Colleges (including B.Ed, Colleges), NGOs, SPO, DPO, BRC, CRC, etc. The State Resource Groups (SRGs) have often included 'good' primary school teachers, who undergo an intensive selection process. The presence of persons with experience of working in primary schools has helped in the development of training programmes that have participatory and experiential training methodologies and content that is more relevant to the school situation.

SCERT

Academic support in the area of school education is provided by the State Councils of Educational Research and Training (SCERTs) and the DIETs in the states. However, deficiencies in human resource and other infrastructural problems have limited the extent of their effectiveness in some states. DPEP has tried to improve the situation by providing additional personnel and infrastructural support in terms of new or additional buildings, vehicles and office equipment.

Presently, in almost all the states, SCERT faculty are involved in the whole range of quality improvement interventions. In states like Maharashtra and Madhya Pradesh and recently in Assam the entire responsibility of pedagogical renewal has been entrusted to the SCERT.

Teacher Recruitment

DPEP initiatives have sped up the teacher recruitment process in the project areas as most states have shortage of teachers to the extent that there are many single teacher schools and multi-grade situation in primary schools. About – additional teachers have been recruited in the project states. DPEP provides funds for appointment of additional teachers, preferably women teachers as studies indicate that presence of lady teachers will enhance participation of girls. On an average only 35 percent of the primary school teachers are female. DPEP states are making conscious efforts to recruit more female teachers. About 51% of teachers newly appointed in DPEP states are women.

Parallely, DPEP has been experimenting with the community selected para teachers who know the local language, specially in remote and tribal habitations. Such teachers are not only effective, but also less costly, as they are paid less than the regular teachers. A large number of such teachers have been recruited in Andhra Pradesh and Madhya Pradesh and are proposed in Rajasthan, Uttar Pradesh and Himachal Pradesh.

SIEMATs

To strengthen the planning and management capacities as also develop the capabilities of the existing staff, DPEP supports setting up of State Institutes of Educational Management and Training (SIEMATs). SIEMATs focus on the management aspects of education including training of functionaries all levels of planning, implementation, research and evaluation.

Distance Education

The Distance Education component in DPEP supports and

supplements on-going training programmes for teachers and other primary education personnel by using distance learning (DL) inputs and materials. The component of open and distance learning was built into the Programme realising that no single approach or model will be able to train about 6,000 to 7,000 primary teachers and over 10,000 primary education personnel in a district. The Distance Education Programme (DEP) was set up under IGNOU as a lead agency, in collaboration with NCERT to provide expertise to project states for strengthening the training efforts by using DL inputs and materials.

Integrating the disabled

Universalisation of primary education cannot be achieved if 10% of the children, who have some physical, intellectual or emotional limitations are excluded from the general mainstream of education. DPEP, therefore, has chalked out a concrete programme to provide for Integrated Education for the Disabled (IED) children. The Programme will fund interventions for integrated education of primary school going children with integrable and mild moderate disabilities. Five categories of disabilities covered under the Programme are – visual, hearing, orthopaedic, and learning impairment and mental retardation.

Early Childhood Education (ECE)

DPEP finances expansion of Early Childhood Education (ECE) centres in village not eligible to be covered by the Integrated Child Development Scheme (ICDS). To improve the quality of ECE, the Programme also develops pre-school materials and impart training to functionaries and ICDS Anganwadi and Balwadi workers. ECE is a vital input in this programme because it prepares children particularly first generation learners for primary school readiness.

Early Childhood Education has an impact on girls' participation in primary education. With the pre-school children in the ECE Centres, the older girls are rendered free to attend school. The effectiveness of ECE Centres is further enhanced if these are situated in or near the primary schools.

In many states DPEP is supporting centres set up by ICDS. In such places, there is close co-ordination with ICDS to ensure that school timings and Anganwadi centre timings match and the Anganwadi centres are located close to the schools. DPEP also takes up capacity building of ICDS functionaries and provides teaching learning material to strengthen the ECE component of Anganwadi centres.

Girls Education

DPEP's commitment to universalise primary education necessarily implies equal and universal participation of all children regardless of religion, caste, creed and sex. Girls, who comprise almost half of the child population, fall into this category of children requiring special attention as their participation in education is not proportionate. Enrolment, retention and achievement levels of girls are low, especially those belonging Scheduled Castes, Scheduled Tribes, minorities and backward and disadvantaged groups.

DPEP, therefore, stresses marked gender focus in all aspects of planning and implementation for improving access, retention and achievement levels of girls, as also to premeate gender sensitivity in training, recruitment of teachers, textbooks and other educational facilities and incentives. The project goals include enrolment of all eligible girls in primary school, retain all girls enroled, ensure minimum levels of learning for girls and reduce gender gap to less than 5%.

There are many deterrents in girls education – household and sibling care responsibilities, non-supportive school environment, natural barriers, distance to school, safety etc. Specific strategies have been designed in the Programme to enhance girls' access, enrolment and retention in the school system.

Thrust of DPEP is to make girls education a community agenda so that the gender perspective is retained even after the project period. This requires high level of community involvement and motivation. Most of the project states have initiated community mobilisation activities including special campaigns, girls enrolment drives, door-to-door campaigns, ma-beti melas, besides generating films, audio-video cassettes, posters, banners, booklets and hoardings highlighting importance of girls education.

One of the major objectives of DPEP is to reduce the disparities between tribal and non-tribal children in enrolment, retention and learner achievement to less than 5 per cent. Since the tribals are not a homogenous group with regard to socio-economic conditions, literacy levels, etc., the approach under DPEP is group/region specific. Access and retention are the issues in tribal areas because of small and scattered habitations, involvement of children in various economic activities/household chores and migration. In many places, the problems are acute as the curriculum and textbooks have little relevance to tribal culture.

Towards this end, efforts are constantly on to increase the tribal community's access to education and development while maintaining their distinctive culture. Education in tribal areas has received a boost with DPEP giving priority to the opening of schools in tribal areas. Some of the interventions include setting up of residential schools, creating a cadre of parateachers within the community, teaching in local dialects and developing culturally-sensitive education material. Several national-level workshops have been organised to facilitate inter-state sharing and networking with resource organisations and institutions working on tribal education.

Strategies include identifying the focus areas and the needs of the states with respect to tribal education and providing the necessary support, ensuring the provision of complete access in tribal areas, targetting the migrating tribes, revision in the method of teaching Language and Mathematics to tribal children, attitudinal and language training for the teachers and identifying pockets with high incidence of child labour and addressing these issues under the DPEP.

Involvement of the community, NGOs and other organisations is the cornerstone of the DPEP initiative in this area. Special community mobilisation campaigns and Kalajathas are organised in tribal areas, using tribal languages. Many project states have textbooks and workbooks in tribal languages and dialects. In some states tribal language dictionaries and bridge language inventories have been developed. Teachers in Tribal districts are given attitudinal training while co-ordinators of BRCs and CRCs are imparted several rounds of training on tribal specific issues.

Similarly, DPEP is in the process of galvanising and mobilising resources for the educational upliftment of the scheduled castes and the minority community for ushering in social equity and justice for all. It is stipulated that VECs must have at least one representation from the SC community. Educational incentives such as free textbooks and reading and writing material are provided to the disadvantaged children to encourage them to enter and remain in school. Demand generation at village level to bring the disadvantaged children to school is definitely encouraged, and increasing emphasis is being laid on pedagogical renewal and new and innovative schemes to enhance child participation rates.

As per the Trend Analysis of NIEPA conducted in 1998, the Index of Social Equity (ISE) for Scheduled Caste population was more than 95 (100 being the ideal measure of equity) in all 42 districts of Phase-I, showing near absence of inequities between Scheduled Caste and general population groups. Though inequities between tribals and others have also narrowed down, more focussed strategy is required to overcome constraints in enrolment and retention of tribal children.

DPEP planning is decentralised, participatory and area – specific. It is also contextual, based on local needs, and priorities.

This has entialed development and management of plan at the micro level. DPEP's planning process evidences a major shift from the conventional planning paradigms. The planning process - unlike blue print planing - is dynamic and continuous, providing for preparation of project plans, annual plans, appraisal and supervision reports. Planning and implementation are regarded as mutually dependent activities that refine and improve each other. Monitoring and evaluation systems are important links in the process of planning and implementation, by providing continuous feedback on impact and field based insights that facilitate fine tuning of the plans. In this way, planning, appraisal, implementation, supervision, monitoring, and evaluation have given room for incorporating course corrections in the original plans.

17

Strategies for Universal Access, Relation, Quality of Elementary Education

From an international perspective, the "new movement" or paradigm shift in primary schooling in developing regions has several elements that can be unified into a central framework that builds on the principle of equal educational opportunity for all children. The framework incorporates seven major principles:

— the inherent right of all children to primary education;

— the commitment to a child-centered concept of education;

— the improvement of quality;

— the provision of a responsive education;

— shared responsibility for provision;

— recognition of the diversity of needs; and,

— commitment to a developmental and holistic approach to education.

Recognition that the improvements in quality of schools and teaching depend on improved professional development.

— Development of national policies for teacher education which cover initial teacher training inservice training, certification, continuous staff development,and address supply and demand problems for teachers and specialists.

— Greater attention to the "hidden population" of the pupils with special needs; those children who need to have significant disabilities, but nevertheless experience serious difficulties in learning.

— Increased flexibility of curriculum practice, teaching methods, and management skill in ordinary classrooms in order to be ore responsive to the needs of individual children.

— Recognition of the value of collaboration among teachers within a school.

— Early identification and screening of all school age children, and culture-free intelligence tests and other diagnostic tools.

Commitment to a developmental and holistic approach to education.

— Educational services are viewed holistically, recognizing the related domains that impact upon educational achievement, including health and physical status, nutritional status, emotional support and supervision, family relations, work demands, employment opportunities, family dislocation and migration, environmental conditions (and disasters), political unrest and conflicts, and stigma and discrimination based on ethnicity or disability.

— Educational programming begins in the first year of life and continues developmentally through the primary years, with particular support provided as the child makes the transition from family to elementary school, and to completion and entry into employment or family life.

Principle 1: Legal Assurances at the International, National and Local Levels: Progress towards universal primary education (UPE) means that primary schools increasingly have to respond to a greater number of children who have never experienced primary education. They must begin to accommodate the different socioeconomic and cultural backgrounds of these children and their broader range of learning styles, behaviors, capabilities, and potential in all sensory domains. Changes in legislation, operations, financial management, and professional training will need to occur to ensure that primary education is provided to all children. Primary education must be delivered with an acceptance of a new norm for the student population, which can no longer be used as a means for exclusion from education.

Principle 2: Commitment to a Child-Centered Philosophy of Education: Under the new paradigm for primary education, educators believe that all children can learn in different ways and to different degrees. There is an expectation that they can learn and progress and that the teacher's responsibility is to assist the child in that process. A powerful and realistic message of confidence in the ability of children to grow is conveyed to them. Teaching is directed toward each child's success. Mistakes and difficulties are viewed as important elements of the learning process and not as failures. For learning to occur, the content, level, and pace of instruction are appropriate, relevant to the life of the child and to his/her individual needs. Children are active participants and teachers use multiple teaching modalities to activate the learning process.

Principle 3: Enhancement of Quality: If primary education is to be more effective in serving a greater diversity of children, then schools need a larger repertoire of teaching strategies and the capacity to conduct responsive curriculum development in order to design educational programs for all children.

Principle 4: Strengthening the Link Between Regular and Special Systems: The concept of a continuum allows educators and parents to realize the possibility and expectation of movement and progression from specialized services into integrated regular settings. The continuum connects special and regular education in a system that shares all students, rather than reinforces the notion of separateness.

Principle 5: Commitment to a Shared Responsibility within Communities: Under the new paradigm for primary education, schools are viewed as an integral part of the community environment. The "community" is not viewed as a separate entity from which children come and to which children are released upon graduation from primary school. Instead, the community becomes a vital.and sustained partner in the planning and implementation of instruction and support services to all children.

Principle 6: Preparing Educators for Diversity: Systematic training of teachers to address a diversity of needs among heterogenous groups of children needs to become a goal throughout the developing world. in many countries already, teacher training institutions are combining training in special educational practices with regular education training programs. Such integrated initial training is expected to help advance the practice and principles of integration at the school level. Teachers need both initial training and continuous practice-based, inservice training to develop and renew their competence for teaching children with special educational needs. Areas of competence that training should address include:

— knowledge of the developmental process and basic principles of early childhood learning;

— skills in recognizing the special needs of students and developing simple assessments of learning problems;

— knowledge of appropriate teaching materials and teaching strategies for adapting curricula and classroom environments for children with special learning problems;

— knowledge of a variety of learning styles of children and skills in adapting instruction to learning, as opposed to the role of authoritarian information giver;

— attitudes to overcome cultural inhibitions to modify the traditional directive and authoritarian teacher role;

— knowledge about the diversity of and continuum of needs among children of school age;

— understanding of the philosophic, economic, and ethical rationale for universal primary education;

— skills in identifying children's need for referral to specialists.

Principle 7: Commitment to a Holistic and Developmental Approach to Educating Children: The principle of the holistic and developmental approach to education is related to, but differs from, the concept of "community shared responsibility" (*Principle* 5). While shared responsibility assumes that a broad range of community agencies and organizations need to collaborate in educating children, holistic and developmental programming refers to assumptions in the design of an educational system that is most responsive to the broad range of needs of children. Such schools are associated with increased enrollment and achievement of children in the primary grades. The holistic and developmental approach is based on the assumptions that:

— many domains of a child's life impact upon educational performance;

— many aspects of the child's early development will determine the extent to which he/she will be able to benefit from education once primary school age is reached; and,

— the effects of a disability and many other life conditions can be cumulative and need to be intervened in as early as possible in the life of the child.

In a school system that applies developmental and holistic principles, educational services address a range of related domains that impact upon educational achievement, including health and physical status, nutritional status, emotional support and supervision, family relations, work demands, employment opportunities, family dislocation and migration, environmental conditions (and disasters), political unrest and conflicts, and stigma and discrimination based on ethnicity or disability.

In countries with adequate educational resources, early sensory stimulation and preacademic programming begin in the first year of life through the coordination of many community agencies. Appropriate remedial support continues in a developmental fashion through the primary years. Special attention and assistance are provided as the child makes the critical transition from family to elementary and secondary school, and from completion of primary school and entry into employment or family life.

Holistic and developmental design means integrating early intervention, health, and nutritional supports with educational services within a developmental continuum of services for the health and development of the child from birth through school age. Many developing countries are realizing that policies and actions to combat malnutrition must occur through "holistic," or integrated, inter-sectoral methods. The integration of primary health care and nutrition education with basic primary education are technical and social necessities. Approaches to malnutrition include providing easily understandable information on proper child-rearing, including suitable caring procedures for good health.

18

EDUCATION FOR ALL

The World Conference on Education For All (EFA) held at Jomtien, Thailand in 1990 affirmed the will of participating nations- including India-to meet the basic learning needs of all children, youth and adults. To achieve this objective a two-pronged strategy was designed, i.e., Universalisation of Elementary Education IUEE) and universal adult literacy, which has since been the priority policy and action areas for the participating nine highly populated countries.

Three years later in December 1993, India's commitment to EFA (Education for All) was reaffirmed in its adoption of the Delhi Declaration and Framework of Action at the EFA Summit. The Declaration calls for ensuring a place for every child in a school or an appropriate education programme according to his or her capabilities, consolidating efforts towards basic education for children, youth and adults from public and private sources, improving and extending literacy and Adult Education (AE) programmes within the context of an integrated strategy of basic education for all people,.eliminating disparities of access to basic education, improving the quality and relevance of basic education, and in all actions and according to the highest priority at national and other levels, ensuring that a growing shore of national and community resources is dedicated to basic education, improving the management of existing resources for education, and collaborating with other notions in the development of distance education.

At a Special Conference convened in February, 1994 following the summit, the Chief Ministers of all the States and Union Territories (UTs) decided that coordinated and concerted action would be needed on the part of the local community, state governments and the central government in the mobilisation of resources for education so that there was a substantial increase in budget allocation and so as to accord higher priority to primary and AE. The process of affirmation of the goals of EFA was reinforced at the Mid Decode Review of EFA which took place in Amman, Jordan in June 1 996, at which various initiatives were discussed in a country-specific context to review achievements of EFA.

MAKING EDUCATION ACCESSIBLE

Ensuring accessibility of educational opportunities has been the principal policy plank of governmental strategy. While special efforts were aimed at educationally disadvantaged groups, particularly, Scheduled Costes (SCs) (comprising roughly 17 per cent of the population and Scheduled Tribes (STs) (constituting about 8 per cent of the population, various measures including monetary and other incentives, and recruitment of more teachers from disadvantaged communities, and flexible school timings provided the fillip to the expanding coverage of enrolment. As on incentive to enrolment, attendance and retention, besides improving the nutrition of children, a nation-wide mid-day meal programme has been launched during 1995-96. More than 33.5 million children benefited from the scheme. By 1997-98 all government run/aided schools in the country would be covered.

The Indian education system is also unique in that it seeks to give due recognition and importance to the social organisation, traditions, customs and value systems of the various communities-particularly SCs and STs. This is supported by the development of materials and curricula in tribal languages, residential schools for tribal children and the encouragement of the young, educated members of the community to participate in the educational process.

Various initiatives have been token to reduce the academic burden on students while improving the quality of education. Not only is curriculum development being decentralised but an increasing involvement of teachers in the development of textbooks, child-centred and activity-based methods of teaching in schools and examination strategies ore being formulated to assess the ability to understand rather than the ability to memorise. The system of examination, too, is continuously under review through introduction of continuous and comprehensive evaluation.

The Government. in 1 996. has renewed its commitment and resolve to UEE and to spend at least 50 per cent of the allocation on education which is to grow to 6 per cent of Gross Domestic Product (GDP) by the turn of the century as against the current level of about 3.23 per cent of GDP. Opening of residential schools for the poor children in each district and Teacher Housing Scheme are the thrust areas of the new policy.

NEW INITIATIVE OF DISTRICT PRIMARY EDUCATION PROGRAMME

The District Primary Education Programme (DPEP) is the major initiative undertaken to effect improvement in the quality and UEE. The programme is distinguished by its holistic approach and the principle of contextuality in planning. This, in effect, implies that education is planned and organised in the specific context of the area concerned-a shift from macro to micro planning with the district as the unit of planning. The programme lays great emphasis on people's participation and management, has a marked gender focus and seeks to enhance school effectiveness by increasing infrastructural facilities, developing instructional materials and training of teachers.

Non Formal Education

The NPE 1986, while taking the enormous challenge of achieving UEE in its entirety [access, retention as well as achievement!, recognised the fact that schools would not reach all children, particularly, millions of girls and working children whose participation in the school system is thwarted by socio-economic conditions. The Policy, therefore, called for a large and systematic programme of NFE as an integral component to achieve UEE with enough flexibility for learners to learn at their own pace and at the same time having quality comparable with formal education.

In keeping with the role of secondary education in preparing students for further academic or professional studies, the policy has been focused on improvement of quality through specific inputs such as the schemes for improvement of Science Education, Environment Education, Population Education and Computer Literacy. Government run schools, Kendriya Vidyalayas (Central Schools) have added to promotion of national identity throughout the country. The Government has accelerated the process of creating infrastructure and teacher training facilities so that these chains of schools act as pace setters for other schools in the country. Residential coeducational secondary schools [Navodaya Vidyalayas] have been established in each district to nourish talent in the rural areas. These schools have a positive bias in favour of girls and currently, about 1,20,000 students are enrolled on the basis of merit, in these schools

A major initiative to expand access of education was to promote distance education. To this end, the Open School system also provides alternative schooling to neo literates who have acquired functional literacy and also to drop-outs from the school and the NFE systems so that their schooling continues at their own pace and at a time convenient to them. The National Open School (NOS) and the State Open Schools provide alternative means to acquire secondary level education in a flexible manner.

Vocational education is the policy framework that seeks to provide diversification of educational options, increase potential employability and reduce the mismatch between demand and supply of skilled manpower. At present, about 10 per cent students take up vocational courses in the last two years of the schooling phase. The endeavour is that 25 per cent students be diverted to the vocational stream by the end of the present century. A Central Institute of Vocational Education (CIVE) under The National Council of Educational Research and Training (NCERT) has been set up to support courses and develop instructional material. The Institute has accomplished this in about 150 vocations. It is also proposed to set up State Institutes of Vocational Education and strengthen existing ones. Pre-vocational education is being introduced at the lower secondary stage (classes IX and X). The scheme aims at covering 1,000 schools during the Eighth Plan 11992-971

Non-formal vocational education and training programmes are also being introduced through Non Governmental Organisations (NGOs), specially, in rural areas. These are intended for girls in the 14-18 age group and are designed to emphasise entrepreneurship and introduce new and emerging technologies to, women

Higher education policy in India has been characterised by upgradation strategies that provide for quality improvement, and consolidation of facilities for existing Universities and Colleges. The higher education sector, considered vital for the national economy, has witnessed a steady growth since Independence in 1947. The enrolment of students too shows an increased share of women and SCs and STs in all stages of higher education. The utilisation of distance education as a cost-effective and easily accessible medium for upgradation of education and skills, particularly in remote areas, forms part of the thrust area in the higher education policy.

Technical education is one of the most significant component of the human resource development spectrum with great potential for adding value to products and services, for contributing to the national economy, and for improving the quality of life of the people. In recognition of the importance of this sector, the successive five year plans laid great emphasis on the development of technical education. Technical education includes courses in engineering, technology management, pharmacy, applied arts and crafts, etc. Policy guidelines in technical education have sought to streamline courses and syllabi in relation to the manpower needs of the country as well as changing technological scenario across the globe.

Policy initiatives to revamp the technical education system include promoting institution-industry interaction, providing continuing education to update the skill and knowledge of technical personnel working in the industry and service sectors, the transfer of technology to the rural sector and setting up Technology Development Missions to meet the emerging challenges in science and technology.

In order to update and upgrade technical education in the Indian Institutes of Technology (IITS), Regional Engineering Colleges (RECs) and other institutions/polytechnics, obsolete machinery and equipment is weeded out, modern machinery and new equipment relevant to curricular needs introduced and opportunities for hands-on experience for student created]

A new policy measure has also been initiated to mobilise funds, particularly, for higher and technical education from non-governmental sources. in tune with the economic liberalisation of the economy, institutions are being encouraged to generate resources, raise fees which often have not been revised in the last three or four decades and embark on judicious financial management with the overall objective of reducing government subsidies.

A National Technical Manpower Information System has been developed by the Government to monitor the absorption of trained engineering and technical manpower and, thereby, create a data base in order to streamline and plan the development of technical education.

During the past few years, the number of institutions in the private sector has increased considerably. A number of industrial houses have also established technical and management institutions. The government, however, has taken suitable measures to regulate education in the private sector to check its commercialisation and maintain standards through setting up All India Council of Technical Education (AICTE).

The National Literacy Mission NLM), set up in 1988 with the goal of helping 80 million persons achieve literacy by 1995, has adopted the Total literacy Campaign (TLC) as the dominant strategy for achieving its literacy goals. This has resulted m a rich and varied experience that has become an international resource. The Mission has now been extended to cover 100 million non-literates by 1997, that is, by the end of the 8th Plan period.

The NPE 1986 recognises that importance should be given to value-based curriculum incorporating the notion of an equitable society, secularism, democracy, and a scientific temper. These are reflected in the core elements of the school curriculum and also include observance of the small family norm, protection of the environment and gender equality. Human rights have also been now included. Both at the national and state levels, textbooks have been reviewed to eliminate passages that were inimical to human rights or that distorted them. Steps have, simultaneously, been initiated to include alternative material which shows sensitivity to human rights issues. Universities are also in the process of introducing courses on human rights. The NCERT has published a Source Book on Human Rights as a guide for teachers. An essential component of EFA is seen as an imperative for the growth of the individual and the nation.

19

ALTERNATIVE SCHOOLING

Universal elementary education is a target, yet to be accomplished in India. Around 3.2 crore children between ages 6 - 11, are still out of school. A sizeable proportion of these children live in villages/habitations where formal schools do not exist. The National Policy on Education (NPE), 1986, and its Programme of Action (POA), gives priority to universal elementary education. The NPE has acknowledged that it may not be possible to provide primary schools in all habitations. Therefore an effective and systematic programme of alternative schools was envisaged for children from these areas

The basic guiding principle of AS programmes in states under DPEP have been:

— Use of microplanning for assessment of needs

— Diversity, flexibility and local specificity of the strategies l Decentralised management system with strong community involvement

— Adoption of appropriate pedagogy, stressing on the quality of the teaching - learning Process

— Cost effectiveness

There has been conscious effort to develop decentralised management practices for implementing the Alternative Schooling programme which includes community involvement, process of selection of instructors and using resource groups in state, district and block levels for decision making and guiding the course of the programme. In the A S programme, priority is given to small and remote habitations with 20 - 30 children, which do not have a school facility within one km. radius. Other strategies have focused on main streaming these children into regular schools and providing alternative schooling facilities that are more flexible and accessible to disadvantaged children.

The various strategies adopted under the A S programme in different states have been broadly classified according to the following six categories of children they address:

— Children of remote/inaccessible habitations
— Children of migrant families
— Children engaged in household chores
— Children engaged as waged labour
— Children to whom access is restrained due to religious beliefs and practices
— Adolescent girls

CHILDREN IN SMALL AND REMOTE HABILITATIONS

EGS of Madhya Pradesh

A state - wide contact programme (Lok Sampark Abhiyan), identified a number of habitations with no access to formal school facilities within a radius of 1 km. The Education Guarantee Scheme (EGS), 1997, was launched to achieve universal education for children in the 6 - 11 age group. Any community with 40 children (25 children in case of tribals), could place a demand for a school to the Janpad Panchayat. The request has to be fulfilled within 90 days of receiving the application. The verification of application, training of the teacher identified by the community, purchase of the material and equipment for the school has to take place in the 90 day period.

The teacher is a local person, proposed by the community who should have passed at least Higher Secondary. The teacher receives training of 20 days and is paid a monthly honorarium of Rs.1000. The Cluster Resource Centre coordinator provides on the spot academic support during school visits. The guruji attends monthly meetings at the CRC and block levels. Teaching - learning materials used in the A S centres are used in the EGS schools as well.

The budget for the school is transferred into the account of the School Management Committee (SMC), comprising of villagers. The community decides the school timings and vacations as per the convenience of the children and the local circumstances. The space for the school is provided by the community (a temporary or permanent structure). The school functions like a formal school, except that it is owned by the community.

The EGS schools are single teacher schools with the TPR ranging from 1:32 to 1:50. Therefore, multigrade/multi-level teaching becomes essential. A second teacher is provided when the number of children in a centre exceeds 50. These schools are operational for at least 200 days a year. Currently there are about 25,000 EGS schools covering more than 9,00,000 children. The estimated cost of one EGS school for 40 children works out to Rs. 14,860.

Community schools of Andhra Pradesh

The community schools in A.P. have helped increase the scope of universalising education since schools can be set up in any habitation, there, with just 15 children. There are tribal areas where children were unfamiliar with formal schooling until the community schools were set up there.

The school is managed through the SMC, formed by the parents. The committee is responsible for the selection and placement of the teacher, providing appropriate space for running the school and also ensures regular attendance of the children.

The teacher, a local, familiar with the language used by the children, is paid an honorarium of Rs. 500 per month through the SMC and in some cases, the community collects money to supplement this fixed amount. There are about 1950 community schools covering 50,000 children in areas with a population of 200 or more. An additional 15,000 schools are proposed to be established in smaller areas having a population of 100 with at least 15 children.

Multigrade centres of Kerala

During the micro planning exercise conducted in the state, some inaccessible tribal pockets were identified from where children had never enrolled in schools. The DPEP functionaries initiated a programme of girl volunteers for communities which were reluctant to send girls to schools and tribal volunteers for the tribal pockets. The volunteers, belonging to these habitations, worked with the community to persuade parents to send children to school. Subsequently, single teacher multigrade centres were set up in many of these pockets. Once enrolled, the volunteers ensured regular attendance of children who were potential drop outs.

The teachers for the multi-grade centres are identified, appointed by the community. Since they are a part of the area themselves, they understand the life and language in the local context. The school has adopted innovative self - learning material with the teacher performing the role of the Facilitator. The self - learning material was developed with technical support from the Rishi Valley School, Madanappalli, A.P. There are 49 multigrade schools in DPEP districts of the state covering 1103 children.

A vocational course of 40 - 60 days is organised for children in Gujarat, who migrate with their parents to the sugarcane fields. The course enables children to cover missed portions during absence from school. In Maharashtra, temporary schools, set up for children at the sites of sugarcane fields or factories, are operational for six months during the sugarcane crushing season. Schools are also set up at brick kiln sites in Maharashtra.

Children engaged in household chores

Aamaar Kendras of Assam

Aamaar Kendras are non-formal educational centres for 6-14 year old children, who are out of school due to difficult circumstances. They function in shifts for a total of four hours, for two years. Their objective is to provide level education to children from tea estates and char areas and to mainstream them in the nearest formal school. A total of 724 kendras are in operation catering to 18,000 children. The kendras can be started in villages and habitations with 25 to 30 children, within a radius of 1 km From the village.

Alternative School Programme in Madhya Pradesh

This programme provides primary education to 1,89,210 children in the age group 6-14 years, through 5179 centres. Most of these centres are located mainly in tribal areas without schooling facilities. The schools function for four hours everyday, 250 days in a year. Each alternative school has two teachers, of the same village, one of them, a woman. The programme is distinct in pedagogy and teaching - learning materials are used. It is activity based, allowing children to learn at their own pace.

A series of textbooks have been designed in language, mathematics, and environmental studies. The programmes are very intensive, with a monthly evaluation system. Strong academic support is provided through a supervisor, for every ten centres.

The management of the centres is the responsibility of the school management committee or the VEC. The supervisor maintains regular contact with the parents. DPEP Madhya Pradesh, has taken a decision to adopt the curriculum, pedagogy and training strategies of the A S programme in the EGS schools.

Working children and street children

" Back to school" camp of Uttar Pradesh

The "back to school" camp in Lalitpur, U.P., based on the learnings from the M.V. foundation,Andhra Pradesh, is set to get children back to schools through a bridge course in a residential mode, for a time period of three months to a year. The teacher and the children stay at the camp, enabling to wean children from activities which keep them out of school. The camp was attended by 75 children, including 19 girls, mostly those working in the stone quarries. The children were then enrolled into formal schools or in the A.S centre in their locality.

"Back to school" camp of Gujarat

Back to school centres have been set up in Gujarat to cater to children in the 7-14 age group, who are either not enrolled or are drop outs. A bridge course is conducted to help children achieve educational levels corresponding to their age. The course duration depends on the age and academic level of the child at the time of admission. The shala sahayaks (teachers) are paid an honorarium of Rs. 50 per child for 20 children and an additional Rs. 10 is paid for every female child enrolled. The teacher is paid instalments - 60 % of the remuneration due is paid every month and a balance 40% is paid if the children achieve the desired educational levels.

Summer schools of Andhra Pradesh

The schools have bridge courses for 6-8 year olds, who are

out of schools. It is operational during the summer vacations in the local formal school. Such a school can be started in any village with a minimum of 20 children. They are mainstreamed into formal school after they are assessed at the end of the course. Around 16,000 summer schools, covering 35,000 children have been conducted in the state during 1999.

Children of specific communities

In Assam, maktabs are used as alternative centres of learning for Muslim children. Maktabs are community initiated centres for religious education, attended by boys and girls. Children who were not enrolled in school have been brought under the fold of primary education by jonabs (maulavis) having a background of formal education. They run A.S centres on a voluntary basis. DPEP Assam provided material support and teaching-learning material for the centres. Jonabs were trained for effective transaction of the curriculum. There are 170 such centres functioning in the DPEP-I districts. The enrolment of girls has been higher in all three districts.

Angana vidyalayas of Bihar

Modelled along the lines of the Jagjagi centres initiated by the Mahila Samakhya programme under the Bihar Education Project, the Angana Vidyalayas target out of school adolescent girls to enrol and go through schooling up to class 3. The instructors of the school are women, the management of the centres also rest with the Mata Samitis, making this a unique intervention. Girls benefited are from the underprivileged groups of society in the age group of 9 years and above. By entrusting the responsibility of the A.S centres to the mata samitis, community involvement in the enrolment and retention of children is ensured. It is also empowering for the women as they take all decisions regarding their childrens' education. The instructor, saheli, is at least middle school pass and belongs to the same community. She undergoes a 30 day foundation training, followed by regular refresher training. The schools have covered more than 10,000 girls from 583 centres and more such centres are to be opened in the coming year.

Prahar pathshalas of Uttar Pradesh

This is a strategy in UP for those 9 plus girls who are non-starters or may have dropped out of school. Though boys have also been enrolled, the emphasis has been on girls. The curriculum is flexible to allow the child to learn at its own pace. The centre is operational for 4 hours during the day. It is possible to start this school in a village with 15 girls of the age group 9-14 years, who are willing to attend it. The school is built with a provision for training in certain local crafts along with the primary school curriculum. This is for attracting the girls to the centre as well as keeping the craft alive. The common crafts include embroidery and stitching, basket weaving etc. Two and a half hours of the day are spent teaching the school curriculum and one and a half hours are devoted to local crafts.

The Bal Shalas of Uttar Pradesh target preschoolers along with their older siblings. While the 3-6 year olds are imparted the school readiness package the older children receive primary education. Through this approach of combining children of two age sets, the problems of non-enrolment and dropout faced by girls is being addressed. Gujarat has initiated similar centres on a pilot basis in Dangs and Panchmahal districts. Each centre has one A S instructor and one Early Childhood Education (ECE) worker so that the needs of both groups of children can be met to satisfaction.

20

DISTRICT INSTITUTE OF EDUCATION AND TRAINING

In order to achieve the goal of Elementary Education for all, the Government proposes to eliminate completely the phenomenon of children dropping out of school and ensure 100% enrolment. The three main components of elementary education for all are as follows:

(a) To ensure cent percent enrolment of all the school-age children from 6 to 14 years.

(b) To ensure retention of all the enrolled children till they complete Std. VIII

(c) To ensure that all these children who complete the Std. VIII achieve the minimum level of learning competencies.

It has been decided to organise a massive movement under the direct supervision of the District Collectors to ensure that drop outs and non-enrolled children join the educational institutions. Education for all (SARVA SHIKSHA ABHIYAN) The Government of India has proposed to implement a new scheme called "Sarva Shiksha Abhiyan" – "Education for All" –from this year in 22 districts of Tamil Nadu. Under this Scheme, all the children of school-age should be enrolled within 2003. All the children within the age group of 6-11 should be given five years of education up to V Std. before 2007. Similarly, all the children in the age group of 11-14 should be given compulsory education up to VIII Std. before the end of 2010. The Government of India have chalked out a programme to impart elementary education to school-age children in the country as envisaged in the Constitution. The scheme is implemented under the Peoples Education Movement. The District Plan is prepared for every school for all the school-age children of all habitations, to ensure 100% enrolment and improvement in quality in education. The District Plan preparation and the Pre-Project activities are in progress with the help of District Institute of Education and Training from the month of October 2000 for all the 22 districts. Rs.3.18 crores have been allotted by the Government of India for these pre-project activities.

Opening of elementary schools: The policy of this Government is to provide elementary schools in all hamlets with population more than 300 within a radius of one kilometer. After ascertaining the status of remaining few hamlets not covered so far, schools will be provided wherever necessary. Additional Enrolment of Pupils: The Government is implementing a number of welfare schemes for children like Puratchi Thalaivar M.G.R. Midday Meals Scheme, free supply of slates, free supply of textbooks, free supply of uniforms and free bus passes to reduce the drop out rate of children in schools.

Orders have been issued prescribing transparent and clear transfer guidelines for the benefits of the teaching community. This has received appreciation from all sections of the society. Teachers posted in schools situated in remote hilly areas are not willing to work there for long. This affects the quality of education in such schools. Considering this aspect, it is proposed to empower the Parent Teacher Associations of such schools to appoint qualified teachers. If qualified trained teachers are not available in the particular locality, graduates or post graduates of that locality can be appointed.

The dropout rate among the school going children up to V Std. is 1 for 7 children (i.e. 14.41%) and further out of these children only 54% of the children attain the required competencies. The required competencies will be enhanced by appointing one teacher for each class, by imparting in-service training to teachers, effective monitoring of the teaching methods and by undertaking remedial measures. To make education a joyful learning for children, proper infrastructure facilities are quite essential. The Government will keep in mind to provide a proper environment suitable for learning by providing proper buildings, drinking water supply, toilets and play area with enough play materials. The textbooks must be made attractive to stimulate the students' interest for learning. The teachers are to be trained in the preparation of additional teaching materials based on the contents of the textbooks.

Three schools in each of the 30 districts are selected every academic year and 90 shields are awarded for the best schools so selected. The Government is incurring approximately Rs.2123 Crores every year for elementary education. This amount is insufficient to provide the schools with basic facilities. Hence with the help of donations from the community and voluntary organisations, basic facilities such as buildings, furniture and Teaching Learning Materials will be provided to schools. Steps will be taken to provide buildings to schools through Rural Development Scheme where there are no buildings. Except the DPEP districts, schools in all other districts, are being paid an annual grant for the purchase of stationery and other materials every year. The school with 3 teachers are paid Rs.300/- p.a. and the schools having more than 3 teachers are paid Rs.500/ - p.a. as grant every year.

In order to protect the overall health of all pupils, the teachers are being given training on health education at the State, District and Panchayat Union levels This will help the children to have a healthy life in future. They identify minor diseases of the children and provide medical treatment with the help of the rural health nurses or health inspectors. Teacher-Pupil ratio will be rationalised. Steps will be taken to provide one teacher for each class. Vacant teacher posts will be filled up soon.

INTENSIVE PROGRAMME FOR EDUCATIONALLY BACKWARD MINORITIES

Under the Centrally Sponsored scheme of Area Intensive Programme for educationally backward minorities, the Gudalur block in the Nilgiris District and Ramanathapuram block in Ramana-thapuram District have been selected for construction of buildings in elementary and middle schools. Out of Rs.150.12 lakhs sanctioned by Government of India, Rs.72.81 lakhs have been released and the construction works are in progress through the Collectors. 15 schools in the Nilgiris district and 3 schools in Ramanathapuram district will be benefited. The Government of India have been addressed to release the balance amount of Rs. 77.31 lakhs.

Supply of RCCP and Television

Under the Centrally Sponsored scheme of Educational Technology scheme of improving the quality of education in elementary schools, 20000 Elementary and Middle schools have been supplied with Radio-cum-Cassette Player. 6100 more schools are to be provided with RCCP and 2000 schools with television in the year 2001-2002..

Instruction through mother tongue The order of the Government for instruction through Tamil or mother tongue in all the schools (except Anglo Indian Schools) in Standards I to V, was not upheld by Madras High Court in its judgement dated 20.04.2000. The Government have therefore filed a special leave petition against the judgement of the Madras High Court and the same is pending before the Supreme Court.

Operation Black Board Scheme

Under the centrally sponsored Operation Black Board Scheme, teaching learning materials are procured and supplied to selected Panchayat Primary and Middle Schools. The fourth phase of the scheme is going on. The Government of India have sanctioned Rs.11.91 lakhs and Rs.633.70 lakhs for the purchase of teaching learning materials for 120 Primary Schools and 1560 Middle Schools. 16 kinds of science articles for schools in plain area and 26 kinds of science articles for schools situated in hilly area, and 80 items of Maps and charts and models are to be supplied to the above schools.

Joyful Learning

Learning by activities, dramas, dances, stories, songs and other play way methods is known as joyful learning. This is also called as child-centred education. It is a bounden duty on the part of the teachers to make the learning a pleasure. To achieve this, practice training of teachers was planned with the assistance of the UNICEF in all the districts except the 8 District Primary Education Programme districts. About 1,75,000 teachers in 22 districts are to be given training with UNICEF assistance. So far 68,149 teachers have been trained in 13 districts. UNICEF has given Rs.5.50 Crores as grant for the above purpose. The government has spent Rs.52 lakhs. The teachers in the remaining 9 districts will be trained in the coming academic year and UNICEF has printed and supplied 42,208 teacher guide books. To assess the impact of the new teaching methodology, 199 Cluster Centres have been formed in the districts where the trainings have been completed.

Model Schools To provide quality education in a changed atmosphere some schools are selected as model schools. Each of the selected schools are placed under the guidance of one officer from the cadre of Assistant Elementary Educational Officer to the Director. Accordingly 838 model schools have been selected and placed under the care of 838 officers at the rate of 1 school per officer.

The officer in charge gives necessary guidance and monitors its functioning. It is the aim of the model school to impart quality education with the existing facilities. These schools will serve as a model both in teaching learning and other activities. Pupils and teachers attend the schools in uniforms.

The teachers whole heartedly involve themselves in teaching process.

In order to make the classroom conducive and attractive for children, an appropriate educational methodology of teaching to promote 'Self-Learning' has been evolved and orders have been issued. As per this scheme, all the elementary school teachers will undergo a refresher course within a period of 3 years.

REGULARISATION OF THE ACTIVITIES OF PARENT TEACHER ASSOCIATION

Under the society of Registration Act of 1975, PTAs are functioning in schools from 1994-1995 onwards. These PTAs function as an institution for improving the quality of education and to secure the co-operation of the parents and teachers. The aims of the PTAs are as follows:

(a) Enrolling all children in school going age;

(b) Undertaking constructive efforts to retain pupil in school without any dropout in the middle; and

(c) Nurturing the development of teaching–learning processes in order to improve the quality of education and efficiency of students

These PTAs are empowered to collect donation for developmental activities of the schools. They collect donations in the form of both movable and immovable properties and provide compound walls, classrooms, electricity, drinking water, toilets, library books and laboratory equipments to the schools. They also take active part in the school improvement conferences and provide the schools with necessary amenities.

The Government of India has now launched a new initiative under EGS&AIE, which replaces the old NFE scheme. The new scheme is based on the review of NFE and also incorporates a number of lessons learnt from the implementation of alternative education programs under the DPEP. It is hoped that EGS & AIE will provide quality educational opportunities with the help of diverse strategies and approached to the millions of children who even today remain out of school for various reasons. It is expected that this scheme would give a fresh impetus to the non-formal education sector in the country and assist in achieving the country's overall goal of Universal Elementary Education.

21

PRE-SERVICE TEACHER EDUCATION IN DIET FOR ADLUT AND NON-FORMAL EDUCATION

There has been a phenomenal growth of teaching profession in India since independence. During 1994-95, about 4.3 million teachers were working in different levels of schools. Of these, 2.7 million (66 percent) were engaged in primary and upper primary schools. Between the period 1990 to 1995, the total strength of teachers at different levels of school education increased from 4.0 million to nearly 4.3 million, marking an increase of 7.5 per cent. If this trend continues, the number of teachers, particularly primary and upper primary teachers will grow significantly over the next decade.

A sex-wise analysis of the teacher force indicates that there are more male teachers than female teachers at all levels of school education. Although the number of female teachers has increased, yet their share in total teaching force is small, particularly, in rural, remote and educationally backward areas. The percentage of women teachers in schools increased from 29.4 per cent in 1987-88 to 32.08 per cent in 1993-94.

A fully qualified primary teacher as recommended by the National Policy on Education 1986, is expected to have twelve years of schools education followed by two years of primary teacher training. However, the practice differs from state to state. There are teachers with ten years of general education and one year of primary teacher training. A large number of teachers recruited before 1986 have had ten years of general education. There are teachers, usually very senior, who have eight years or less of general education. While data on teachers' pre-qualification is not adequate, it is estimated that there are about 0.24 million teachers who are not fully qualified.

The National Policy on Education 1986, and also as revised in 1992, placed significant emphasis on pre-induction training as well as on inservice continuing education of primary teachers. Over the years, India has developed a multi-tier infrastructure for teacher education. At the national level, National Council of Education Research and Training (NCERT), set up in 1961, leads the county in designing exemplar instructional material on teacher education and providing training through innovative programmes. National Council for Teacher Education (NCTE) was set up in August' 1995 under an Act of Parliament for planned and co-ordinated development of teacher education.

Indira Gandhi National Open University (IGNOU), through its School of Education offers teacher education programmes in the distance mode. State Councils of Educational Research and Training (SCERTs) were set up in 20 states and State Institutes of Education (SIEs) in nine other states as the state counterpart of the NCERT to provide direction and leadership to reforms in school education including teacher education. Below the state level there are elementary teacher training institutions which are continuously being upgraded since 1987 under a Centrally Sponsored Scheme (CSS).

TEACHER EDUCATION SCHEME

As envisaged in the National Policy on Education, the Centrally Sponsored Scheme of Restructuring and Reorganization of Teacher Education was taken up in 1987 to create a viable institutional infrastructure, academic and technical resource base for orientation, training and continuous upgradation of knowledge, competence and pedagogical skills of elementary school teachers in the country. The scheme has the following five components:

— Setting up of District Institutes of Education and Training (DIETs) to organise pre-service and in-service courses for elementary school teachers and for personnel working in non-formal and adult education.

— Strengthening of Colleges of Teacher Education(CTEs) and development of about 50 of them as Institutes of Advance Study in Education (IASEs)

— Revitalization of State Councils of Education Research & Training(SCERTs)

— Mass Orientation of school teachers under a planned programme to be implemented under the supervision of NCERT.

— Establishment and Strengthening of Departments of Education in the Universities through Universities Grants Commission (UGC).

Establishment of DIETs under Centrally Sponsored Scheme of Teacher Education is a major intervention as there did not exist facilities for continuous Teacher Education at district level before the launch of this Scheme. It has been envisaged that DIETs would provide for training and resource support to Elementary Education (both formal and non -formal) and Adult Education systems at the grass-root level. A DIET has three main functions

— Training both induction level as well as inservice.

— Resource support extension/guidance, development of materials, teaching aids, evaluation tools etc.

— Action research.

All programmes of pre-service and in-service teacher education are so designed as to train the teacher/instructor in transacting curriculum, keeping the learner at the centre of the teaching learning process.

DIETs have been established through out the country either by upgradation of the existing Primary Teachers Training Institutions (PTTIs) or by establishment of a completely new district level institution. In both the cases central assistance is provided for either upgrading the existing physical infrastructure of a PTTI or for setting up of a new building with adequate facilities of class rooms, hostels, administrative block and staff quarters. As per the norms approved for the VIII Plan, non-recurring assistance up to Rs. 5.8 million could be sanctioned for additional civil work of an upgraded DIET and up to Rs 10 million for a completely new building.

Besides this, an amount up to Rs 1.7 million could be sanctioned for procurement of necessary equipment and other teaching aids. As far as recurring assistance is concerned, the central government undertakes to reimburse the full expenditure on pay and allowances of faculty and administrative staff sanctioned for various DIETs along with the expenditure incurred on training programmes and contingencies. By the end of last financial year 451 DIETs have been established/upgraded, out of which 380 are operational and organizing training programmes.

The Secondary stage is a vital one in the educational system. It is the terminal stage of school education which prepares students either for higher education or for going into a vocation of their choice. With the introduction of the 10+2 system throughout the country and the objective of introducing vocational courses at the +2 stage, secondary stage of the school system has acquired an even greater significance, and so naturally has the education of secondary school teachers. With the setting up of District Institutes of Education and Training for elementary school teachers, it also became necessary to produce good quality elementary teacher educators.

Thus selected secondary teacher education institutions combined twin functions of education of secondary school teachers as well as of elementary teacher educators. The system of secondary teacher education, therefore performs the following broad functions:

— Imparting of quality pre-service and in-service education to the secondary school teachers;

— Preparation of personnel for the faculties of elementary teacher education institutions, and their continuing education;

— Provision of general resource support to the secondary schools and elementary teacher education institutions; and

— Research, innovation and extension work in the field of secondary education and elementary teacher education.

To facilitate the training of secondary level teachers and teachers educators of DIETs, 76 Colleges of Teacher Education (CTEs) and 34 Institutes of Advanced Studies in Education (IASEs) have been setup throughout the country under teacher education scheme. In all about 2600 teacher training institutions are functioning both in government and private sectors which provide pre-service and in-service training to teachers and teacher educators.

Strengthening of State Councils of Educational Research and Training (SCERTs) is an important component of teacher education scheme. These councils are expected to perform multifarious role and responsibilities relating to research, development, training, extension, documentation and consultancy. Though majority of States have established these councils the status of most of them requires upgradation in terms of better infrastructure and faculty to enable them to come up to the level of vibrant state level organisations, capable of playing an effective role as lead institutions. Efforts are on to make the state level institutions autonomous and independent with over all responsibilities to supervise and guide functioning of DIETs, CTEs and other teacher education institutions in the state.

The National Council for Teacher Education (NCTE) has been established as a National level statutory body by the Government of India in August, 1995 with the objectives of achieving planned and coordinated development of teacher education system, regulation and proper maintenance of norms and standards of teacher education and for matters connected there with. Some of its major functions are laying down norms for various teacher education courses, recognition of teacher education institutions, laying down guidelines in respect of minimum qualifications for appointment of teachers, surveys and studies, research and innovations and prevention of commercialisation of teacher education.

As per the provisions of the NCTE Act, four Regional Committees for the Northern, Southern, Eastern and Western regions have been set up at Jaipur, Bangalore, Bhubneshwar and Bhopal respectively. These Regional Committees consider the applications of institutions of teacher education for recognition/permission in accordance with the provisions of the NCTE Act. The Council has laid down norms and standards for pre-primary, elementary and secondary level teacher education institutions and for B.Ed course through correspondence/ distance education mode. Besides a number of useful publications on the subject of teacher education, a new curriculum Framework on Teacher Education has recently been brought by the Council.

SOME OF THE INNOVATIVE INTERVENTIONS IN TEACHER EDUCATION

Shiksha Karmi Project : Shiksha Karmi Project (SKP) is being implemented in Rajasthan since 1987 with assistance from Swedish International Development Co-operation Agency (SIDA). The project aims at Universalisation and qualitative improvement of primary education in remote and socio-economically backward villages in Rajasthan with primary attention to girls. The project identifies teacher absenteeism as a major obstacle in achieving the goal of Universalisation of Elementary Education (UEE). It was realised that a primary school in remote villages, with the teacher not residing there, often tended to become dysfunctional, and parents as well as children failed to relate to such an institution, leading to high drop-out rates. Under SKP, regular teachers are replaced by local teachers who are less qualified but specially trained.

The Shiksha Karmi (SK) is a local person with minimum educational qualification of Class VIII for men and Class V for women. To overcome the basic lack of qualification, Shiksha Karmis are given intensive training through induction programme as well as periodic refresher courses. : Shiksha Karmi Project (SKP) is being implemented in Rajasthan since 1987 with assistance from Swedish International Development Co-operation Agency (SIDA). The project aims at Universalisation and qualitative improvement of primary education in remote and socio-economically backward villages in Rajasthan with primary attention to girls.

The project identifies teacher absenteeism as a major obstacle in achieving the goal of Universalisation of Elementary Education (UEE). It was realised that a primary school in remote villages, with the teacher not residing there, often tended to become dysfunctional, and parents as well as children failed to relate to such an institution, leading to high drop-out rates. Under SKP, regular teachers are replaced by local teachers who are less qualified but specially trained. The Shiksha Karmi (SK) is a local person with minimum educational qualification of Class VIII for men and Class V for women. To overcome the basic lack of qualification, Shiksha Karmis are given intensive training through induction programme as well as periodic refresher courses.

Major achievements under Shiksha Karmi Project are as follows :

— A six fold increase in enrolment of children in the age group of 6-14 years in Shiksha Karmi Schools and Prehar pathshalas (School of convenient timings).

— Enrolment of children in the age group 6-14 years in primary education in SKP villages has improved significantly from 37% to 83% at present

— Enrolment of boys has gone up from 50% to 93% enrolment of girls has increased from 21% to 76%.

— Monthly attendance of children in SK schools has improved from 58% to 84%.

— Retention of children in schools which have been with the project for more than five year has improved considerably.

— 1979 disabled children have been integrated in SK schools.

— 55% of the children in SK schools belong to the Scheduled Castes and Scheduled Tribes and 19% to Other Backward Classes (OBC).

— One of the outstanding achievements of SKP is 100% enrolment of children in the age group of 6-14 years in 576 villages i.e., more than one-fourth of project villages.

— The SKP has constituted 2600 Village Education Committees (VECs) in villages to promote community involvement in primary education and encourage village level planning, supervision and management in improving effectiveness of schools.

— A number of strategies have been tried out and implemented in the SKP for the promotion of girl education.

— Prehar Pathshalas have enabled out of school children, especially girls in the remote areas to avail of opportunities for primary schooling at their own pace and with sufficient flexibility. At present 22,138 girls who constitute 68% of learners in PPs are benefiting from this facility.

— Angan Pathshalas (Courtyard Schools) for small children, particularly girls who cannot travel long distances to attend schools, have been started. At present, 97 APS centers are in operation with 4023 children.

— In order to facilitate and increase the enrolment of girls in villages where literate women are not available to work as SKs, 14 Mahila Prakshishan Kendras (Women Training Centers) have been set up in interior rural areas in which 334 women are being trained.

MV Foundation Programme : MV Foundation programme is being run in the Ranga Reddy district of Andhra Pradesh for Universalisation of Elementary Education. It was started neither as a low-cost alternative to regular government teachers in schools, nor in response to teacher absenteeism. It has its origin in the organisation's concern for eradication of child labour. The MVF strategy is to release children from labour and put them into the regular government schools. The role of the para teacher, a local youth, is;

— To campaign against child labour,

— To mobilise children, parents and the community in favour of schooling,

— To run bridge courses for children released from labour for giving them basic literacy and numeracy skill and getting them used to the school life , and

— To assist the government teachers in teaching, and to retain the new entrants recently released from labour and put in to school after an intense campaign.

These para teachers have also helped in sensitising the government teachers to take a stand against child labour, and towards larger educational reforms, which is the MVF agenda. More than 1600 para teachers are active in Ranga Reddy district at present. The programme which started in 1991 has grown rapidly. It has already succeeded in putting 50,000 children back into schools.

Volunteer Teacher Scheme : The Himachal Pradesh Volunteer Teacher Scheme (HPVTS) was introduced by the state government of Himachal Pradesh in 1984. The HPVTS was formulated to provide an additional volunteer teacher to the single teacher primary school. This was needed because there was an increase in the enrolment in government schools. Further, the scheme was started to provide work to educated unemployed youth for a short period of time. After completion of 10 years service VTS are regularised as Junior Basic Teacher. The Teachers appointed under this scheme must live within a radius of 5 Km. of the single teacher primary school. S/he receives points in the selection process for being local and his/her educational qualifications can range from The Himachal Pradesh Volunteer Teacher Scheme (HPVTS) was introduced by the state government of Himachal Pradesh in 1984.

The HPVTS was formulated to provide an additional volunteer teacher to the single teacher primary school. This was needed because there was an increase in the enrolment in government schools. Further, the scheme was started to provide work to educated unemployed youth for a short period of time. After completion of 10 years service VTS are regularised as Junior Basic Teacher. The teachers appointed under this scheme must live within a radius of 5 Km. of the single teacher primary school. She receives points in the selection process for being local and his/her educational qualifications can range from Matric to B.A./B. Ed. The candidates also undergo a personal interview and are awarded points based on their performance.

ACTION PLAN TO INCREASE OPPERTUNITIES FOR PROFESSIONAL DEVELOPMENT OF TEACHERS

Electronic media has a time-tested, large and definite role to play in the field of Distance Education. In fact, the latest innovations in the arena of teachers' training through distance education are based on electronic media. Educational Television is more than 35 years old in India. Educational Radio is still older. In terms of response of the students, it is in favour of educational television which broadcasts both image and voice. Teachers and students have graduated from pure audio to the image and voice learning media. Next logical step is two way interaction - and expectation will be interaction with image and voice - preferably two way video - otherwise at least one way video and two way audio.

Indira Gandhi National Open University (IGNOU), with a national jurisdiction, state of the art media production facilities, fairly well-established student support services and expertise in teacher education has been making attempts to provide teacher education/training packages for teachers in the institutions of higher education and primary education through distance education. With the aim to cater to the training needs of the primary sector, the School of Education, IGNOU went into a collaboration with National Council of Educational Research and Training (NCERT) in 1993. It is offering a Certificate Programme in Guidance for primary school teachers and parents and is in the process of developing a comprehensive programme titled "Diploma in Primary Education (DPE)", following a modular approach, for training the untrained primary school teachers in the North-Eastern States of India. There is also a plan to extend this programme in other State in subsequent years.

The University makes use of self-instructional print materials, audio and video programmes, theoretical and activity oriented assignments, tutorials and academic counselling, contact session and internship, Radio and TV broadcast and teleconferencing for its professional programmes. At the Centre level, Government of India has funded a successful experimentation in introduction of distance education mode in delivering training packages to the primary teachers under the existing "Special Orientation Programme for Primary School Teachers"- a training programme with cascade model. This distance education mode has made use of the interactive video technology. Two pilot projects have been taken up by the implementing agency - the National Council of Educational Research and Training (NCERT).

The first pilot project was taken up during January, 1996 in the state of Karnataka. 850 primary school teachers who had been assembled in 20 centres, were trained. The learning centres were almost at a distance of 2500 kms from the Teaching Centre. The seven day programme had 14 sessions, each of which was on various topics such as Minimum Levels of Learning, Teaching Aids, Multi-Grade Teaching and strategies for teaching Mathematics, Environmental studies and Languages. Each of the sessions was of about 210 minutes (120 minutes of live interaction and 90 minutes of individual and group activities). Each session comprised of self-study, presentation and demonstration (live and pre-recorded) by experts, panel discussions, teachers interaction with panelists through telephone and fax and also group activities.

NCERT's Central Institute of Technology (CIET) had also conducted a Classroom 2000+ experiment in May 1993 which demonstrated the potential of Interactive Video Technology in direct teaching of Physics and Mathematics concepts to group of students spread at various distant locations in the country. It made use of Television set, a telephone and computer key pads for trainees making responses. The similar mode had now been tried for teacher training. Keeping these developments in mind, India's National Action Plan (NAP) for Inservice Education of Primary Teachers through Distance Education - a perspective plan to integrate all the ongoing programmes in this direction, has been prepared. In this plan it has been felt that only by pressing into service the distance education mode, equipped with modern training technology, it will be possible to provide inservice training to all primary teachers every year and their trainers and supervisors every second year.

Thus the technology aspect has to play a big role in implementing this plan. Therefore, it has been also felt necessary to test-run yet another pilot project to train teachers through distance mode using interactive technology. With the collaboration from UNESCO and the International Telecommunication Union (ITU), Government of India has taken up a pilot programme on Inservice Primary Teacher Training (IPTT) through application of interactive television (ITV) in distance education. The project will aim at designing and pilot testing a continuing inservice education of primary teachers and teacher educators (DIET Staff). It will simultaneously validate and standardise technology specifications for interactive television system for application in distance education in the developing countries. The major objectives of the project are:

— to design and implement an interactive distance education programme for primary teachers and DIET staff throughout a wide geographical area in the selected States,

— develop print, audio and video software according to the requirements of the proposed distance education programme,

— to use interactive television (ITV) to improve quality of interactivity in distance education programme and standardise technology specifications for ITV for application in distance education,

— to gain insight into the organisational managerial and technical constraints and problems to interactive distance education for inservice training of primary teachers, and consider the trade off between large number of learners and the level/quality of interaction.

Some of the major outputs of this project will be standardisation of ITV technology for application in distance education; training of at least 8000 teachers and teacher trainers; gain of experience and insight during the implementation, learning centres would get equipped with reception facilities in addition to the existing educational technology aids and equipment.

INDEX